THE RELATIONAL POWER OF GOD

THE RELATIONAL POWER OF GOD

Considering the Rebel Voice

Eleanor O'Donnell

PICKWICK *Publications* · Eugene, Oregon

THE RELATIONAL POWER OF GOD
Considering the Rebel Voice

Pickwick Publications
An Imprint of Wipf and Stock Publishers
199 W. 8th Ave., Suite 3
Eugene, OR 97401

www.wipfandstock.com

PAPERBACK ISBN: 978-1-6667-3368-6
HARDCOVER ISBN: 978-1-6667-2855-2
EBOOK ISBN: 978-1-6667-2856-9

Cataloguing-in-Publication data:

Names: O'Donnell, Eleanor, author.

Title: The relational power of God : considering the rebel voice / Eleanor O'Donnell.

Description: Eugene, OR : Pickwick Publications, 2023 | Includes bibliographical references and index.

Identifiers: ISBN 978-1-6667-3368-6 (paperback) | ISBN 978-1-6667-2855-2 (hardcover) | ISBN 978-1-6667-2856-9 (ebook)

Subjects: LCSH: Power (Christian theology).

Classification: BT738.25 .O36 2023 (paperback) | BT738.25 .O36 (ebook)

VERSION NUMBER 011923

In memory of my parents, with love

CONTENTS

ACKNOWLEDGMENTS

Uneasy lies the head that wears a crown.
—William Shakespeare, *Henry IV,* Part II, Act III, Scene 1

My grace is sufficient for you, for power is made perfect in weakness.
—Second Corinthians 12:9 (NRSV)

This book is the result of a journey in theology which began when I was twelve and I have been blessed with many generous companions on the way. Friends and colleagues in the Anglican Diocese of Tasmania have encouraged my efforts over the years to think through issues of power in conceptions of God and how they affect relationships in the world and the church. I thank them all, especially those who are, or have been, associated with ministry in the Parish of Channel and Cygnet.

I warmly acknowledge the ongoing interest of the faculty and staff of St Mark's National Theological Centre in the Australian Capital Territory. Special thanks to Heather Thomson, who taught me in the first year of my Bachelor of Theology at St Mark's before going on to supervise both my honors dissertation and doctoral thesis. Her wisdom and guidance over the years has been invaluable. I must also mention the support of Anna Case-Winters of McCormick Theological Seminary, who was unequivocal in her view that my thesis must become a book. I am grateful for her wise advice.

Considerable thanks are due to family members who have graciously given me space and time during the school holidays to focus on the contents of this book, when I could otherwise have been spending time with them. This is especially so of my sons Michael, Toby, and Paul and their partners, along with my sister Sarah, her husband Phil, and their children. I acknowledge their collective forbearance with love and gratitude.

A big thank-you is also due to friend and fellow priest, Tony Bretherton, who has unfailingly read, considered, and discussed each chapter and draft. His ongoing support and enthusiasm for the project has helped me enormously.

Finally, I must acknowledge the quiet, unswerving commitment of my husband, Dennis, who has faithfully walked the entire journey with me. Without his ongoing patience and gentle encouragement over many years this book could never have been conceived, let alone completed.

Eleanor O'Donnell
All Saints Day 2021

INTRODUCTION

The abuse of greatness is when it disjoins remorse from power.
—William Shakespeare, *Julius Caesar*, Act II, Scene 1

For I am convinced that neither death, nor life, nor angels, nor rulers, nor things present, nor things to come, nor powers, nor height, nor depth, nor anything else in all creation, will be able to separate us from the love of God in Christ Jesus our Lord.
—Romans 8:38–39 (NRSV)

I did not begin studying theology seriously until I was middle-aged, according to the biblical lifespan of three score years and ten, but I began to think deeply about God when I had just turned twelve. In 1977, on a January morning in Sydney, Australia, my father caught his usual train from the Blue Mountains to the city but did not arrive at his intended destination. He died along with eighty-two others after the train derailed and crashed into a bridge as it approached Granville station. The bridge collapse, mostly over two carriages of the train, injured two hundred and ten people in addition to the death toll. The Granville Train Disaster remains the worst rail disaster in Australia's history, was my first experience of personal tragedy, and changed the community of the Blue Mountains where I lived forever. It was the catalyst for me of a search for meaning, which included an exploration of the possibility of the existence and nature of God.

The God I met through my local Anglican Church after my father's death was all-powerful and all-knowing and directed the course of the world in every respect. He (for God was a "He") had a plan and was in charge of everything. I lay awake at night wrestling with God as God had been explained to me, and even though I could not reconcile God's purported love and goodness with what had happened, nor, indeed with the way in which God apparently operated in general, eventually I succumbed to a greater power. Due to my strong conviction that God was a reality, I felt that I had no choice but to give in and believe and do all I could to shape my life according to the will of God as revealed in the Bible and in the life of the Church—which at that stage I understood to be coterminous with the brand of theism I had been taught.

What I did not realize at age twelve, nor later in my teens and twenties, was that the tightly bound package of belief that had been bestowed on me needed to be loosened and investigated both to make sense and to be life giving. I began the formal study of theology at university some twenty years after being convinced about the reality of God. It was a difficult step, my main fear being that the application of my mind to the model of faith I had been taught would cause it to dissipate like a morning mist when the sun rose. I knew that a lot of it did not make rational sense, and I also knew that I was living and thinking in ways that did not cohere with what I said I formally believed. For instance, by this time I was living in the state of Tasmania and leading services and preaching at the local Anglican Church despite my femaleness—that particular handicap obviously unchanged from my time in other Anglican communities where it had been deemed so great that any leading and teaching capacity I had was restricted to Sunday School and the occasional women's bible study.

The first year of my Bachelor of Theology was a revelation. Choosing to do a double major in biblical and theological studies I explored sacred text and faith for the first time in genuinely open and academic ways. The transition from learning the right answers to learning to ask the right questions was both exciting and empowering. Having finally found the courage and energy to open the theological jack in the box I realized that things were never going to fit back together in the same way again.

The critiques of mainstream theology that excited and interested me in my early years of study were to do with the exercise of power—God's power and ours. Feminist theology, ecological theology, liberation theology, and pluralist theology all protest against power being used "over" others in patterns that have become socially normal according to certain ways of understanding God. Current social and ministry issues in the church are also to do with power: the sexual abuse crisis, the position of women in the church, whether homosexuals are allowed a voice and a place, who is in charge of whom in terms of hierarchical leadership, and what it actually means to be a leader, whether lay or ordained. Even notions of the interpretation of scripture and tradition are associated with power. Questions about which voices should be heard, the challenge of postmodernism alongside the nature of core religious truth—indeed truth in general—all come back to where we locate power and how we understand it.

The way God exercises power is called into question by the very processes of the world in which we live. My honors dissertation explored the difference a scientific understanding of the origin and development of the natural world makes to the way we understand God. It arrived at the conclusion that the power of God in the world is not omnipotence and control, but rather non-coercive strength and goodness.

Two themes have continually emerged and re-emerged throughout my theological studies and my movement into the ordained ministry of the Anglican Church. The first theme was the Social Trinity and the associated notion of shared leadership. The idea of God as a community of equals, particularly as represented in the work of Jürgen Moltmann, provided a rationale for my participation in the formal ministry of the church after many years of adherence to a headship model of God and therefore a headship model of church ministry—a model which had not only prevented me from taking up leadership in the church because I am a woman, but had caused me to redefine myself as less than I could otherwise have been.

The second theme was that of God as peaceable and persuasive rather than militant and coercive. This theme finds its most developed form in process theology, which has been on the fringes of my research interests throughout my studies. Regularly dismissed as sub-Christian, certainly on the edge of mainstream theology, process thought has some fascinating insights into the potential nature of God in a contemporary, scientific, and postmodern world. Not insignificantly, the model of God which grows from process theology provides some answer, at least a feasible response, to the problem of evil and suffering. It certainly provides a better response than the one given to my twelve-year-old self after the death of my father. This is because process theology sets aside a notion of God as all-controlling and as the sole determiner of everything that happens in the universe. In a process view the future is genuinely open, and it is not possible for God to have complete and exact knowledge of the entire future, significantly reducing God's responsibility for evil.

Either of my two themes could be a study in its own right, but together they open an even more interesting possibility. Having reached the conclusion that our understanding of the nature of God shapes everything about the way we live our lives, whether that shaping is conscious or unconscious, it is rather disconcerting to then arrive at the conviction that there is something very wrong with the most mainstream model of God. It is even more disconcerting to admit that there is also something wrong with our conception of God as Trinity when it is conceived in hierarchical terms with power exercised "over" others and the world, rather than "with" others and the world. I hasten to say at this point that in my efforts to bring trinitarian and process theology together I seek to arrive at a recognizably Christian understanding of God. It must, however, be one that makes sense in the world in which we live: a world that evolves, a world in environmental crisis, a world where much evil and greed is seen to prosper and good is trampled down. To achieve this I am quite prepared to work on the liminal fringe of the faith, but I am not keen to abandon it altogether. Nor do I believe that what I am proposing would logically require that.

The questions at the heart of this project ask: What model of God best explains God's exercise of power in the world, taking both metaphysics and the Christian tradition seriously? Can a synthesis of process theology and trinitarian theology through a mutual panentheistic understanding of God, offer such a model? If it does, what might it then contribute to a reconsideration of the theology of power and of suffering? What I seek, therefore, is to bring process theology and trinitarian theology together to develop a coherent contemporary panentheistic understanding of God. The aim is to contribute to the way we understand the power and providence of God in the face of evil and suffering in the world and, further, explore what that might mean for human relations generally.

Essentially, I am defending panentheism, which, in the simplest terms, understands God to be in the world and the world to be in God—this without reducing God *to* the world.[1] In more complex terms, God can be described panentheistically as a perfect knower of the world; a world in which freedom and change are real elements. For freedom and change to be genuine, and for God's knowledge of this reality to be perfect, God's knowledge must itself change and develop. As new facts come into being, God comes to know these new facts, and God's knowledge grows. A perfect knower includes within itself the object which is known. God, as a perfect knower, therefore, includes the world within Godself, and as the world grows, God grows and becomes. God is the supreme effect through perfectly knowing and including the world, and everything that happens affects God and changes God. There is, however, an element in God which remains the same whatever happens in the world, an eternal, non-abstract element. This means that God retains God's own integrity and wholeness in this ongoing process.[2]

1. Kung, *Beginning of All Things*, 106.
2. Franklin, "Panentheism," 818–19.

The process thinking I draw on principally is Charles Hartshorne's translation into theology of Alfred North Whitehead's process philosophy. In regard to the panentheistic nature of God, Hartshorne asserts that God is absolute, yet related to all,[3] and is not omnipotent in the traditional sense.[4] Hartshorne was convinced that classical theism as a model of God was an incorrect rendering of the central religious idea. He claimed that panentheism "is an appropriate term for the view that deity is in some real aspect distinguishable from and independent of any and all relative items, and yet, taken as an actual whole, includes all relative terms."[5]

Hartshorne's panentheistic understanding of God developed through process philosophy bears a striking resemblance to Jürgen Moltmann's panentheistic understanding of God developed through a focus on the Trinity in Christian theology. The trinitarian theology brought to bear on Whitehead and Hartshorne's process idea of God will therefore be indebted to the work of Jürgen Moltmann. In Moltmann's social trinitarianism "the triune God is at home *in* his world, and his world exists *out of* his inexhaustible glory."[6] Moltmann looked to the experience of God "in, with and beneath each everyday experience of the world,"[7] and his notion of immanent transcendence[8] is key to the relationship of the Trinity to the universe. As he points out, if God having created the world, also dwells in the world and the world God has created exists in God,[9] any doctrine of domination that requires God's coercive power "over" the world loses coherence.[10] In turn, if the triune God is a panentheistic community of equals, a community immanent in the world and affected by it; if the Triune God participates in the destiny of creation, suffering and experiencing "annihilations,"[11] and influences the world by peaceful persuasion, then implications for relationships in the Church and in the world are significant. A monarchical view of the power of God will be very difficult to defend. There will be no justification for the domination or marginalization of women, children, homosexuals and gender diverse people, or people of color. Hierarchical and gender

---

3. Hartshorne, *Divine Relativity*.

4. Hartshorne, *Omnipotence and Theological Mistakes*.

5. Hartshorne, *Divine Relativity*, 89.

6. Moltmann, *Trinity and the Kingdom*, 128.

7. Moltmann, *Spirit of Life*, 34.

8. Moltmann, *Spirit of Life*, 31.

9. Moltmann, *God in Creation*, 98.

10. Moltmann, *God in Creation*, 99.

11. Moltmann, *God in Creation*, 97.

biased leadership models in the Church will be reshaped, and any attempt to explain evil, suffering and disaster as the will of God will be set aside.

A challenge for this study is the difference between the languages of philosophy and theology. Process thinking, certainly that of Whitehead, is essentially philosophy. Although Hartshorne sought to theologize aspects of Whitehead, and developed his own system that overlapped Whiteheads', in many ways he continued with a metaphysic as much as a theology. Hartshorne could see that process philosophy could be advantageous for Christian theology in ways that earlier naturalistic and idealistic philosophies were not, because process thinking recognizes the qualitative discontinuities in human existence and does not identify God with any natural process.[12] Hartshorne recognized the metaphysical/philosophical[13] nature of the ideas he was working with, even as he sought to use the language of theology in their consideration, and this issue will be exacerbated as trinitarian theology is brought into the mix. As process thinking is properly a philosophy and notions of Trinity are properly theology, finding a vocabulary that bridges the gap between the two disciplines will be necessary in giving due consideration to a potential understanding of God as a Trinity in process.

It would be naïve to think that any theology at all could be done without an involvement with power and its interactions, whether power and God's exercise thereof was intended to be a key factor. The feminist theologian Elisabeth Schüssler Fiorenza challenges the theological endeavor by pointing out that no theology materializes out of nowhere but is located in socio-political contexts which are "always already implicated" in power relations.[14] In other words, structures and strategies of domination or emancipation are already socially established and our theologies can either support them or seek to change them for the better. Following Michel Foucault, Fiorenza notes the connection between knowledge and power in academic discourses (particularly in theology), and further that language itself is a form of power.[15] This means that "language is not a mere vehicle for the transmission of social and historical context but the producer of meaning."[16]

Focusing on language about God and power from different contexts may well assist the aforementioned bridge building between the vocabularies

---

12. Reves and Brown, "Development of Process Theology," 34.

13. As metaphysics is the branch of philosophy that deals with the nature of reality, in this book the terms metaphysics and philosophy will be used interchangeably.

14. Fiorenza, *Politics of Interpretation*, 4–5.

15. Fiorenza, *Politics of Interpretation*, 14.

16. Fiorenza, *Politics of Interpretation*, 16.

of metaphysics and theology, specifically those of Hartshorne and Molt-mann. It will also be important in my critique, analysis, and curation of some of the ongoing discourses of the Christian Church regarding power and its relationship to the way God has been modelled over the Christian centuries, along with how these discourses have played out in power relations within the church. As Fiorenza observes, the time of the early Jesus movement was not some halcyon age where there was a perfect and unambiguous understanding of what it was to be a discipleship of equals. Rather, from its earliest days and continuing now, there is conflict within the discipleship of equals between "those who understand Christian identity as radically inclusive and egalitarian and those who advocate *kyriarchal* domination and submission," such domination and submission being grounded in gender, and in class and race and other features of human identity.[17]

Important for this book is how the manner of our talk about power and God has implications for social relations within church and society, and how these have effects on the bodies and lives of individuals and groups when power is abused.[18] On this account my work is both practical and relevant, for without a deeper awareness of the real connection between theologies of power and the outworking of human relations, people will be bound to continue having to bear the scars of the misuse of power. I'm keen, therefore, to make clear from the outset that I am concentrating specifically on power and God, and how understandings about God's power do have practical application to life in social contexts. Further, that the understandings of power I criticize are not just inadequate theologically or theoretically, they are also morally wrong and harmful to relationships in the world and in the church. They result in bad pastoral care at one end of the scale of harm right through to physical, sexual, and emotional abuse and violence at the other. It is, in fact, this array of harmful outcomes in human society that has compelled me to attempt to right the "wrong" at the heart of this book, the wrong being to define God's power as dominant control.

---

17. Fiorenza, *Politics of Interpretation*, 49.

18. Foucault noted the role of the human body in power relations, insisting that discipline (which for him is one and the same as exercising power) "produces subjected and practiced bodies, 'docile bodies.'" *Discipline and Punish*, 146. Examples of power as discipline/domination having effects on bodies are found in any penal system. In such a context people can be incarcerated and/or their physical actions regulated. In the church, power can affect bodies through the forming of doctrines and legislation regarding human sexuality and through associated directives from church leaders. Confining sexual relations to heterosexual marriage is one example of this.

1

POWER, GOD, AND CREATION

Then everything includes itself in power: power into will, will into appetite, and appetite, an universal wolf, so doubly seconded with will and power, must make perforce an universal prey, and last eat up himself.

— William Shakespeare, *Troilus and Cressida*, Act 1, Scene 3

Then the Lord answered Job out of the whirlwind: "Who is this that darkens counsel by words without knowledge?"

— Job 38:1–2 (NRSV)

P ower is the capacity to act or do. Anyone or anything that has strength or potency to take any action, to do anything at all, has power. The words most often used as synonyms for power are control, domination, authority, and force.[1] These words and the expectations about the exercise of power that lie behind them are often hung on our notions of God: the formal notions that emerge from theology and the colloquial notions that stem from a general idea of, or wondering about, the divine. This chapter explores how

---

1. Weber (translated by Keith Tribe in 2019) defines power as "every *Chance*, within a social relationship, of enforcing one's own will even against resistance, whatever the basis for this *Chance* might be." He notes that the idea of power is "socially amorphous" in that "any conceivable quality of a person, and all conceivable constellations, can place someone in a position of being able to enforce one's own will in a given situation." Weber then broadens the semantic field to connect the concept of power with "rulership," "command," "discipline," and "obedience." Weber, *Economy and Society*, 134–35.

concepts of power are intricately linked with the way God is and has been conceived, both philosophically as an idea and religiously as a position of faith. It begins with an overview of two highly influential visions of God, classical theism, and deism, both of which explain God as omnipotent over the world and separate from it. From perceptions of power connected to notions of the rule of an almighty and transcendent God, two key theories about power in human relationships, those of Max Weber and Michel Foucault, are then briefly examined to demonstrate that power understood as domination is culturally embedded. This analysis of power as a concept within society concentrates on the social wrong that understands God's power as domination and control, and what meaning that understanding produces for human relationship.

The next focus of this chapter is on theologians of power who, due to their collective dissatisfaction with power understood as domination, have been working on at least three fronts simultaneously. They have been working against theologies that cast God as omnipotent in the traditional sense, against theologies that remain in a prescientific worldview and do not take current science seriously, and against the cultural norm which continues to associate power with domination and control. It explores what theologians must consider so that emerging theologies of power are not immersed in and determined by previous theological and cultural assumptions. Instead, by critically engaging with older views, the idea is to develop an understanding of God's power that is compatible both with scripture and contemporary science.

The solution proposed in this chapter, and explained in this book, to problems associated with God's power understood as traditional omnipotence is to move beyond both theism and deism to understand God and God's exercise of power panentheistically. This shift in thinking requires a willingness to embrace a balance between the immanence and transcendence of God, and to challenge the established view that true power exerts coercive control. The chapter concludes with the questions in the book of Job which have given voice to the persistent wondering of people of faith over centuries about God's exercise of power.

GOD AND POWER

Classical theism is the conventional view of God in the history of philosophy and has made an indelible imprint on a Christian vision of God. Its ancestry can be traced through Plato, Aristotle, Middle Platonism and Neoplatonism, and it can be detected in Christianity as early as Irenaeus and Clement of Alexandria. By the time the Roman Empire was on the wane classical theism had been widely accepted as Christian orthodoxy. Although increasingly challenged from c.1300, it remains at the center of the mainstream understanding of God in Christianity. Classical theism unfolds from the claim that God is the ultimate reality, and includes the divine attributes of omnipresence, omniscience, and omnipotence. This view of God as the ultimate reality is also associated with other attributes of God, including aseity (self-sufficiency) and simplicity (being without parts). Further, God is immaterial (not made of matter), without accidents (non-relational), immutable (unchanging), impassible (beyond suffering), eternal (beyond time) and necessarily existent (immune from non-existence). Thus, in classical theism, God is infinite or unlimited. This manifests in God being completely independent of anything else.[2]

With its emphasis upon the utter transcendence, immutability and impassibility of God, classical theism leaves process thinkers (among others) unconvinced. Process theology looks instead to a both/and: the transcendence of God alongside the active involvement of God in the world. Through the eyes of Whitehead, who viewed God as primordial, God is in the strict sense complete, eternal, unchanging and contains all possibilities. Yet in God's consequent nature, which is inseparable from his primordial nature, God is in some sense incomplete, due to being involved in every historical and creative process, luring each process by a primordial vision of truth, beauty, and goodness.[3] Hartshorne went on to argue actively and overtly throughout his career against classical theism. On his view, the absence of any relativity or dependence in God inherent in classical theism is illogical and does not match up with either the nature of reality or with religious experience.[4] In the conclusion to his *Omnipotence and Other Theological Mistakes*, with the telling sub-heading "What Went Wrong in Classical Theism,"[5] Hartshorne insists that God is not separate from us or from the world, rather that:

> The whole cosmos must everywhere directly communicate with God, each member furnishing its own psychical content (its feelings or thoughts) to the Soul. In turn, the member, in whatever way its own type of individuality makes possible, and

---

2. Leftow, "Classical Theism."

3. Long, *Western Philosophy of Religion*, 382; Whitehead, *Process and Reality*.

4. Hartshorne, *Divine Relativity*.

5. Hartshorne, *Omnipotence and Other Theological Mistakes*, 6.

across the two-way bridge of sympathy or feeling of feeling, receives influences from divine feeling or thought.[6]

Moltmann similarly rejects classical theism. In his case, he finds that
its essential concepts are insufficient to support a satisfactory trinitarian
theology. At the beginning of *Trinity and the Kingdom of God*, he flags a
question about how the "specifically Christian doctrine of the Trinity" fits
in with the "general concepts of God as supreme substance and absolute
subject," and indeed whether the Trinity can "provide us with the matrix
for a new kind of thinking about God, the world, and man."[7] Moltmann
explains his intentions thus:

> In distinction to the trinity of substance and to the trinity of
> subject we shall be attempting to develop a social doctrine of
> the Trinity. We understand the scriptures as the testimony to the
> history of the Trinity's relations of fellowship, which are open to
> men and women, and open to the world. This trinitarian herme-
> neutics leads us to think in terms of relationships and commu-
> nities; it supersedes the subjective thinking which cannot work
> without the separation and isolation of its objects.[8]

For Moltmann, therefore, classical theism denotes an idea of God that
is far too static and invulnerable; an idea of God that fails to do justice to the
testimony of the Bible.

Considerations such as these from process thought, from Hartshorne,
and from Moltmann as he developed his Social Trinity have not prevented
the ongoing influence on theology by the classical view, particularly when it
comes to the way God's exercise of power is understood. The otherness and
might of God that the classical view espouses goes hand in hand with the
notion of omnipotence, and the idea of a dominant and controlling God.
This idea of God is bound up in hymns, prayers, and liturgies that reinforce
the idea that God is unremittingly in charge of every aspect of the course
of history. Take the first three verses of the well-known hymn by Walter
Chalmers Smith (1824–1908) as an example:

> Immortal, invisible, God only wise,
> In light inaccessible hid from our eyes,
> Most blessed, most glorious, the Ancient of Days,
> Almighty, victorious, thy great name we praise.
> Unresting, unhasting, and silent as light,

6. Hartshorne, *Theological Mistakes*, 135.

7. Moltmann, *Trinity and the Kingdom*, 16.

8. Moltmann, *Trinity and the Kingdom*, 19.

Nor wanting, nor wasting, thou rulest in might.
Thy justice like mountains high soaring above,
Thy clouds which are fountains of goodness and love.
To all life Thou givest, to both great and small;
In all life Thou livest, the true life of all;
We blossom and flourish as leaves on the tree,
And wither and perish, but nought changeth Thee.[9]

The hymn summarizes key elements of the classical view of God. It focuses on the transcendence of a Holy Other in terms of inaccessibility, separation, and hiddenness. The word almighty is synonymous with omnipotence, and the kingly and high court images of rule and justice (albeit tempered with love) in the hymn connect strongly with the idea of overarching power to direct and to discipline. The third verse affirms a God who does not change in any manner at all, a God unmoved and unaffected by the created order.

During the lifetime of the hymn writer, Walter Chalmers Smith, the prevailing worldview was changing. The change was associated with new thinking about the origins of the world surrounding the work of Charles Darwin (1809–1882) and others on natural selection and the concomitant rise of a scientific worldview in the mid-to-late-nineteenth-century. Effectively a modern spinoff from classical theism, deism sought to explain the divine in relation to a world quite differently understood. It separated culture and science from God, which resulted in the idea of a divine being necessary only in explaining the world's contingent beginning.[10] Deism therefore emphasizes the transcendence of God even more than the classical theism from which it developed. The earlier deterministic and reductionist principles of Newtonian physics leant support to the idea of a deity of awesome power, sovereign and absolute, the "Lord of Dominion" and "Ruler Supreme." In the context of the Industrial Revolution God was regarded as the "Great Mechanic," the one who set the world in motion before retiring to rule over it from the heavenly realms. This powerful God of "First Cause" remained resolutely separate from the world. His dominion was the universe, the divine sensorium. Deism gave God a very limited role indeed, one which involved ensuring that the celestial bodies continued to spin in what

9. Smith, "Immortal, Invisible," vv. 1–3.

10. Moltmann, "Reflections on Chaos," 218. Hartshorne agreed with Moltmann (and others) about the inadequacies of deism. Both Hartshorne and Moltmann argued for the middle ground of panentheism between the two extremes of pantheism and theism/deism. As Hartshorne explains, "traditional theism or deism makes God solely independent or noninclusive," while in pantheism "God is merely the cosmos." Hartshorne, *Divine Relativity*, 89–90.

was understood to be a mechanized universe. This limited role eventually gave rise to the controversial idea of a "God of the Gaps": a God who takes care of that for which no scientific explanation has been developed. The deist model, even more than classical theism, eventually left the Christian thought based on it stranded and defenseless against the arguments of atheists; even an all-knowing, all-powerful God who has nothing to do is no God at all.[11]

In the contemporary era, an emergent view of the world has overtaken the view espoused by deists at the beginning of the scientific revolution.[12] This is due to a mainstream acceptance of evolutionary theory and its grounding in the understanding that random change is an integral part of the processes of the world. Such a change in established worldview continues to raise important questions of purpose and meaning in the universe and has a significant impact on how it is that the Christian tradition understands and articulates God as Creator.[13]

There can be no underestimating the impact of natural selection on the way the world of nature is understood to operate. Charles Darwin, who first articulated the concept of natural selection and is on that basis the father of evolutionary theory, himself once said that going public with his ideas was like confessing to murder.[14] Due to natural selection's reliance on processes such as predation, disease, and starvation, Darwin referred to it as the "war of nature" and was disturbed and compelled by the darker side of the becoming of the world and its range of species, particularly what this might mean theologically.[15] Certainly, any attempt to rely on natural selection alone to understand the power of God at work in the world is profoundly unsatisfactory.[16] If God is seen as the external director and controller of evolution, with humans the planned end purpose, then human sin and natural evil necessarily become part of God's plan from the beginning.

---

11. Campbell, *Many Faces of God*, xvii.

12. Gregersen, "Primer on Complexity," 14. Deism is much more than a nineteenth-century phenomenon, finding its roots in sixteenth-century Poland. Campbell, *Many Faces of God*, 121. Key proponents of deism in Great Britain include Matthew Tindal (1657–1733) and William Wollaston (1659–1724); in the United States of America, Benjamin Franklin (1706–1790) and especially Thomas Jefferson (1743–1826); and in France, Voltaire (Francois-Marie Arouet, 1694–1778) and Maximilien Robespierre (1758–1794).

13. Edwards, *God of Evolution*, 45–46.

14. Flannery, *Here on Earth*, 7.

15. Sideris, *Environmental Ethics*, 3.

16. King, "Interpretations of Complexity in Nature," 57.

It would also mean that the suffering and perpetual perishing that is the lot of created beings was deliberately built into nature by God.[17]

Instead of casting God as an outside force compelling the species of the world into being, it is far more helpful to view the interface of chance and natural law over time as that which brings about the right conditions for natural selection to operate. This perspective enables the processes of evolutionary biology to begin to explain the origin of evil. Evil and suffering become the logical consequence of creaturely freedom to develop and become in an ongoing, open system. On this view the system of the world operates in an unfinished universe with creatures necessarily imperfect.[18]

The system of contingency, lawful constraint, and abundant time that typifies Darwin's natural selection is fully emergent. It allows entities, characterized by their distinctive properties and processes, to emerge out of the processes that constitute the entities, properties, and processes of the levels below them.[19] This points to an inherent openness in the evolutionary process in which God can legitimately act. It is not a deist-type "God of the Gaps" action because God is not directly breaking into the natural world and intervening in evolution. Instead, God is already immanent in the world, and is therefore acting within the openness that God gifted to the universe in creation.[20]

Quantum theory also offers ways of conceptualizing God's exercise of power in the world. "Bottom-up" causality originates at lower levels and gives potential for God's exercise of a continuous influence on the course of evolution. "Top-down" causality is where higher level events impose boundary conditions of chemical and physical processes at lower levels. God could work in this way to constrain the possibilities on the world. There are also the changing probability patterns according to the theory of autopoietic processes, a theory which proposes that systems are both self-organizing and produce or change their own elements.[21] Physicists who have a Christian faith hold a range of views about the scope of God's possible action in the world on the basis of quantum theory, but there is wide agreement among them that a God who creates a world governed by quantum processes must be understood as a God of both law and chance.[22]

---

17. Haught, *Christianity and Science*, 51.

18. King, "Models of Invisible Realities," 40.

19. Campbell, "Process Ontology of Activity," 152.

20. Russell, *Cosmology, Evolution, Hope*, 28.

21. Barbour, "God's Action," 113; Gregersen, "World Made to Flourish," 110–11.

22. Wegter-McNelly, "Atoms May Be Small," 98.

Cosmologists point out that, had the basic characteristics of matter been different even in very tiny ways, life in general and specifically the lives of conscious human beings could not have existed. This is known as the Anthropic Principle, and, in its weak form it is widely accepted in the scientific community. The Anthropic Principle simply affirms that the universe is able to produce human beings, but it is a remarkable affirmation given the exquisite sensitivity required of the initial conditions and characteristics of matter at the beginning of the universe.[23] While anthropic balances are consistent with the Christian claim of a Creator God who calls the universe to be fruitful in terms of human life, there is no warrant for an over-attribution of the idea of design to God, as if God were a finite subject. Such an anthropomorphic concept of God wrongly reduces God's personal agency to that of a "spatio-temporal planner" rather than recognizing God as the continuously creative life behind the self-organized complexity of the universe.[24] Proponents of Intelligent Design Theory go down this unhelpful anthropomorphic track based on an amalgamation of a pre-scientific theist and a modernist deist conception of God. The resulting omnipotent, disconnected "Director of Design" approach makes God both fully responsible for all natural evil and overtly interventionist in terms of constantly working outside the laws of nature.[25] For this reason, Intelligent Design Theory is unacceptable both scientifically and theologically.

Contemporary cosmology, evolutionary and quantum theory, reveal characteristics of the world and the universe in which it is situated. These characteristics point to revised ways of understanding God in relation to the world as we know and experience it. A worldview shaped by contemporary science recognizes that the universe evolves at all levels and that natural processes have their own integrity such that they can be explained scientifically.[26] This does not mean that natural theology is all there is, or that special revelation is somehow defunct in the order of things. What it does mean is that there is no need for a "God of the Gaps" to temporarily fill in pieces of the puzzle until our understanding of the cosmos is clearer. It also means that we know already that the universe is directional and that it is moving toward greater complexity through a process of chance and lawfulness. On this basis, the power of God in creation is far better understood as a process of open development rather than a fixed divine plan ordained in

23. Edwards, *God of Evolution*, 48.

24. Gregersen, "World Made to Flourish," 83.

25. King, "Models of Invisible Realities," 34.

26. Edwards, *How God Acts*, 2–8.

every detail from all eternity.[27] The science associated with the existence of life and fecundity in the world is open to Christian interpretation at a range of levels. This can include an understanding of divine activity that operates *with* the grain of the universe, effectively a non-interventionist model of God's action in the world.[28] When all reality, including God, is conceived to be process as well as substance, God can certainly be seen as the ground of order, but it is a changing and developing order.[29]

The model of God and God's relationship with the world that functions best theologically in the light of what we are learning from science is panentheism. For the purposes of this book, the specific focus is the panentheism characteristic of Hartshorne's take on process theology, based on the philosophy of Whitehead. Central to Whitehead's thinking is the idea that God is responsible for ordering the world, but not through direct action. Instead God provides the various possibilities that the physical universe is then free to actualize. In working in this manner, God does not compromise the openness and indeterminism of the universe but is still able to encourage a trend towards good through subtle and indirect influence. This panentheistic, process vision of the God/world relation makes us participants in an unfinished universe and in God's continuing work.

Process thought fits well with an ecological and evolutionary understanding of nature as a dynamic and open system, characterized by emerging levels of organization, activity and experience.[30] In it, God's action in the world is represented as a single conceptual scheme that includes both the human and the non-human sphere. Although both process theology and a panentheistic vision of God have been criticized for departing too far from classical theology and from theism, chiefly for their rejection of the omnipotence of God and the resulting limitation of God's power in the world, it is this feature which enables evil and suffering in the world to be viewed as something that is not directly caused by God.[31] Process theology deserves high marks for internal coherence as it is consistent with what we

27. Polkinghorne, "Quantum Theology," 138.

28. Russell, *Cosmology*, 28; Haught, *Christianity and Science*; Edwards, *How God Acts*, 35.

29. Birch, *On Purpose*, 90–93.

30. Barbour, "God and Nature," 269.

31. Reducing the power of God (rather than the goodness of God) is a well-documented response to the problem of evil and suffering. For process thinkers, and some others, finding that evil can be outside of God's direct control in this way makes God *more* worthy of worship than the alternative, namely that God cannot be fully good if God has the power to curtail evil but chooses not to do so. The standard options in the dilemma are that either God is not all-powerful, not all-good, or simply does not exist.

know about cosmic, biological, and human history.[32] Due to this coherence and consistency it has the respect of many scientist theologians, even those unable or unwilling to relinquish more traditional theism.[33] Process theology, along with Hartshorne's associated panentheistic model of God, will be more fully explored in chapter 2.

HUMAN RELATIONSHIPS AND POWER

Max Weber has been described as "the last great polymath of nineteenth-century social thought"[34] due to his contributions to scholarship ranging across the theory of law, political science, sociology, economics, comparative religion, history, and the philosophy of history.[35] Most well known as a sociologist, Weber's consideration of how power operates in human relationships is such that some theologians of power preface their God-talk with reference to Weber's ideas. He located power firmly in relationships rather than seeing it as a quality of an individual. For Weber, "power is the probability that one actor within a social relationship will be in a position to carry out his will despite resistance, regardless of the basis on which this probability rests."[36] In an essay about power and the social order, Weber said:

> In general we understand by 'power' the chance of a man or of a number of men to realize their own will in a communal action even against the resistance of others who are participating in the action. . . . Man does not strive for power only in order to enrich himself economically. Power, including economic power, may be valued 'for its own sake.' Very frequently the striving for power is also conditioned by the social 'honor' it entails.[37]

When people exercise power, they use the resources they have to influence others. It is, nevertheless, the motives and evaluations of *the other* that determine whether those resources actuate as negative or positive sanctions, along with how much purchase the sanctions will have over the actions of the other.[38] This social exchange theory recognizes that the resources deployed

32. Barbour, "God and Nature," 125, 266.

33. Russell, *Cosmology*, 106.

34. Wrong, *Max Weber*, 8.

35. Wrong, *Max Weber*, 1.

36. Weber, *Economy and Society*, 53.

37. Weber, *Essays in Sociology*, 180.

38. Mennell, *Sociological Theory*, 102.

in the exercise of power are countless. They include whatever constitutes inducements and deterrents to those subject to them. Examples include income, property, sacramental and religious practices, bureaucratic office, and access to information, knowledge, skills, and charisma. Weber demonstrates the intimate connection between the established values and interests of a society and the forms of domination found in it.[39] Resources can yield domination to which people may comply without necessarily considering it legitimate. Domination which those dominated regard as legitimate or morally justified is usually referred to using the term "authority".[40]

"Authority" is a term behind which the stronger words "power" and "domination" can be hidden. This is due to "authority" generally being deemed a more benign word, one that carries with it a sense of the legitimate and appropriate exercise of power over others. For this reason it is better suited to association with religion, for notions of raw power and domination are particularly difficult in theology.[41] Weber separates power into two basic types: the domination of others resting on the ability to influence their interests, and the domination of others resting on authority, which, for him, is the power to command and the duty to obey. In Weber's schema, the foundational criterion of authority "is a certain minimum of voluntary submission".[42] So, the distinctive feature of power exercised through authority is a belief system that describes the application of social control as legitimate. The same is true of control exercised in a religious framework.

There are three types of authority/domination distinguished by Weber grounded in the differences between the legitimizing belief systems that validate them.[43] They are traditional authority, charismatic authority, and rational-legal authority. Together they form Weber's threefold topology of legitimate authority, or legitimate domination. Whether the term used is authority or domination depends on the way the German word *Herrschaft* is translated into English.[44] The three types of legitimacy are in effect

39. Mennell, *Sociological Theory*, 103.

40. Mennell, *Sociological Theory*, 104.

41. Sykes makes just this point, suggesting that if the word "power" could be made a scapegoat for the "unacceptable negative connotations" associated with it, then the word "authority" would be free from them. He also notes that the relationship between "power" and "authority" has tended to be the domain of sociology rather than theology. Sykes, *Power and Christian Theology*, 4.

42. Weber in Blau, "Critical Remarks," 147.

43. Blau, "Critical Remarks," 150.

44. Wrong, *Max Weber*, 41. In his 2019 translation of Weber's Economy and Society, Keith Tribe affirms that "the standard English translation of *Herrschaft* . . . has been 'domination,'" although he prefers and uses "rulership" or "leadership." He points out that *Herrschaft* emerged in old German and, at least until the seventeenth century, was

normative principles which can be repeatedly and publicly invoked to justify compliance with the directives of an authority far more than they are terms of genuine and heartfelt motivations to obedience. As ideological construc-tions, rather than psychological constructions, Weber's threefold topology of legitimate domination can be described as a "political formula".[45]

Traditional authority, the first of Weber's three types, rests on a belief in the sanctity of long-established traditions and the legitimacy of those ex-ercising authority under them.[46] The current social order is seen as part of a sacred, eternal, and unbreakable trajectory. The dominant person, or group of people, most often defined by heredity, is understood to have been pre-ordained to rule over the rest. Subjects are bound to the ruler/s by personal dependence and a sense of loyalty, and their obedience to the ruler/s is fur-ther reinforced by cultural beliefs such as the divine right of kings. Systems of government developed prior to notions of the modern state exemplify traditional authority. The power of the rulers may be limited by the tradi-tions that legitimate it, but this is not a severe restriction given that some unpredictability on the part of those who rule is traditionally expected and therefore built into the system. In general, traditional authority preserves the *status quo*, making it unsuited to much social change. In fact, historical change undermines its very foundation. One idea of traditional authority is illustrated through an old saying derived from the machinations of French monarchy in the thirteenth century: "the king is dead, long live the king."[47]

Charismatic authority, Weber's second type, rests on dedication to the exceptional sanctity, valour, or exemplary character of an individual, and the normative patterns they reveal or proclaim. Such power has brought about a succession of social movements in history,[48] generally with a leader as head of a new cause followed by disciples and converts. There is a sense of calling to spread a new message, and a sense of rejecting the past and heralding the new future. Devotion to the leader, and the conviction that the declarations of the leader embody the spirit and ideals of the movement, are

---

an indeterminate term translatable into English as "dominion," but also as "authority," "command," "empire," "lordship," "mastery," "reign," "rule," and "sovereignty." Further, that *Herrschaft* "designates the manner in which social, economic, and political orders are characterized by a governing hierarchy in which decisions are made and executed by a ruling person, or group of persons." Tribe in Weber, *Economy and Society*, 471–72.

45. Wrong, *Max Weber*, 41.

46. Mennell, *Sociological Theory*, 105.

47. Blau, "Critical Remarks," 150. The origin of the saying is in the French *Le roi est mort, vive le roi!* which was first declared upon the accession to the French throne of Charles VII after the death of his father Charles VI in 1422.

48. Mennell, *Sociological Theory*, 105.

the source of the willing obedience of the group to follow commands and directives. Charismatic leaders can appear in practically any area of social life. Religious prophets, military heroes, or political icons are significant examples, but it is true to say that an element of charisma is involved whenever and wherever someone inspires others to follow their lead. Charismatic authority generally acts as a revolutionary force in that it involves a rejection of traditional values and something of a rebellion against the established order of things. Charismatic movements are often in response to a crisis, and there is, therefore, an anarchistic streak within them. There can be a certain distain for routine tasks and the minutiae of organization and administration, due to a keen desire that the leader's inspiration and the cause at hand are not diminished by mundane considerations. Weber suggested that the spirit of innovation that defines charismatic authority is captured in Jesus' words: "It is written . . . but I say to you . . ."[49] It is noteworthy that charismatic authority inevitably becomes reduced to the far more customary procedure represented by one of the other typologies when the charismatic leader disappears.[50]

The third type, rational-legal authority, finds its legitimization in a belief in the supremacy of the law regardless of the specific content of that law. It is founded on the acceptance of the idea that the law has been established intentionally to further the rational pursuit of collective goals. In a system like this, obedience is not owed to a person, to neither king nor charismatic leader, but to the principle of law. This principle includes an obligation to follow directives coming from those who have a higher office in the system, regardless of who occupies that office. All organizations that have been formally established illustrate rational-legal authority structures. The prototype is modern government, which has a monopoly over the legitimate use of physical coercion. The same principles are reflected in the various executive agencies of government, such as the defense forces, and in private corporations, like a business, for example. While managers have authority over workers, both are subject to the authority of the law. The idea of "a government of laws, not of men," well sums up rational-legal authority.[51]

When it comes to social organization, Weber recognized that if a leader or ruler is to permanently dominate large numbers of people, they

49. Blau, "Critical Remarks," 150–51. Matthew 5:44 (NRSV) and the beatitudes are examples of this phraseology of Jesus in the gospels.

50. Mennell, *Sociological Theory*, 105.

51. Blau, "Critical Remarks," 151. "A government of laws, not men" is most famously attributed to John Adams in 1780 as the Massachusetts Constitution was set in place. The desire was for the rule of law as a principle, rather than governance by the whims of individuals, whether they be elected leaders or traditional monarchs.

need a special inner group to carry out the will of the leader.[52] Stability will result if the inner group accept the leader's dominance as legitimate, be it on rational, traditional, or charismatic grounds. The power of the inner group is conceptually different to that of the leader in the view of those subject to it, but as power resources are gathered the span of power exercised is increased. Organization formalizes chains of command and improves co-ordination. This stabilization of power resources increases the probability of success in the intended outcomes of those who have social power to exercise.[53] In discussing how power is distributed in the political community, Weber focused particularly on the organization of power resources of three types: the economic, the honorific, and the politico-legal.[54] He spoke elsewhere of military and religious power resources and their corresponding social organizations.[55]

Two general effects of the overall social organization of power are worth noting briefly here. The first is that organizations formed to express the ideals and interests of one group often stimulate the organization of groups whose ideals and interests are the antithesis of theirs. This is as true of protest political parties as it is of competing religious ideologies. The second is that social organization based around one kind of power resource may make possible the acquisition of other resources. For instance, military and political power may be the stepping-stones to economic resources, or groups with economic power may find themselves entitled to a level of social honor. It is, of course, social, and historical circumstances that determine which power resources enable others to be gained; Weber was quite cautious about generalizing about the sources of power across all societies.[56]

Weber's theory of power is one among many, but any theorizing about power is entwined with definitions of authority, legitimization, and force. As already revealed in the translation from German to English of Weber's thought, it is not at all uncommon for the word "authority" to be used as a euphemism for "power" and a synonym for "domination." This is so even when it is properly power that is at stake rather than the legitimization of power that the word authority invokes. It is so when power could be exercised in ways other than domination. This cultural norm makes it very difficult to name power differently to authority and domination; ironically, it also compounds the exploitation of those who have less of it. A cultural

---

52. Weber, *Economy and Society*, 212.

53. Mennell, *Sociological Theory*, 106.

54. Weber, *Economy and Society*, 927–37.

55. Mennell, *Sociological Theory*, 106.

56. Mennell, *Sociological Theory*, 107.

norm of power understood as authority and domination can also lead to negative understandings of, and feelings about, power as an overall concept. Whenever power is used *over* others, or *against* others, in manipulative ways, negative feelings are invoked. There are certainly positive ways to experience or think about power, and these include power *to be* and power *to do*,[57] that essential agency that rightly belongs to individuals, groups, and organizations. When power is regularly couched as domination, however, these positive aspects of power can very easily be overlooked.

Game theory investigates the strategic behavior of those who have power to exercise in social relationships and who are aware that their decisions and choices affect others. This theory has had a significant impact on the social sciences and related fields. It is summarized here in a very simple form as a potentially useful contributor to ways of thinking about power in relationships, divine and human, and particularly to our norms and expectations about relational power.

While any social interaction may be termed a game with rules and a set of players, game theory is marked by its analysis of the logic and strategic behavior of the players, especially in regard to the responses of players to the moves or decisions of each other.[58] It emerged from the economic theories of the nineteenth and twentieth century and was enhanced by mathematicians such as Emile Borel and Ernst Zermelo in the early twentieth century.[59] The earliest theorem of game theory is named after Zermelo and relates to a game of chess. It asserts that in a game of chess played in perfect conditions there are three possible outcomes. Black can win, white can win, or there can be a draw. In this respect, Zermelo argued, chess is strictly determined. The theory does not suggest correct strategies for play, nor a correct outcome, but applies to two-person zero-sum games conducted under the aforementioned perfect conditions: namely that all relevant information including payoffs and the possible strategies of all players is known to all players. Games such as chess, checkers and Chinese checkers are zero-sum. In this kind of game, the victory of one player is the loss of the other.[60]

The creation and distribution of social power may be conceived as either "zero-sum" or "non-zero-sum." As just explained, zero-sum in games

57. Ogden, "Power," 128–29.

58. Calhoun, *Dictionary of the Social Sciences*, 183.

59. Calhoun, *Dictionary of the Social Sciences*, 184. Von Neumann and Morgenstern's *Theory of Games* is widely considered to be the foundational text of game theory. Game theory has become a term denoting a wide-ranging body of work on a range of social issues including cartel behavior, conflict resolution, and collective bargaining, for example.

60. Calhoun, *Dictionary of the Social Sciences*, 184.

theory describes a system in which the winner gains what the loser loses, so that the sum of gains and losses is zero. It applies exclusively to closed systems in which the players gain nothing from, nor lose anything to, people outside the game, and in which the game itself provides no additional benefits like the enjoyment of playing. The zero-sum notion of power can be summarized by a simple equation: if one person or group has thirty units of power (for example), then those over whom power is exercised must therefore have *minus* thirty units of power. While a zero-sum game is artificially closed most real relationships are, however, open. In a non-zero-sum system, the support of allies can be enlisted, which makes the amount of power resources in play indeterminate and fluctuating. The value of the winner's gains may exceed the value of the opponents' losses, or, in a pyrrhic victory, be less. It is much less straightforward in the complex network of social relationships reflected in a non-zero-sum system to work out how gains and losses add up overall.[61]

The terms zero-sum and non-zero-sum work as metaphors representing different aspects of power relationships. Sociologists who are interested in the zero-sum idea are focused on how power resources are distributed in society at any given time and whether one person or sector can achieve its will in the face of opposition. This is effectively a "power *over*" model. In contrast, those who are more interested in the non-zero-sum support a "power *with*" model which focuses on the possibility of attracting the consent and support of enough people to achieve collective objectives.[62]

Game theory further describes the seeking of objectives that benefit a group, rather than the individual, as the coalitional or cooperative approach. Such cooperative games favor examining the possibilities for agreement among a group and the division of available payoffs among members or coalitions within the group depending on their various contributions. In contrast, the strategic or non-cooperative approach generally disallows any group coordination, emphasizing instead the individual player and the strategies that are optimal for them. The basic terminology of game theory is increasingly being used in theology to describe relationships, especially regarding aspects of theologies of power.[63] Before turning to power and

61. Mennell, *Sociological Theory*, 108.

62. Mennell, *Sociological Theory*, 108.

63. See, for example, Nowak and Coakley, *Evolution, Games, and God*. In this essay collection the authors use game theory to inform mechanisms through which cooperation (which they define as "a form of working together in which one individual benefits at the cost of another") arises through natural selection. Johnson also references the non-zero-sum aspect of game theory to describe God's exercise of power in the world as "a saving, healing, restoring power that benefits human beings." Johnson, *Ask the*

theology, I will give an overview of Michel Foucault's philosophy of power. In the language of game theory, Foucault's notion of power as discipline, much like Weber's sociological model, can be explained almost exclusively in zero-sum and non-cooperative terms.

A French philosopher, Michel Foucault was preoccupied with power as a social and political concept and wrote extensively on it in the middle of the twentieth century. He insisted that power in and of itself is neither good nor bad. In fact, he leans in his earlier writings at least, towards power as a positive rather than a negative force:

> We must cease once and for all to describe the effects of power in negative terms . . . power produces; it produces reality; it produces domains of objects and rituals of truth.[64]

The ethics of power is, for Foucault, grounded in the way it is exercised and in what it produces. His philosophical approach to power famously holds no seamless consensus on its meaning and significance from the beginning to the end of his career.[65] What it does do consistently is to "name" power rather than hiding it behind apparently benign notions of authority as previously discussed in the overview of Weber. Foucault's approach to power importantly shows how it links to knowledge and how this connection can be used to marginalize the other.[66]

The aphorism "knowledge is power," often attributed to Sir Francis Bacon (1561–1626), reminds us that knowledge is a *source* of power, but equally significant is the understanding that power is used to construct knowledge claims.[67] In Foucault's words, "we are subjected to the production of truth through power and we cannot exercise power except through the production of truth."[68] Put simply, those with the most power are those who create the truths of any culture or people group, and these cultural truths become things simply *known to be right*. An example of this in a patriarchal society is the accepted truth that it is inappropriate for men to

---

Beasts, 157. Her insistence that God's power does not play out as a zero-sum game in which the gain of one protagonist is the other's loss is developed in chapter 5.

64. Foucault, *Discipline and Punish*, 194.

65. Elden, *Birth of Power*, 185–89.

66. Ogden, "Power," 129. Ogden finds Foucault's approach to power particularly helpful for his essay exploring the relationship between difference and power and how it manifests in the Anglican Church. He suggests that it is an "Anglican inclination" to avoid the use of the word "power" in favor of the gentler sounding "authority," as if power is purely a secular issue. He further contends that this refusal to properly name power in the Anglican Church compounds the exploitation of others.

67. Ogden, "Power," 129.

68. Foucault, "Two Lectures," 93.

undertake menial domestic tasks. In certain parts of the Christian Church the knowledge claim that "we have always known homosexuality is wrong" is another example of power being used to create a "truth."[69] Foucault insisted that the relationship between the three distinct elements of truth, power and the subject of knowledge is absolutely pivotal, and that none of the three elements can ever be reduced to the others.[70] He states:

> The political and economic conditions of existence are not a veil or an obstacle for the subject of knowledge but the means by which subjects of knowledge are formed, and hence relations of truth. There cannot be particular types of subjects of knowledge, orders of truth, or domains of knowledge except on the basis of political conditions that are the very ground on which the subject, the domains of knowledge, and the relations of truth are formed.[71]

In his writings and lectures Foucault used this power/knowledge/truth dynamic to demonstrate a multifaceted understanding of power covering everything from prison reform and psychiatric practise to population studies. In its early stages his work considered the notion of power *over* people. Later his understanding developed into a strong sense of the inherent power *of* people. An enduring theme is that power is dynamic and is expressed in relationships, so that no one institution, group or individual ever has a monopoly on power. Every person or group has some power, even if it is expressed as compliance or submission.[72] In moving from an understanding of power as sovereignty to this more dispersed model, Foucault understood power to be less possessed than exercised and not emanating from a centralized source. He also came to describe power predominantly as discipline.

Power as discipline is not concentrated in a named and visible individual, but instead it is power that produces an effect on its target, and particularly on the body and the person of that target.[73] Two key sources of this new form of power as discipline were religious practices and the military. Foucault suggests that through the fourteenth and fifteenth centuries the emergence of disciplinary measures can be traced in everyday life, in pedagogy, and in the generalized discipline of the convent and asceticism. This spread through society in the ensuing centuries, taking center stage in the nineteenth. Foucault discusses earlier models of discipline in the Cistercian

69. Ogden, "Power," 130.

70. Foucault, *Courage of Truth*, 8–9.

71. Foucault in Elden, *Birth of Power*, 39.

72. Ogden, "Power," 132.

73. Elden, *Birth of Power*, 115.

monasteries and the orders of Cluny and Citeaux of the eleventh and twelfth centuries in his work and describes the colonization of South America by the Jesuits as effectively the creation of "disciplinary microcosms."[74]

So, Foucault believed that power exercised in the social ordering of human life through politics and government, the family, the church, or any other authority was always power as discipline. Furthermore, he asserted that all disciplinary systems are an occupation of the time, the life, and the body of the individual.[75] This relationship between power effected and the body is most important in terms of the exercise of power/discipline in the creation of normalcy and the shunning of difference in human societal groupings. Foucault said of discipline:

> The sentence that condemns or acquits is not simply a judgement of guilt, a legal decision that lays down punishment; it bears within it an assessment of normalcy and a technical prescription for a possible normalization.[76]

The human body therefore plays a role in power relations. Foucault insisted that discipline (which for him is coterminous with the exercise of power) "produces subjected and practiced bodies, 'docile' bodies."[77] He said that the body is *always* at issue, the body and the forces of the body, their usefulness and their compliance, their distribution, and their submission.[78] For Foucault, then, the make-up of the human individual is a product of the exercise of power as discipline. On his view there are two ways of looking at any individual. The first is to see the individual as an abstract subject with rights that no power can remove unless they consent by contract. The second is to see the individual as an historical reality, subject to productive and political forces. This individual is a subjectified body held in a system of surveillance and submitted to procedures of normalization.[79]

In his writing and thinking overall, Foucault considers power to be something like a matrix that pervades society and is conveyed in a range

---

74. Elden, *Birth of Power*, 115.

75. Elden, *Birth of Power*, 117.

76. Foucault, *Discipline and Punish*, 21–22.

77. Foucault, *Discipline and Punish*, 146.

78. Foucault, *Discipline and Punish*, 24. An example of power as discipline occupying the time, life, and particularly the body of an individual is to be found in any penal system, where people can be incarcerated and/or their physical actions regulated. An example in the Church is the forming of doctrines regarding human sexuality and associated directives from Church leaders.

79. Foucault in Elden, *Birth of Power*, 118–19.

of ways.[80] In describing human individuals as abstract subjects rather than objects, and recognizing the human rights that attend this description, he captures a key contemporary understanding of what it is to be a person in church and society; he captures the way we like to think of ourselves in democratic societies and in voluntary associations with such organizations as the Church, as free and equal and having a certain power. At one and the same time as acknowledging that humans are abstract subjects with rights, Foucault insists that the exercise of power in the systems of human society not only discipline, shape, and seek to normalize us, they also produce our knowledge and truths.

Although Foucault did move over time from an understanding of power purely as sovereignty to a more dispersed model where, if not exactly shared, power of some sort was at least held by all, he continued to use the language of domination and control to speak of the exercise of power throughout his career. Despite his insights about the relation of power to knowledge, to accepted truths and normalcy, the language of discipline and punish and domination suggests that Foucault remained firmly in a non-cooperative zero-sum framework in his thinking about power. Kyle A. Pasewark, whose theology of power includes a significant analysis of Foucault, insists that Foucault's influential mature theory of power can only be understood according to a model of domination.[81] It is to Pasewark I now turn to begin considering some theologies of power.

THEOLOGIES OF POWER

Pasewark proposes an ontological account of power that seeks to bridge any perceived gap between love and power in God.[82] His attempt to make a fully benevolent understanding of God sit comfortably with what he sees as the reality of domination by God relies on the success of his stated aim in writing. His aim is to steer a course between a complete transvaluation of power, which eliminates any relationship between sovereignty and power, and a complete identification of power with domination.[83] It is an uneasy balance. For Pasewark, domination is without doubt a blighted manifestation of

---

80. Ogden, "Power," 132.

81. Pasewark, *Theology of Power*, 33.

82. A perceived gap between power and love in traditional models of God is a major concern of process thought. See Whitehead, *Science and the Modern World*, 222–23, and Hartshorne, *Man's Vision of God*, 14. Power in process thought will be more fully explored in chapter 2.

83. Pasewark, *Theology of Power*, 5.

power. At the same time, it is a manifestation derived, although alienated from, the way things are in God, whom he sees as the source of all power. He insists that the power of being originates in God as the "communication of efficacy,"[84] and that God is essentially beneficent. God exercises sovereignty through the ability to constitute being and make it productive, but such a conferral of power depends on a critical moment of encounter "at the borders" between God and other.[85]

In developing a theology of power, Pasewark acknowledges that in Foucault the balances of power are considerably more malleable than in many other theories but insists that the stubborn alternatives of victor and vanquished in the exercise of power has not been changed or developed effectively by him. Tapping into what he sees as key evidence of a zero-sum framework in Foucault's thinking about power, Pasewark says:

> If power is dangerous, if its balances must be worked out in terms
> of victory and defeat, and if, additionally, power is ubiquitous,
> it seems to follow that existence is a perpetual and meaningless
> battle. This is an intolerable alternative for Christian theology.[86]

He concludes that understanding power as domination or control, as both Weber and Foucault have done is ultimately destructive of being.[87] Noting the growing dissatisfaction in the latter part of the twentieth century with power defined as domination in sociology, philosophy, and theology, Pasewark offers a theological interpretation of power with the following main features. Firstly, agreeing with both Weber and Foucault, he affirms that power is indeed both ubiquitous and unavoidable, and is the fundamental description of being itself.[88] He then seeks to go beyond the insights of sociology and philosophy, insisting that our understanding of power cannot remain captive to political power, especially when we are considering the power of God.[89] Drawing on the thinking of the protestant reformer, Martin Luther, and the Christian existentialist philosopher, Paul Tillich, he postulates a basic definition of power as a communication of efficacy that is expressed at the border of encounter.[90] For Pasewark:

84. Pasewark, *Theology of Power*, 5.
85. Pasewark, *Theology of Power*, 5.
86. Pasewark, *Theology of Power*, 34.
87. Pasewark, *Theology of Power*, 3.
88. Pasewark, *Theology of Power*, 336.
89. Pasewark, *Theology of Power*, 5.
90. Pasewark, *Theology of Power*, 6.

> Instead of power's being completed in exclusive possession, it
> is fulfilled only as a unity of universal and deep power. Power,
> insofar as it is essential power, is saving power. The ethical im-
> plications of this view emerge from within power itself, rather
> than being placed in the impossible situation of attempting to
> control power from the outside.[91]

To describe God's power as a communication of efficacy is to recognize that
the power of God is only truly divine power because it is *used for us.* Pasewark further claims that human power is only truly power, rather than a
destructive distortion, when it produces power *for others.*[92] For him, the life
and power of God is founded in the benefits provided believers, which then
appears as power provided for the good of the neighbor.[93] Keen to avoid a
theology of power that only *pretends* to escape the identification of power
with sovereignty, Pasewark looks to God's activity in creation:

> Nowhere could an identification of power and sovereignty be
> so much in evidence in Christian theology as in the doctrine of
> creation *ex nihilo.* What is created is a sovereign and exclusive
> decision of divine will. In the originating moment of creation,
> however it is understood, power must be purely external because
> there is no creaturely 'inwardness' in existence, and it must be
> exclusive because there is no other power. This is significant not
> only for our examination of the relation between power and
> creation but also because it indicates how far from the usual
> political understanding of power Christian thought that takes
> the doctrine of creation out of nothing seriously should be. In
> political theory, the logical aim of power, identified with ex-
> ternal sovereignty, is an ever-increasing dominion over one's
> opponents. Possibilities of increase in one's own power depend
> on corresponding decreases in power for all other participants
> in the power game. The quest for power is finally a quest for
> omnipotence. The striving to acquire more power has its logical
> completion in one's becoming the only power.[94]

Pasewark notes that the appropriation by theology of an equivalence
between power and domination, and the implied zero-sum and non-cooperative character of power, should be significantly limited by the Christian
notion of creation *ex nihilo,* but that it very rarely is. He argues that if the

---

91. Pasewark, *Theology of Power,* 336.

92. Pasewark, *Theology of Power,* 197. Emphasis mine.

93. Pasewark, *Theology of Power,* 198.

94. Pasewark, *Theology of Power,* 199.

objective that power seeks is pure domination, that objective already belonged to God before creation. He explains that "if nothing is except God, then by definition God has all power by virtue of being the only power."[95] Furthermore, he points out that the action of God creating power not identical with God, even if that creation stands under God, is the complete antithesis of what one would expect if the starting point is the usual political identification of power and domination.[96]

Regarding this contradiction between the purpose of power in sovereignty theory and the action of God in creation, Pasewark notes three possible conclusions. He first points out that any claim that God is omnipotent in the traditional sense, in the light of God creating something other than God, is senseless. The most one could say about this is that God is potentially omnipotent and dominant over all things but engages in a self-limitation of divine power.[97]

Second, Pasewark explains that it could be proposed that power requires an other in order to be exercised; in order to show itself fully. While claiming a level of truth in this proposal, he recognizes that if it is coupled with an equation of power as domination/control/sovereignty, an irresolvable ontological conflict is created:

> On the one hand, power as domination requires an other in order to dominate it. On the other, it must seek the destruction of that other, since the other is always a threat to domination because it constitutes a non-identical center of power which robs and decreases one's own power. Domination seeks to create puppets, but the puppet is never utterly controlled by the puppeteer. If it were, the other would cease to be an other, being either destroyed or completely identical with the dominator, the latter of which is impossible. The subsumption of power within domination is self-defeating and self-contradictory, for if it reaches its own inner objective, it eradicates its own power in eliminating the power of all others.[98]

The third conclusion presented, and the one which represents Pasewark's own thought, is grounded in the already accepted notion of the ubiquity

---

95. Pasewark, *Theology of Power*, 199.

96. Pasewark, *Theology of Power*, 200.

97. Pasewark, *Theology of Power*, 200. This notion of the self-limitation of power in God is the position of Gilkey, *Reaping the Whirlwind*, 248–50 and a range of other theologians including Fretheim, *Suffering of God*, and *What Kind of God?* However, as Pasewark rightly points out in a footnote, if power is not essentially domination, God's creation of free beings cannot be an act of self-limitation but must be an act of power.

98. Pasewark, *Theology of Power*, 200.

of power. It is that the complex of power and control/domination as a basic conceptual identification must be broken. If it is not, Pasewark asserts, then God can only be conceived of as our greatest enemy, and as the perpetrator of a vicious and meaningless hoax. [99] Pasewark therefore reaches the over-all conclusion that a God who exercises power as domination and control cannot be the generous, liberating, renewing and reconciling God of fully articulated Christian thought. He reaches this conclusion in concert with a range of contemporary theologians who agree that understanding divine power as operating only in a model of domination and control is not only incorrect, but it has also led to an impasse in the theodicy problem and has extraordinarily negative implications for human relationships. [100]

In her exploration of God's power, Anna Case-Winters works from the overall thesis that the underlying meaning of power that the classical view of omnipotence presupposes is the crux of a huge problem. [101] She points out that the most common definition of omnipotence is "God can do all things," but that this definition is not sufficiently nuanced even to go close to proper-ly expressing the power of God in a contemporary worldview. She illustrates her point through describing what she calls the classical model of God and God's power through the thinking of another key protestant reformer, John Calvin. Case-Winters asserts that in Calvin power is always described in the mode of domination and control, and that he understands the power of God to be conterminous with the will of God. She suggests that in Calvin's model God is an agent very similar to a human agent. In this personal model Cal-vin relies almost exclusively on the sovereignty metaphors of Father, Lord, and King for God, and operates on the basis that creation and governance are inseparably joined. [102] Case-Winters assesses Calvin's position on God's exercise of power as "domination and control," and goes on to assert that the outcome is disastrous when this understanding of power becomes "omni" and is applied to God. [103]

For Case-Winters, this disaster unfolds on three main fronts. Firstly, in a denial of human freedom; secondly, in an aggravated theodicy problem

---

99. Pasewark, *Theology of Power*, 201.

100. Case-Winters, *God's Power*, 10–19. Migliore agrees that God's power must be understood differently to domination and control. He describes it as "the power of self-giving, liberating, renewing, and reconciling love." Migliore, *Power of God*, 35. Sykes finds no necessary connection between power and force. Sykes, *Power and Christian Theology*, 103,

101. Case-Winters, *God's Power*, 7.

102. Case-Winters, *God's Power*, 39–53.

103. Case-Winters, *God's Power*, 63.

due to the freewill defense being untenable;[104] and thirdly in oppression in human community through the divinization of power understood as dominion. She points out that Calvin did discuss theodicy, and that his two main points were that God uses evil in the execution of good purposes and that the guilt for evil is to be attributed to the evil motives of humans.[105] Case-Winters insists, however, that both of Calvin's points are unsuccessful, citing "a fundamental inconsistency in Calvin's maintaining a compatibilist framework and at the same time proposing a freewill defense as a resolution to the theodicy problem."[106]

Case-Winter asserts that Calvin operates on a "might makes right" basis, and that he finds in the sovereign will of God the source of all that is and the reason for things being the way they are.[107] She locates his thought in what she describes as a "classicist worldview."[108] Case-Winters rightly notes that the modern/postmodern world has rejected many of the elements that make up the classicist worldview that shaped and limited Calvin's doctrine of omnipotence. These include the scripture principal, the prescientific notion of divine intervention in world processes, substance metaphysics, the hierarchy of being, and pre-democratic political theory.[109]

Any conclusion about God's exercise of power that relies on the model of power as domination and control we have inherited from theologies developed in a classicist worldview and more recently from sociology and philosophy will be unsatisfactory. This is because conclusions that reflect a worldview that no longer has currency and/or are based on a limited cultural norm cannot provide a holistic vision of anything, least of all God. Case-Winters finds that a synthesis of process thought, especially that of

104. The freewill defense is a well-known theodicy. It argues that evil is the result of human freewill and that God cannot make people with freewill act for good. If, however, God does exercise power in a model of domination and control (as in Calvin's model, for example) then human freedom is denied and cannot be called upon to ameliorate God's responsibility for the effects of evil in the world. In other words, the veracity of the freewill defense depends on one's understanding of the manner of God's exercise of power and the level of freedom creatures therefore have.

105. Case-Winters, *God's Power*, 64.

106. Case-Winters, *God's Power*, 78. Effectively, the understanding of compatibilism is that the free will defense, as described above, alongside determinism (the idea that all happenings are completely governed by pre-existing causes) is logical.

107. Case-Winters, *God's Power*, 80–81.

108. Case-Winters, *God's Power*, 89.

109. Case-Winters, *God's Power*, 93.

Hartshorne,[110] with feminist perspectives,[111] provides a constructive proposal for beginning to come to terms with the kind of power we attribute to God.[112] Rising to the challenge of recalibrating our thinking about God and power is important because, wherever and whenever our relationships and motivations *are* characterized by coercion and a desire to dominate and control, this human power play subliminally validates a model of God that is unsound and inadequate both theologically and scientifically.

Daniel Migliore finds that God's power, and the exercise thereof, must be understood differently to the power we know and exercise as human beings.[113] In setting out his theology of power within the framework of the different power of love,[114] he asserts that questions about God arise from our own experiences of power and powerlessness, and further that questions about God are essentially the same as questions about the nature of ultimate power.[115] In discussing the power of God who freely loves, Migliore explains why the doctrine of the Trinity is crucial for a fully Christian understanding of the power of God in three succinct points. First, that the one God who created the heavens and the earth cannot be separated from the crucified and risen Jesus or from his renewing Spirit. Second, that God's own life is communal, therefore God is not the will to power but the will to communion in freedom. Third, that the deepest meaning of God's triune life-in-relationship is that God is the power of self-giving love. In Migliore's thinking, the triune God is eternally open for costly relationship with the world because God is fully love and therefore exercises power differently:[116]

> Trinitarian doctrine describes God's power as altogether different from our finite and sinful human experience and exercise of power. God's power is communicative power, shared power, both in God's own eternal life and in God's relationships to the

---

110. While Case-Winters is of the view that Hartshorne has not altogether eradicated from his system of thought instances of divine power exercised in the mode of domination and control, she sees these as "lapses." Overall, she describes his process interpretation of God's exercise of power as "promising and persuasive." Case-Winters, *God's Power*, 168–70.

111. Case-Winters notes that there is not one overarching feminist perspective on which to draw and assesses the thinking of a range of feminist theologians. She also finds that power is both a male preoccupation and a male defined term. Case-Winters, *God's Power*, 171–74.

112. Case-Winters, *God's Power*, 201.

113. Migliore, *Power of God*, 20–35.

114. Migliore, *Power of God*, 35.

115. Migliore, *Power of God*, 2–9.

116. Migliore, *Power of God*, 78–83.

world. The power of God is different from mere power to transcend the world and exercise absolute control over the world.[117]

The doctrine of the Trinity affirms that God's own life includes
otherness,[118] and so is intricately connected to any Christian theology of
power. Chapter three of this book therefore focuses on power within the
Trinitarian theology of Moltmann, as a precursor to an exploration of the
possibilities of his Social Trinity. The different power of love is an important crossing over point for a potential understanding of a Social Trinity
in a process framework, the subject of chapter four, as Hartshorne and the
process movement more generally is also keen to articulate the power of
God in terms of love. Whitehead, in fact, roundly critiques the Church for
fashioning God as an imperial ruler, or a personification of moral energy, or
as an ultimate philosophical principle, rather than as love. He states:

> There is, however, in the Galilean origin of Christianity yet an-
> other suggestion which does not fit very well with any of the
> three main strands of thought. It does not emphasize the rul-
> ing Caesar, or the ruthless moralist, or the unmoved mover. It
> dwells upon the tender elements in the world, which slowly and
> in quietness operate by love; and it finds purpose in the present
> immediacy of a kingdom not of this world. Love neither rules,
> nor is it unmoved; also it is a little oblivious to morals. It does
> not look to the future, for it finds its own reward in the immedi-
> ate present.[119]

This goes to the heart of Whitehead's process view that the power of
God is only and always described as non-coercive love. Hartshorne agrees,
stating that "God's power simply is the appeal of unsurpassable love."[120]
Hartshorne explains this different power of God with reference to Whitehead reading Plato and Aristotle and arriving at the view that it is divine
beauty that moves the world. Hartshorne said that, since the beauty beyond
all others is the beauty of love, God is best described as love. Life has meaning with love and none without it, and so for him, love is both the ultimate
principle *and* the Divine Other. Hartshorne notes with regret that, for the
ancient Greek philosophers, love could not be the ultimate principle because

---

117. Migliore, *Power of God*, 129.

118. Migliore, *Power of God*, 130.

119. Whitehead, *Process and Reality*, 343.

120. Hartshorne, *Omnipotence and Other Theological Mistakes*, 14.

in their view love implies that one does not have in oneself all possible value and so must look to another for further value.[121]

Theism of the classical type discussed at the beginning of this chapter has changed and developed over time, but even in contemporary theistic models of God divine power is generally understood as omnipotence. This is widely taken to mean that God has ultimate power in every respect.[122] Further, due to God possessing all power, all things that happen do so according to the will of God. Other individuals can and do have power, but it is always subordinate to the power of God who exerts power over all. Omnipotence as it is understood within theistic models of God, ancient and modern, therefore remains essentially a "power over" concept. It is associated with God's dominion over the world, which it understands as domination.[123]

In the critique of modern theism and its relation to God's power as omnipotence made by Paul Tillich, the influential twentieth century existentialist philosopher and theologian, the link between a better understanding of the exercise of divine power and divine love is central:

> Love and power are often contrasted in such a way that love is identified with a resignation of power and power with a denial of love. Powerless love and loveless power are contrasted. This, of course, is unavoidable if love is understood from its emotional side and power from its compulsory side. It was this misinterpretation which induced the philosopher of the 'will-to-power' (i.e. Nietzsche) to reject radically the Christian idea of love. And it is the same misinterpretation which induces Christian theologians to reject Nietzsche's philosophy of the 'will-to-power' in the name of the Christian idea of love. In both cases an ontology of love is missing and in the second case power is identified with social compulsion.[124]

Simply assessing power in the social realm leads to understanding it as domination and control. This has been demonstrated through a brief overview of Weber and Foucault. Tillich understood power much more broadly

---

121. Hartshorne, *Omnipotence and Other Theological Mistakes*, 14–15.

122. See Fretheim, *Suffering of God*, 17. Fretheim points out that the standard portrait of God is grounded in the Judeo-Christian tradition regnant in synagogue or church. Namely, that God is understood in terms of traditional categories: freedom, immutability, omniscience, and omnipotence. He says that if they are not explicitly stated, they are commonly assumed.

123. Christ, *She Who Changes*, 94.

124. Tillich, *Love, Power and Justice*, 11.

than did Weber and Foucault describing it as the power of being.[125] Further-more, he understood God to be *being itself*, thus linking power to God as an attribute in a very different way to the application of standard notions of divine omnipotence. For Tillich to assert that God is not *a* being, not even the *greatest* being, but *being itself*, is to assert that the world and God are more intimately related than a theistic position would suggest.[126] In fact, Tillich is concerned to transcend theism altogether to enable a more helpful notion of God.[127] He says that theism as a concept has three meanings, and the first one simply affirms God in an unspecified way. Tillich insists that, used in this first sense, theism is empty and does not even mean what it says when the name of God is invoked. He points to politicians and rhetoricians and those who wish to make an impression on an audience as those who like to use the word "God" in this way, which is simply to generate the feeling among their hearers that the speaker is serious and ethically dependable.[128]

A second meaning of theism, according to Tillich, is the name we give to a personal relationship with God:

> In this case it points to those elements in the Jewish-Christian tradition which emphasize the person-to-person relationship with God. Theism in this sense emphasizes the personalistic passages in the Bible and the Protestant creeds, the personalistic image of God, the word as the tool of creation and revelation, the ethical and social character of the kingdom of God, the personal nature of human faith and divine forgiveness, the historical vision of the universe, the idea of a divine purpose, the infinite distance between creator and creature, the absolute separation between God and the world, the conflict between holy God and sinful man, the person-to-person character of prayer and practical devotion. Theism in this sense is the non-mystical side of biblical religion and historical Christianity.[129]

While, for traditional believers in God, it can be difficult to see what is wrong with this view, Tillich links this meaning of theism to atheism. He finds that unbelief is generated from this explanation of belief due to a very human attempt to escape the divine/human encounter. He describes this as an existential rather than a theoretical problem.[130]

125. Tillich, *Love, Power and Justice*, 45.

126. Long, *Western Philosophy of Religion*, 330.

127. Tillich, *Courage to Be*, 176.

128. Tillich, *Courage to Be*, 176.

129. Tillich, *Courage to Be*, 177.

130. Tillich, *Courage to Be*, 177.

The third meaning of theism for Tillich is purely a theological one. He says that, like every theology, it depends on the religious ideas it conceptualizes. It is dependent on the first type of theism described above as it seeks to prove God in some way, looking to the traditional arguments or proofs of the existence of God. Further, it is dependent on the second type of theism in as much as it seeks to establish a doctrine of God that transforms person-to-person encounter with God into a formula about two persons, yet the two persons have a reality different and an independence from each other. Tillich declares that the first understanding of theism must be transcended because it is irrelevant, and the second understanding of theism must be transcended because it is one-sided. Even more emphatically, he insists that the third understanding of theism must be transcended because it is patently incorrect. Tillich describes it simply as "bad theology."[131]

The reason that theism, particularly in Tillich's third sense, is not good theology is that it couches God as a being rather than being-itself. A being is bound to the subject-object nature of reality, and this is an unacceptable way to conceive of God:

> For (the idea of) God as a subject makes me into an object which is nothing more than an object. He deprives me of my subjectivity because he is all-powerful and all-knowing. I revolt and try to make *him* into an object, but the revolt fails and becomes desperate. God appears as the invincible tyrant, the being in contrast with whom all other things are without freedom and subjectivity. He is equated with the recent tyrants who, with the help of terror, try to transform everything into a mere object, a thing among things, a cog in the machine they control. He becomes the model of everything against which Existentialism revolted. This is the God Nietzsche said had to be killed because nobody can tolerate being made into a mere object of absolute knowledge and absolute control. This is the deepest root of atheism. It is an atheism which is justified as the reaction against the theological theism and its disturbing implications. It is also the deepest root of the Existentialist despair and the widespread anxiety of meaninglessness in our period.[132]

Tillich is seeking the courage to transcend theistic notions of God entirely. He calls it the courage to be,[133] a courage that is to be found in

---

131. Tillich, *Courage to Be*, 178.

132. Tillich, *Courage to Be*, 179. It is noteworthy that both Moltmann and Hartshorne make a similar link between theism and atheism. See Moltmann, *History and the Triune God*, 28 and Hartshorne, "Formally Possible Doctrines," 205.

133. Tillich, *Courage to Be*, 180. Which is also the title of his 1952 book.

the "God above God" who transcends every religious category, including mysticism.[134] In Tillich's view, the God above the God of theism is present, although hidden, in every encounter between the divine and the human. He says that both biblical religion and Protestant theology are aware of certain key things, the first of which is the paradoxical nature of this divine-human encounter. Second, they are aware that if God encounters humanity, God is neither object nor subject, so God is above the structure into which theism as a concept has forced the divine. Third, biblical religion and Protestant theology are aware that personalism in God is balanced by a trans-personal presence of the divine. Fourth, they are aware that only if the power of acceptance or grace is effective in humanity can forgiveness be a reality. Fifth and finally, they are aware of the paradoxical nature of every prayer, of speaking to somebody to whom you cannot speak because they are not "somebody"; of asking somebody of whom you cannot ask anything as they give or do not give before you ask; of saying "thou" to somebody who is nearer to the I than the I is to itself. Each of these five paradoxes, according to Tillich, drives the religious consciousness toward a God above the God of theism.[135]

What Tillich is seeking to capture in his notion of a God above theism is a conception of God that avoids casting deity into the role of an invincible tyrant that objectifies and subjugates all else. Of all the models available to us to articulate the nature of a non-tyrannical God, panentheism is the one that best carries Tillich's God-above-God ideal. Given its transcendent/immanent balance, panentheism is also the model of God that has the most to contribute to a consideration of God's exercise of power in creation when we take known world processes into account.

Classical theism and the idea of God as eternal unchanging and timeless mystery located vertically, based on prescientific theological metaphysics,[136] closely followed by the aloof deist God of first cause, arguably remain the dominant models of God in Christianity. In many branches of the Church these pre-scientific notions of God are promulgated as a test of true religion and remain remarkably robust in popular Christian piety. Both belong to an obsolete worldview that is incompatible with what we now know about the world in which we live. Panentheism, in contrast, is a helpful way of understanding God in our current scientific paradigm, as it allows for God's presence and creativity in an evolving universe. It unites the transcendence of God found in both theism and deism with a full and deep understanding

---

134. Tillich, *Courage to Be*, 180.
135. Tillich, *Courage to Be*, 180–81.
136. Haught, *Christianity and Science*, 4.

of the immanence of God. God is in the world and the world is in God, but God and the world are not one and the same. Panentheism allows God to maintain an appropriate sense of otherness, while at the same time imbuing the entire created order with the presence of the divine. It is a conception of God that changes an intractable power dynamic and goes a considerable way towards breaking the impasse in the theodicy problem associated with either a fully transcendent or an external God. As a key link and crossover between the process theology of Hartshorne and the trinitarian theology of Moltmann, panentheism will be further developed and explained in chapters 2 and 3 on process theology and the Trinity respectively. It is also a key feature of chapter 4 which seeks to present a cohesive understanding of a Social Trinity in process, a fully relational theology.

Pantheism, by contrast, is the view that the world is one and the same as God. Quite distinct from panentheism, pantheism essentially describes the world as fully divine, which leaves no room for a separate divine entity not coterminous with everything that is. Pantheism is effectively animism. It is therefore as old as human history and the associated history of religion and is a well-known heresy of Christian thought. Individual process theologians and the process movement in general have regularly been accused of letting go of any sense of the transcendence of God that is a feature of both panentheism and theism, and articulating pantheism instead, thus finding themselves outside of a properly Christian conception of God.

In *Becoming and Being*, his study of the doctrine of God in the thinking of Charles Hartshorne and Karl Barth, Colin Gunton, for example, describes Hartshorne's process theology as "a superstitious form of idolatry, in that it divinizes the world, both as the creator of itself and God and as the body, coeternal and consubstantial, of God who is its soul."[137] This is effectively a charge of heresy, but it is a charge based on an unfair assessment of Hartshorne's overall thinking. To suggest that Hartshorne espoused pantheism is to ignore Hartshorne's own opposition to the idea. Hartshorne was always at pains to draw a distinction between his own panentheism and pantheism, which he described as "the view that deity is the all of relative or interdependent items, with nothing wholly independent or in any clear sense nonrelative."[138] Hartshorne points out that:

---

137. Gunton, *Becoming and Being*, 223. See also Tanner, *God and Creation*, 162–65. In a similar manner to Gunton, Tanner finds that Hartshorne sees the creature as God. She insists that "a theologian should stress God's sovereignty and talk of the creature with a constant thematic reference to God's direct creative agency for it." Tanner, *God and Creation*, 161.

138. Hartshorne, *Divine Relativity*, 89.

The error of most pantheists has been to deny the externality of concrete existence to the essence of deity. They have not realized that the inclusive actuality of God, which includes all de facto actuality, is as truly contingent and capable of additions as the least actuality it includes. This is the freedom both of God and of the creatures. For since the essence of God is compatible with any possible universe, we can be allowed some power of decision, as between possibilities, without infringing the absolute independence of God in his essential character or personality. And God's own freedom is likewise safe-guarded, since freedom means a personal character with which alternative concrete experiences or states are compatible.[139]

Pantheism is an error in Christian theology because it empties God of any kind of power at all, even the non-coercive power that process theology argues for, as the god of pantheism has no level of separation from the created order and therefore no capacity to invite or influence towards the good.

The panentheistic understanding of God associated with process theology is not entirely modern, nor does it find its validity only from a scientific worldview. The questions that have given rise to this way of understanding God have been explored over time in a variety of ways and are even embedded in the Old Testament. In his book *When Bad Things Happen to Good People,* Harold Kushner turns to the ancient book of Job to reflect on the nature of God and the problem of evil. He writes from a Jewish perspective, although notes in his introduction to a twentieth anniversary edition indicate that it was Christian clergy who turned his modest consideration of the attributes of God in the face of human suffering into a runaway bestseller after its original publication in 1981. He wrote the book after the death of his teenage son because Kushner believed in God and the goodness of the world. As a Rabbi, he had spent most of his life trying to help others believe, but found himself compelled by personal tragedy to reassess everything he had been taught about God and how God acts in the world.[140] Kushner contends that the book of Job is a struggle with the very same issue, and, more controversially, he comes to the conclusion that the writer of Job arrives at an understanding of God that, as process theology has done, forgoes the notion of divine omnipotence:

> Let me suggest that the author of the Book of Job takes the position which neither Job nor his friends take. He believes in God's goodness and in Job's goodness, and is prepared to give

139. Hartshorne, *Divine Relativity,* 89.
140. Kushner, *When Bad Things Happen,* xix.

up his belief . . . that God is all-powerful. Bad things do happen to good people in this world, but it is not God who wills it.
God would like people to get what they deserve in life, but He
cannot always arrange it. Forced to choose between a good God
who is not totally powerful, or a powerful God who is not totally
good, the author of the Book of Job chooses to believe in God's
goodness.[141]

The book of Job is not strictly a theodicy as it does not seek to vindi-
cate God's justice in the face of innocent suffering.[142] It is rather a profound
analysis of human suffering, tapping into the physiological, psychological, social, and spiritual dimensions of existential anguish. It also makes a
pointed critique of traditional formulations of the nature of God.[143] Some
Old Testament scholars contend that Job is two books in one cover and refer
to them as Job I and Job II. The first book refers to an ancient folktale that is
the story of Job, and the second to "the rebel Job."[144] The voice of the rebel is
totally different to the Job of the folktale.[145] The rebel voice says that God is
not all-powerful, and that lived reality belies the idea of divine retribution.
Evildoers have their wealth and power and are unimpeded in their manner
of living. The rebel Job does not fear the God of his three challengers, nor
does he seek to repent before him, as for the rebel this type of God does not
exist, despite the shadow of this type of God haunting him continually and
clouding the issue. The rebel voice is an important one in that it speaks for
all humans in their suffering.[146]

In his recent commentary on Job, Loren R. Fisher suggests that the author of the rebel Job was a Jerusalem scribe well-versed both in the ways that
the miseries of life were usually described and in how others had dealt with
the subject previously. The words of the rebel Job form an angry response
to the ancient folktale of Job, debating three so-called "friends" who defend

141. Kushner, *When Bad Things Happen*, 45. Notably, Hartshorne also points to
the story of Job as illustrative of the invalidity of the notion of a divine omnipotence
that oversees and orchestrates each event and circumstance. Hartshorne finds that "the
religious value of such a notion is more negative than positive. It is the mother of no end
of chicanery (see the book of Job for some examples), of much deep feeling of injustice
(the poor unfortunate being assured that God has deliberately contrived everything as
exactly the best way events could transpire), and of philosophical quagmires of paradox
and unmeaning verbiage." Hartshorne, *Divine Relativity*, 23–24.

142. Terrien, *Job*, 39; Fisher, *Many Voices of Job*, xviii.

143. Terrien, *Job*, 39.

144. Fisher, *Many Voices of Job*, xii.

145. Fisher, *Many Voices of Job*, xv. The folktale is told in Job 1–2; 27–31; and 38–42.
The voice of the rebel is found in Job 3–36.

146. Fisher, *Many Voices of Job*, xv.

the position and the beliefs of Job I.[147] Fisher contends that the voice of the rebel Job was hidden in the ancient story, and that the book of Job was then edited in an attempt to ensure that traditional formulations of the nature of God remained intact:

> We are fortunate the words of the rebel Job have survived, even though they were buried within the old story. This melding of the two books made the book of Job impossible to understand for most readers. In case anyone did understand the words of the rebel Job, the orthodox establishment added the 'Speeches of Elihu' at a later time to confuse the arguments of the rebel Job.[148]

Fisher believes that the orthodox establishment succeeded in its aim of maintaining a particular view attesting to an all controlling God in the book of Job, stating somewhat sadly that "the rebel Job is so surrounded by verbiage and hate that his gift to us has been lost."[149] Fisher's conclusion is that, to get to the heart of what the book of Job really seeks to say about the nature of God, we must avoid finding within it a final and decisive scene in the drama of the story in favour of creating an enduring scene where the rebel Job finds his voice and speaks again.[150] It could be argued that Christian theology generally finds more value and comfort in treating potentially evolving scenes as final and decisive, and that this makes it difficult to develop deeper and more nuanced understandings of God and God's relationship with the world. Allowing and expecting the rebel Job to speak again may well change our conception of God's exercise of power in the lives of human individuals and in the ongoing life of the world itself.

Another commentator on Job who also eschews the view that the book exclusively validates a model of God as all-powerful controller of every aspect of the life of the world is Gerald Janzen.[151] In his commentary on chapters 38–41 of Job, the section of the book in which God finally responds to Job through a series of questions, Janzen contends that we are incorrect to understand these questions within the domain of courtroom procedure and logic. If we do, he says we operate within the logic of a zero-sum game, where for one party to be declared in the right the other party must be declared in the wrong. As the divine speeches have primarily to do with the dynamic processes at play in God's creation and seem therefore to move

147. Fisher, *Many Voices of Job*, 29.
148. Fisher, *Many Voices of Job*, 30. The speeches of Elihu are in Job 32–37.
149. Fisher, *Many Voices of Job*, 100.
150. Fisher, *Many Voices of Job*, 101.
151. Janzen, *At the Scent of Water*.

out of the domain of law and its courts into the domain of *Shadday*[152] (the domain of cosmic and human blessing) Janzen suggests that what God is doing is asking Job to relinquish his zero-sum understanding of justice. Janzen proposes a paraphrase of the second question from God which turns it into an explanatory statement:

> Job, you don't have to put me in the wrong in order for you to be vindicated against the charges of your friends. But in order for you to appreciate this, you have to relinquish your understanding of ultimate divine justice and see it rather in terms of the dynamic thrust toward life that you see manifest in the world around you. This understanding of my justice does not rule out the possibility of undeserved suffering; but it places it within a context which will free you from the logic of your friends.[153]

Janzen emphasizes the idea of God answering Job *out of* the whirlwind (38:1 NRSV) meaning that it is both *in* and *through* the whirlwind that Job finally hears God. He contends that the whirlwind is not a symbol of the blustering power of God seeking to intimidate or subdue Job,[154] but is rather evidence of God acting in and through natural processes to render the earth fertile and life-sustaining,[155] something along the lines of the streams in the desert image in Isaiah.[156] The wasteland of human suffering is transformed in the gift of water, and with the weather that renews the earth also comes a message to Job and to humankind generally. It is a message with a twofold character: it comes for correction, and it comes for love.[157]

> First, the whirlwind and its following rain address Job. And clearly, insofar as the rain is life-giving, it is not a punishing 'correction.' Rather, it corrects Job in respect to his assumption that God's justice is a zero-sum game locked within the logic of reward and punishment. But finally, the whirlwind and all that follows it carry to Job a message concerning God's 'love,' God's *hesed* or faithful, steadfast loyalty to both creation and Job

152. *Shadday* is part of an ancient Hebrew term for God found in the book of Job and other parts of the Old Testament. It was eventually superseded by the term Jehovah. A variety of meanings have been suggested, one relating *Shadday* to the noun *shad* (breast or udder) pointing to the nourishing, supplying, or nurturing aspects of God. This very early meaning implies benefit or blessing. Good, "*El Shadday*: Meaning and Implications," 67.

153. Janzen, *At the Scent of Water*, 97.

154. Janzen, *At the Scent of Water*, 96.

155. Janzen, *At the Scent of Water*, 100.

156. Isaiah 41:18 and Isaiah 43:19.

157. Janzen, *At the Scent of Water*, 103.

himself. He who had briefly hoped for the scent of water now experiences it, in and through the renewal of the natural world around him.[158]

The book of Job addresses the most fundamental issues of human life: justice, goodness, suffering, and the reality of God.[159] It is a key witness in the bible to theological understandings of power in relation to God and the world. As has been demonstrated briefly through Kushner, Fisher, and Janzen's interpretation of the message of the book, Job makes no open and shut case for an omnipotent, controlling God. Through the rebel, or questioning, voice in Job we tap into a long standing and insistent wondering on the part of people of faith about the logic and the justice inherent in any model of God in which power is exercised as domination and control. This chapter ends with this questioning voice. In the next chapter I will seek to unpack the "rebel voice"[160] of process thought within Christianity. The persistent voice of process thinkers, beginning with Whitehead nearly a century ago, has questioned many of our inherited notions of God, especially those regarding divine omniscience, omnipotence, and immutability.[161] I therefore turn to issues of power in process theology next.

---

158. Janzen, *At the Scent of Water*, 104.

159. Janzen, *At the Scent of Water*, ix.

160. Janzen, *At the Scent of Water*, 29.

161. Ford, *Lure of God*, 1.

2

POWER AND PROCESS THOUGHT

O thou dull god, why li'st thou with the vile in loathsome beds,
and leav'st the kingly couch a watch-case, or a common "larum-bell?"
—William Shakespeare, *Henry IV*, Part II, Act III, Scene 1

So we have known and believe the love that God has for us. God is love,
and those who abide in love abide in God, and God abides in them.
—John 4:16 (NRSV)

Classical theism as a way of understanding God has arguably held much sway over the centuries because we have operated on the basis that omnipotence, understood as the power to direct and control, is a basic criterion for worship and honor. Process thinkers question the validity of this view and argue against the idea of an omnipotent God. The way process theology has articulated the power of God in relation to the world, more than any other aspect of its extensive scholarship, has made it a "rebel voice"[1] in Christian theology as it speaks against long-accepted models of God grounded in ancient and medieval philosophy and theology. This chapter considers the implications of the power aspect of process theology for a contemporary Christian understanding of God, inviting the rebel voice in from the fringes to the center of the conversation. The majority of the chapter considers the adequate power of God in the discourses of process thought

1. Janzen, *At the Scent of Water*, 29.

and traces the motivations and main ideas of Whitehead and Hartshorne and some of their contemporary interpreters in the process movement. Then follows a section which briefly outlines how process thinking about the power of God can contribute to properly Christian notions of incarnation, resurrection, eschatology, theodicy, and justice.

Process thinkers certainly argue for adequate power in God, but this is understood to be less comprehensive and overt in the panentheism espoused than in more traditional models of God. Hartshorne asserted that adequate cosmic power is simply "power to do for the cosmos (the field of divine social relationships) all desirable things that could be done and need to be done by one universal or cosmic agent."[2] Process theology has not arbitrarily reduced or limited the power of God to suit its purposes. It has instead formulated an idea of adequate cosmic power which is not burdened with the logical deficiencies of a traditional view.[3] Hartshorne explains:

> It has become customary to say that we must limit divine power to save human freedom and to avoid making deity responsible for evil. But to speak of limiting a concept seems to imply that the concept, without the limitation, makes sense. The notion of a cosmic power that determines all decisions fails to make sense. For its decisions could refer to nothing except themselves. They could result in no world; for a world must consist of local agents making their own decisions. Instead of saying that God's power is limited, suggesting that it is less than some conceivable power, we should rather say: his power is absolutely maximal, the greatest possible, but even the greatest possible power is still one power among others, is not the only power. God can do everything a God can do, everything that could be done by 'a being with no possible superior.'[4]

Despite the common assumption that process theology argues for a weak and/or limited God, in fact process theology looks to a God with the "greatest possible power."[5] The greatest possible power is not omnipotence as it is usually conceived, for this expectation limits God far more than a recognition of the logic of the adequate power of God. Hartshorne made clear that the God of life, movement, and creativity must not be limited by omnipotence understood as a zero-sum equation of domination and control. He said: "No worse falsehood was ever perpetrated than the traditional

---

2. Hartshorne, *Divine Relativity*, 134.

3. Hartshorne, *Divine Relativity*, 138.

4. Hartshorne, *Divine Relativity*, 138.

5. Hartshorne, *Divine Relativity*, 138.

concept of omnipotence. It is a piece of unconscious blasphemy, condemning God to a dead world, probably not distinguishable from no world at all."[6]

Essentially, process thinkers view reality as both temporal and creative, and insist that becoming is more fundamental than being. This runs counter to the metaphysics of being which has dominated both Western philosophy and Christian theology, and therefore challenges long established ways of understanding God's exercise of power and the extent to which God controls or directs events.[7] For process thinkers, because becoming *includes* being, there is a partly new universe each time it is referred to, and the future really is open or partly indeterminate—even for God. Creative freedom is real, there is no absolute causal determinism, and the laws of nature evolve. God is always in some aspect in process and is influenced by the creatures. Experience, both human and non-human, is coextensive with reality—and so memory, as the givenness of the past, is basic. Social relations are all important in both experience and reality, and there are both internal and external relations, both dependence and independence for all things. This relatedness means that self-interest is neither the principle of all motivation nor the justification of altruism, for us or for God.[8]

THE FOUNDERS OF PROCESS THOUGHT

Process thought emerged from the thinking of Alfred North Whitehead (1861–1947), the mathematician and philosopher who famously described God as "the great companion—the fellow sufferer who understands."[9] Whitehead was born in 1861, two years after the publication of Darwin's *Origin of the Species*. He was brought up in an Anglican vicarage and studied at Sherborne School, one of the public schools of England, where he was immersed in Anglican piety and tradition. He then went to Trinity College at Cambridge University to study and eventually teach mathematics.[10] He was at Cambridge from 1880 to 1910, and, as an undergraduate, he talked openly about his interest in religion and in Christian missionary work overseas. These early religious convictions faded into doubt and uncertainty relatively quickly, quite possibly due to the problem that faced many Victorians—the problem of God's omnipotence and the presence of evil in the world. The proposal, if God is all-powerful then God must be negligent in

6. Hartshorne, *Omnipotence and Other Theological Mistakes*, 17–18.

7. Brown et al., *Process Philosophy*, v.

8. Hartshorne, "Ideas and Theses of Process Philosophers," 100–101.

9. Whitehead, *Process and Reality*, 351.

10. Long, *Western Philosophy of Religion*, 367.

doing anything about evil in the world, was keenly topical in the academic milieu of late-nineteenth-century England against the backdrop of the work of Charles Darwin. During this time Whitehead took up the study of theology. After some eight years, he gave up the subject, packed up and sold all his theological books and turned his full attention to science and philosophy.[11]

As the nineteenth century gave way to the twentieth, a revolution was taking place in physics. The special and general relativity theories of Einstein turned the foundations of physics which Whitehead knew upside down. He was of the generation that had been totally assured of the set principles of physics, the same since the time of Newton and expected to remain so. With the entire theory underpinning what had seemed to be a stable science now up for grabs, there came a reluctance in Whitehead to take too fixed a view on the final foundations of things ever again. Despite this element of tentativeness in his thinking from this point, he remained fascinated with the fundamentals of reality. In the early nineteen twenties Whitehead undertook a series of studies on the foundations of natural science, the last a critique of Einstein's theory of relativity in which he proposed an equivalent theory to replace it. After thirty years at Cambridge Whitehead moved to London where he became the Dean of the Faculty of Science at the Imperial College of Science and Technology. It was not until he was approaching retirement that he developed the process metaphysics for which he is best known. After a career of teaching mathematics, with publications in mathematics, logic, and the philosophy of nature, he was offered a chair in philosophy at Harvard University. It was therefore from America and Harvard that his formed view of the process nature of God and reality developed.[12]

Whitehead envisaged a metaphysical system of the world in which the basic fact of existence is always and everywhere a process of self-realization—one that grows from previous processes and itself adds a new pulse of individuality and a new value to the world. This makes the fully independent existence of anything at all logically impossible. Whitehead often used the phrase "requiring each other" to sum up his understanding of the nature of all reality including that of God.[13] He explains this interdependence of all things with God in the conclusion to *Religion in the Making*:

> He is the binding element in the world. The consciousness which is individual in us, is universal in him: the love which is partial in us, is all-embracing in him. Apart from him there could be no world, because there could be no adjustment of individuality.

11. Ford, *Lure of God*, 2.
12. Ford, *Lure of God*, 3.
13. Lowe, "Whitehead's Metaphysical System," 3.

His purpose in the world is quality of attainment. His purpose
is always embodied in the particular ideals relevant to the actual
state of the world. Thus all attainment is immortal in that it fash-
ions the actual ideals which are God in the world as it is now.
Every act leaves the world with a deeper or a fainter impress
of God. He then passes into his next relation to the world with
enlarged, or diminished, presentation of ideal values.[14]

Although Whitehead did not use the word panentheism in his writing,
his above description of God fits very closely with the immanent/transcen-
dent balance inherent in the term. In short, Whitehead was no pantheist
and his thought, especially once fully developed, is far too rigorous to be
dismissed as a form of scientific or philosophical paganism. As in Gunton's
criticism of Hartshorne's view of God, in which he dismissively described
Hartshorne as a pantheist,[15] it has been standard practise to emphasize
the phrases in Whitehead that appear to collapse God fully into the world,
without attending to the phrases which seek to ameliorate such an all or
nothing approach. For example, to take up Whitehead's phrase "He is the
binding element in the world,"[16] while leaving aside his phrase "He is not
the world,"[17] makes a blanket assessment of Whitehead in particular, and
process theology in general, as necessarily outside properly Christian orthodoxy axiomatic. This unfortunate tendency has made it difficult for contemporary process theology, all of which draws on Whitehead's foundational
thought, to be fully accepted in mainstream Christianity.

Despite this there is always the possibility, if not the presumption, of
a God that is not fully coterminous with the world running behind Whitehead's thought about the nature of reality. He first presented a metaphysical synthesis, the beginning of his process ideas, in the Lowell Lectures of
1925 which were later incorporated into his book *Science and the Modern
World*.[18] The lectures themselves make an uncompromising criticism of the
scientific materialism prevailing at the time,[19] a reminder that Whitehead
consciously and consistently left room for both the metaphysical and the
spiritual, making him far more than merely the purveyor of a Godless

14. Whitehead, *Religion in the Making*, 152.

15. See Gunton, *Becoming and Being*, in which Gunton cannot differentiate between Hartshorne's stated panentheistic view of God and his own understanding of
pantheism.

16. Whitehead, *Religion in the Making*, 152.

17. Whitehead, *Religion in the Making*, 152.

18. Whitehead, *Science and the Modern World*.

19. Ford, *Lure of God*, 4.

philosophy of nature. In the 1925 preface to his book based on the Lowell Lectures, Whitehead says:

> If my view of the function of philosophy is correct, it is the most effective of all the intellectual pursuits. It builds cathedrals before the workmen have moved a stone, and it destroys them before the elements have worn down their arches. It is the architect of buildings of the spirit, and it is also their solvent:—and the spiritual precedes the material.[20]

When Whitehead delivered the Lowell Lectures, he examined the interaction of science and religion in a manner relatively neutral about the existence of God. When the lectures were published as part of the aforementioned book, however, Whitehead made several additions. A key addition was a chapter entitled "God" which both argued for the existence of God and described God's nature as he then understood it.[21] It is notable that, even in this early stage of his process thinking about the God/world relationship, Whitehead alluded to the philosophical problem of evil that just won't budge when God is understood as the ultimate director of history:

> Among medieval and modern philosophers, anxious to establish the religious significance of God, an unfortunate habit has prevailed of paying to Him metaphysical compliments. He has been conceived as the foundation of the metaphysical situation with its ultimate activity. If this conception be adhered to, there can be no alternative except to discern in Him the origin of all evil as well as of all good. He is then the supreme author of the play, and to Him must therefore be ascribed its shortcomings as well as its success. If he be conceived as the supreme ground for limitation, it stands in His very nature to divide the Good from the Evil, and to establish Reason 'within her dominions supreme.'[22]

Whitehead thus cautions philosophers against casting God as the supreme controller of everything, for the outcome of ascribing to God the kind of power traditionally believed necessary for God to function religiously and be worthy of worship is an insurmountable theodicy problem. Through commenting that philosophers ancient and modern have paid God "metaphysical compliments"[23] in a desire to protect God's religious significance,

20. Whitehead, *Science and the Modern World*, x.
21. Ford, *Lure of God*, 4.
22. Whitehead, *Science and the Modern World*, 222–23.
23. Whitehead, *Science and the Modern World*, 222.

Whitehead is criticizing the tendency in philosophy to push God outside the creaturely reality of the world into a realm of absolutes. For Whitehead, at the center of reality there is *both* plurality *and* unity, and this is what denies the implicit monism of the classical view of God as the ground of being. In Whitehead's view the eternal objects are not created by God but rather have within themselves the principle of their eternal existence as possibilities. That the role of God is therefore "to divide the Good from the Evil"[24] does not incriminate God when undesirable possibilities are actualized, for events in the world are self-creating. As already mentioned above, for Whitehead, a proper conception of God holds in tension God's immanence as much as God's transcendence. True to his more developed thought, Whitehead here breaks down dualisms into polar pairs. Plurality and unity come together; immanence and transcendence come together; and rather than each pair being ontologically separate, the polar pairs instead depend on each other and in fact describe the same reality.[25]

Whitehead was utterly convinced that religious ideas needed to be transformed through philosophical reasoning to make sense in his own day and into the future. A year after the Lowell Lectures and the ensuing book *Science and the Modern World,* Whitehead published *Religion in the Making,* that book consisting of four lectures he gave on religion at King's Chapel in Boston early in 1926.[26] He explains the aim of the lectures and therefore the book in the preface:

> The aim of the lectures was to give a concise analysis of the various factors in human nature which go to form a religion, to exhibit the inevitable transformation of religion with the transformation of knowledge, and more especially to direct attention to the foundation of religion on our apprehension of those permanent elements by reason of which there is a stable order in the world, permanent elements apart from which there could be no changing world.[27]

Religion in the Making is in some ways a companion volume to *Science and the Modern World* as Whitehead applied the same train of thought to religion as he had to science the previous year.[28] These volumes only hinted at Whitehead's eventual theory that God was more than the principle of

---

24. Whitehead, *Science and the Modern World,* 223.
25. Bowman, *Divine Decision,* 30.
26. Whitehead, *Religion in the Making,* 7.
27. Whitehead, *Religion in the Making,* 7.
28. Whitehead, *Religion in the Making,* 7.

limitation previously discussed. [29] His full schema was expressed in *Process and Reality*, Whitehead's magnum opus of process metaphysics originally published in 1929. In his earlier thought Whitehead understood God as a source that limits possibilities; later on he came to understand God as the ultimate source *of* the possibilities for any event. So, at least from the time he wrote *Process and Reality*, Whitehead described the role of God in terms of providing the origin of any occasion's subjectivity. This is important because Whitehead is clear about each event enjoying its own subjectivity, but, until *Process and Reality*, he had not explained how that subjectivity is acquired. How does an event have the capacity to prehend its numerous causal data and bring them together to create the future?[30] In his developed thought, Whitehead proposes that it happens due to an ideal of what it can become, given its specific circumstances. It is this ideal that is received from God, and it achieves its own actualization by the manner in which it melds together all of its efficient causes by means of this ideal of itself. The event is therefore not determined by God, as it is capable of using the past causes it inherits to adjust that aim, nor is it determined by its past, as it can also use that aim to adapt and to influence the way in which it will appropriate the past. Thus, the previously discussed balance of polarities in Whitehead's thinking allows spontaneity and freedom in the God/world relationship rather than domination and control.[31]

Whitehead eventually decided that, in order to make his metaphysics logical, God would need to be understood as one actual entity among other actual entities, and have physical prehensions, thus directly experiencing the world. On this view, God and the world form an ecosystem where both contribute to the other. God provides each event with the aim towards which it moves. Each event actualizes itself, influenced by the possibilities provided by God, and by appropriating elements out of its own past. The result of this process is then experienced by God, and in this way, God is enriched by the world.[32] For Whitehead:

> The universe, thus disclosed, is through and through interdependent. The body pollutes the mind, the mind pollutes the body. Physical energy sublimates itself into zeal; conversely, zeal stimulates the body. The biological ends pass into ideals of standards, and the formation of standards affects the biological facts. The individual is formative of the society, the society is

29. Ford, *Lure of God*, 8.
30. Ford, *Lure of God*, 7.
31. Ford, *Lure of God*, 8.
32. Ford, *Lure of God*, 11.

formative of the individual. . . . The individuality of entities is just as important as their community. The topic of religion is individuality in community.[33]

In Whitehead's system, God's action in the world is purely persuasive. God's primordial nature is "the divine persuasion, by reason of which ideals are effective in the world and forms of order evolve."[34] God functions as the "Principle of Concretion" in that God initiates the move toward a definite outcome from an indeterminate situation. The initial aim only partially defines the goal which is best in any given situation, and the temporal occasion does the rest.[35] Thus the ultimate creative purpose is "that each unification shall achieve some maximum depth of intensity of feeling, subject to the conditions of its concrescence."[36] Each concrescence is an undividable creative act, so the temporal advance of the universe is not continuous, but distinct. In retrospect and as potential for the future, however, the physical side of each atom of process is infinitely dividable. This taps into theories of space and time, and, for Whitehead, space and time are features of process, an abstract system of perspectives, for feeling is always perspectival. Space-time is not a fact previous to process, it is all part of one whole. Each actual occasion therefore prehends the space-time continuum in its infinite wholeness, and "actual fact includes in its own constitution real potentiality which is referent beyond itself."[37]

As far as Whitehead is concerned, the ultimate character pervading the universe is creativity. Neither a thing nor an entity, creativity cannot be understood in terms of the other three categories of existence (shortly to be discussed) that Whitehead explicates in *Process and Reality*; it forms its own.[38] Creativity is "that ultimate notion of the highest generality which actuality *exhibits*."[39] It is "that apart from which nothing can be . . . the actuality of every actual entity."[40] This is an essential feature of Whitehead's thought. The interdependence of God and the world, along with his final emphasis on creativity, is right at the center of his understanding of the nature of reality.[41] Indeed, it was largely on the basis of interdependence and

33. Whitehead, "Religion and Metaphysics," 68–69.

34. Whitehead, *Adventures of Ideas*, 214.

35. Lowe, "Whitehead's Metaphysical System," 12–13.

36. Whitehead, *Process and Reality*, 381.

37. Lowe, "Whitehead's Metaphysical System," 17–18.

38. Whitehead, *Process and Reality*, 22.

39. Lowe, "Whitehead's Metaphysical System," 3–4.

40. Cobb, "Whiteheadian Doctrine of God," 240.

41. Lowe, "Whitehead's Metaphysical System," 20.

creativity that Whitehead completely rejected the notion of an omnipotent God, insisting that "the presentation of God under the aspect of power awakens every modern instinct of critical reaction."[42] For him, both a religious faith and a scientific understanding of the world was integrated into an ever changing cosmos pulsating with life and possibility:

> Religion is the vision of something which stands beyond, behind, and within, the passing flux of immediate things; something which is real, and yet waiting to be realized; something which is a remote possibility, and yet the greatest of present facts; something that gives meaning to all that passes, and yet eludes apprehension; something whose possession is the final good, and yet is beyond all reach; something which is the ultimate ideal, and the hopeless quest.[43]

Whitehead's adventuring with ideas undoubtedly did not exclude overtly religious ones, although, as the above quote suggests, he felt a deeper level of certainty in the realm of philosophy than he did in the realm of religion, particularly regarding personal faith. It is relevant to note here that his metaphysical schema seeking to explain the nature of all reality (which, on his view, necessarily included, but did not entirely subsume, God) was begun to be developed in the years after the Great War. In this tragically dubbed "war to end all wars,"[44] the flower of British youth perished, including many young men whom Whitehead taught at Cambridge and London. Whitehead's younger son, Eric, also died, killed in air combat in 1918.[45] It was a time of great suffering, and a context in which traditional religious views about the power and providence of God could well be called into question. For Whitehead, the religious quest always remained quietly compelling. Eight years after the death of his son and the end of the war he wrote:

> The fact of the religious vision, and its history of persistent expansion, is our one ground for optimism. Apart from it, human life is a flash of occasional enjoyments lighting up a mass of pain and misery, a bagatelle of transient experience.
> The vision claims nothing but worship; and worship is a surrender to the claim to assimilation, urged with the motive force of mutual love. The vision never overrules. It is always

42. Whitehead, "Religion and Science," 439.

43. Whitehead, *Science and the Modern World*, 238.

44. The "war to end all wars" is a term for World War I (1914–1918). Originally coined to state a positive ideal, it is now used almost exclusively in the sardonic sense.

45. Ford, *Lure of God*, 8.

there, and it has the power of love presenting the one purpose whose fulfilment is eternal harmony. Such order as we find in nature is never force—it presents itself as the one harmonious adjustment of complex detail. Evil is the brute motive force of fragmentary purpose, disregarding the eternal vison. Evil is overruling, retarding, hurting. The power of God is the worship He inspires.[46]

In the development of his process metaphysics Whitehead was quite prepared to go out on a limb to test the fullest possibilities of his logic, and he has rightly been described as one who dared to esteem adventure more than safety.[47] As just noted, he did not shy away from referencing God at certain points in his speculative commentary on the nature of reality, but it is true to say that the language he used and the method he employed was principally forensic and philosophical. Whitehead did, however, use terms that he borrowed from poetry. Examples of these include his metaphorical use of expressions like "society," "feeling," or "satisfaction"[48] to denote certain aspects of his categories of thought. Add this to his coining of neologisms like "prehension" or "actual entity"[49] and we begin to see more clearly how his particular brand of speculation enlarged the metaphysical dictionary. Whitehead's terminology for process thinking, although difficult to understand and not used in a consistent manner throughout his writing, has nevertheless filled in some of the many gaps in our linguistic representation of the texture of experience.[50]

The developed process thought of Whitehead is best explained in *Process and Reality*, a book described in the editor's preface as "one of the major philosophical works of the modern world."[51] Whitehead's system of thought consists of four categories. The first is the Category of the Ultimate, which contains only one thing, creativity. Creativity is both the universal of universals and the principle of novelty.[52] The second is the Category of Existence, and there are eight Categories of Existence including Actual Entities, Prehensions, and Eternal Objects.[53] These three terms are used constantly

---

46. Whitehead, *Science and the Modern World*, 238.
47. Solch, "Metaphysical Creativity," 15.
48. Whitehead, *Process and Reality.*
49. Whitehead, *Process and Reality.*
50. Solch, "Metaphysical Creativity," 15.
51. Whitehead, *Process and Reality*, v.
52. Whitehead, *Process and Reality*, 21.
53. Whitehead, *Process and Reality*, 22.

by Whitehead, and have become part of the language of process thought, so it is worth defining them here:

> Actual entities—also termed 'actual occasions'—are the final real things of which the world is made up. There is no going behind actual entities to find anything more real. They differ among themselves: God is an actual entity, and so is the most trivial puff of existence in far off empty space. But, though there are gradations of importance, and diversities of function, yet in the principles which actuality exemplifies all are on the same level.[54]

To describe the term "prehension" as a feeling or an experience is to oversimplify, but it does take us into the constant movement of process thought. A prehension is a relating or transition which carries an object into the makeup of the subject. For Whitehead, a subject's enjoyment of an experience does not exist beforehand, nor is it created externally. Instead, it creates itself in the very process of the experience. The important point in this is that an actual entity (defined above), in a state of process or becoming, during which it is not fully defined, determines its own ultimate definition. Indeed, any organism determines the eventual characteristics and combination of its own parts; the brief progression of each pulse of experience being steered by an internal teleology.[55]

The meaning of the term "eternal objects" changed somewhat for Whitehead as his schema developed. In *Process and Reality* an alternate term offered for eternal objects is "Forms of Definiteness."[56] So the eternal objects can be described as those things of definite form. The best synonym for "eternal" seems to be "atemporal," as it picks up the sense of existing outside of time, rather than "everlasting," in the simple sense of being ongoing.[57] Whitehead explained the meaning of eternal objects using color as an example: "A color is eternal. It haunts time like a spirit. It comes and it goes. But when it comes, it is the same color. It neither survives nor does it live. It appears when it is wanted."[58]

Eternal objects are often described as permanent possibilities, things that everlastingly subsist because they are envisaged by God from time immemorial. The idea is that eternal objects endure as possibilities because God is always prehending them. This doesn't do full justice to eternal objects

54. Whitehead, *Process and Reality*, 27.
55. Lowe, "Whitehead's Metaphysical System," 7.
56. Whitehead, *Process and Reality*, 22.
57. Ford, "Whitehead's Differences from Hartshorne," 59.
58. Whitehead, *Science and the Modern World*, 126.

as a category of existence, however, because in Whitehead's worldview the primordial God "is not *before* all creation, but *with* all creation."[59] The import of this is that there never was a time in which God was enthroned in solitary splendor before the world was created, rather that the primordial nature itself is emergent with creation, nascent when relevant and as required. This non-temporality of God is hard for us to envision, for we are bound by time. God, in contrast, is not time-bound, and so God's pure conceptual prehensions of the eternal objects need not be in a particular place in time and space. The ontological principle demands that they must be somewhere, but in this case the "somewhere" is the non-temporal actual entity—the primordial mind of God, which does not refer to a particular space or time, nor indeed to all space-time.[60]

The third category of Whitehead, after the Category of the Ultimate and the eight Categories of Existence, are the Categories of Explanation. There are twenty-seven of them, each seeking to explain the nature of reality according to Whitehead's metaphysics. The first three of the Categories of Explanation lay the groundwork of his thinking:

> That the actual world is a process, and that the process is the becoming of actual entities. Thus actual entities are creatures, they are also termed 'actual occasions.'
>
> That in the becoming of an actual entity, the *potential* unity of many entities in the disjunctive diversity—actual and non-actual—acquires the *real* unity of the one actual entity; so that the actual entity is the real concrescence of many potentials.
>
> That in the becoming of an actual entity, novel prehensions, nexus, subjective forms, propositions, multiplicities, and contrasts, also become; but there are no novel eternal objects.[61]

Even without laboriously defining all of Whitehead's terminology separately, it is clear that he understands reality as cumulative. When an actual occasion is completed the creativity of the universe moves on to the next birth, and it carries that occasion with it as an object which all future occasions are obliged to prehend. They will feel it as an efficient cause, that is, as the immanence of the past in their immediacies of becoming. The end of an occasion's private life is, in Whitehead's language, its perishing.[62] Whitehead explains:

59. Whitehead, *Process and Reality*, 521.
60. Ford, "Whitehead's Differences from Hartshorne," 59–60.
61. Whitehead, *Process and Reality*, 22.
62. Whitehead, *Science and the Modern World*, 8.

If you get a general notion of what is meant by perishing, you will have accomplished an apprehension of what you mean by memory and causality; what you mean when you feel that what we are is of infinite importance, because as we perish we are immortal.[63]

The fourth and last of the categories into which Whitehead ordered his system is called Categoreal Obligations. There are nine of them, the last of which is The Category of Freedom and Determination. It gives an insight into the philosophical reasoning Whitehead employs to inform the view in process thought that God shares power with the world and always operates non-coercively:

> *The Category of Freedom and Determination.* The concrescence of each individual actual entity is internally determined and is externally free. This category can be condensed into the formula, that in each concrescence whatever is determinable is determined, but that there is always a remainder for the decision of the subject-superject of that concrescence. The subject-superject is the universe in that synthesis, and beyond it there is nonentity. This final decision is the reaction of the unity of the whole to its own internal determination. The reaction is the final modification of emotion, appreciation, and purpose. But the decision of the whole arises out of the determination of the parts, so as to be strictly relevant to it.[64]

Working out how decisions about the direction of the universe might be made, and the relationship between all there is and what is contributed by "the parts,"[65] is the heartland of the process thought of Whitehead. It is also intimately connected to notions of the exercise of power, particularly regarding God and God's manner of operation in the world. Whitehead's experience of loss in the war was a key to this, his suffering indivisible from the development of his thinking about the possibility of God in the processes of reality, and the potential of good over evil in his vision of the world. As previously mentioned, for Whitehead, a religious vision grounded in a history of constant becoming is cause for optimism. Without it, he says that human life is at best a flash of occasional joy in a mass of pain and misery. The vision of Whitehead is grounded in power as love and fulfilled in eternal harmony, and it is on this basis that the order found in nature is never force. For Whitehead, force is evil, and the use of force disregards the

63. Whitehead, *Essays in Science and Philosophy*, 117.

64. Whitehead, *Process and Reality*, 27–28.

65. Whitehead, *Process and Reality*, 28.

eternal vision for good. Ultimately, on Whitehead's view, the essence of the power of God is the worship inspired by God.[66] It is true to say that process philosophy was not his life's work in one sense, as Whitehead had had a full academic career predominantly in mathematics before he fully embarked on his extraordinarily ambitious project. In another sense, his refined system of thought variously referred to as process philosophy, process metaphysics, even process theism,[67] represents a culmination of the thinking, the concerns, and the experiences of Whitehead's entire life. Far from being a cold process of "incipient rationality,"[68] Whitehead's vision of an interdependent universe in process had a distinct spiritual aspect and was deeply personal.

To translate the metaphysical/philosophical language of Whitehead into theology we now turn to Charles Hartshorne (1897–2000). In his obituary in the New York Times, Hartshorne was described as "a philosopher, theologian and educator who wrote more than 20 books and 100 articles in a lifelong mission to prove that God was a participant in cosmic evolution rather than the supreme composer."[69] In the tribute, one theological commentator summed up the import of Hartshorne's work in colloquial, but very effective, terms. He proposed that God can no longer and never again be imagined to look like Charlton Heston, for now we understand that God suffers with us.[70] By making process thought more accessible to Christian theology, Hartshorne makes an important contribution to the way in which Christians can think about and describe God and God's relation to the world, and thus the related issues of power and suffering.

From the publication of his first book in 1934 no thinker has matched Hartshorne in the elaboration and adaptation of Whitehead's philosophy.[71] As his thought is so closely associated with that of Whitehead, and as they were both connected with Harvard University, it is often assumed that Hartshorne was Whitehead's student, but this is not the case. While mediating Whitehead for theology, Hartshorne was also an original contributor to a panentheistic, process understanding of God: one that emphasizes God's dynamic nature as both acting upon and being affected by the world.[72] In acknowledging the influences of William Ernest Hocking and Charles S.

66. Whitehead, *Science and the Modern World*, 238.

67. Ford, *Lure of God*.

68. Whitehead, *Religion in the Making*, 23.

69. Martin, "Charles Hartshorne, Theologian Is Dead."

70. Charlton Heston (1928–2008) was the American actor especially well known for taking the lead roles in Hollywood biblical epics. His brand of chiseled manhood represented a white, Anglo-Saxon, male vision of an all-powerful God.

71. Reeves and Brown, "Development of Process Theology," 27.

72. Long, *Western Philosophy of Religion*, 372.

Pierce, along with that of Whitehead, on this thinking, Hartshorne insists that "with or without their influence, I would probably have had beliefs like theirs, but much less well articulated and argued for."[73]

In an academic career spanning two thirds of the twentieth century Hartshorne served on the faculties of Harvard, Chicago, Emory and the University of Texas.[74] In his early writing Hartshorne expressed an understanding of God that found a middle way between the absolutism of classical theology and the atheistic humanism adopted by many of his contemporaries in the nineteen thirties.[75] He initially described his view of the God/world relation as theistic naturalism, or naturalistic theism, and argued that he is not a supernaturalist in any ordinary sense of the term. For him, supernaturalism and humanism are two facets of the same error.[76] Hartshorne insists:

> (It is a) mistaken notion that nature, in her non-human portions and characters, is wholly subhuman. Not finding the superhuman in nature, the supernaturalist seeks it 'beyond' nature; the humanist, in the unrealized potentialities of man. . . . Only an improved understanding of the higher aspects of nature can enable the doctrine of a natural but super-human—and even, in a sense, perfect—God to take the place of the other two doctrines.[77]

For Hartshorne, nature is in effect an individual with a quality that is divine. The term he gave to the relationship between God and creatures was panpsychism.[78] Whitehead did not use this particular word, but his notion of actual occasions had a very similar import, as actual occasions can feel

73. Hartshorne, *Creativity in American Philosophy*, 104.

74. Long, *Western Philosophy of Religion*, 372.

75. Reeves and Brown, "Development of Process Theology," 28.

76. Long, *Western Philosophy of Religion*, 373.

77. Hartshorne, *Beyond Humanism*, 3–4.

78. Hartshorne, *Beyond Humanism*, chapter 2. Panpsychism is a somewhat flexible concept that predates Hartshorne and can be found in Baruch Spinoza (1632–1677) and in the sympathies of Gottfried Wilhelm Leibniz (1646–1716). Nadler, *Best of All Possible Worlds*, 221–23. Hartshorne in fact refers to Spinoza's panpsychism as "pantheism" and is at pains to distance his thinking from that of Spinoza. In making clear his own view is that of panentheism rather than the pantheism/panpsychism of Spinoza, Hartshorne expresses his opposition to "any doctrine which, like Spinoza's, asserts that there is a premise from which all facts are implied conclusions." Hartshorne, *Divine Relativity*, 90. "For Spinoza, God is nothing but nature—*Deus sive Natura*, 'God or Nature,' in his famous phrase—the infinite, necessarily existing, eternal, and active substance of the universe. There is nothing good or bad, perfect or imperfect about God or Nature; it just *is*." Nadler, *Best of All Possible Worlds*, 222.

an environment and respond both creatively and with purpose.[79] Both Hartshorne and Whitehead defend a cell theory of "compound individuals" where macroscopic objects are constructed as aggregates of sentient occasions of experience. The idea is that, while rock and similar substances are not sentient, the simplest physical entities of which they are composed are. On this basis, everything has some degree of willing, feeling, and mentality. The world, indeed, the entire universe, is therefore a vast system of organisms and non-organic societies of organisms, from microscopic physical events to God. In this system there is significant continuity between levels of existence because every level is constituted by social relationships. For Hartshorne, this contrasts sharply with more traditional views of the world and God, because traditionally matter is regarded as too inferior to be social and God too superior to be truly social.[80] In Hartshorne's thinking reality is social at all levels and therefore so is God. God alone is directly related to all other creatures, both to influence them and be influenced by them. Since to prehend others is to include them, God includes all others in such a manner that their freedom is protected and God's responsibility for their action is limited. As far as Hartshorne is concerned, it is only if genuine creaturely freedom is upheld, and with it the logically implied restriction of divine power and knowledge, that the notion of God as love can be upheld.[81]

The headings of the three main parts of Hartshorne's 1948 analysis of the nature of God, *The Divine Relativity*, give an overview both of his understanding of the social nature of reality and his desire to avoid charges of pantheism in his view. The first part describes God as supreme yet indebted to all. The second part describes God as absolute yet related to all. The third part explains the attributes of God as types of social relationship.[82] In the conclusion to his reflection on the balance between the supremacy and the indebtedness of God, Hartshorne writes:

> If God can be indebted to no one, can receive value from no one, then to speak of serving him is to indulge in equivocation. Really it must, on that assumption, be only the creature who is to be served or benefited. God would be the cause and protector of value; but the value caused and protected must be simply ours. On this time-hallowed view, God was the mine and the miner from and by which the wealth was dug; but the ultimate consumer was ourselves. God was the policeman and

79. Reeves and Brown, "Development of Process Theology," 28–29.

80. Reeves and Brown, "Development of Process Theology," 29.

81. Reeves and Brown, "Development of Process Theology," 30.

82. Hartshorne, *Divine Relativity*, 1–115.

judge and ruler, but man was the citizen, for whose sake the commonwealth existed. It is time that we consider the possibility that it may be just as blasphemous to suppose ourselves the ultimate recipients, as the ultimate makers, of achieved good. We are intermediate and secondary makers of value, intermediate benefactors; are we not likewise intermediate and secondary recipients of value, intermediate beneficiaries? The supreme source, and as well the supreme result, of the entire process of value-making is, I suggest, the divine life, in its originative and its consummatory phases, and these phases are genuinely distinct.[83]

As Hartshorne sought a balance between the supremacy and indebtedness of God, so he also sought a balance between the transcendence and immanence of God. He describes how God can be absolute and yet related to all. In this he specifically articulates the difference between his own panentheistic view of God and pantheism. In referring to pantheists he uses the term "they," thus distancing himself from the view that God is merely the cosmos and is in all respects inseparable from the system of dependent effects:[84]

> The error of most pantheists has been to deny the externality of concrete existence to the essence of deity. They have not realized that the inclusive actuality of God, which includes all de facto actuality, is as truly contingent and capable of additions as the least actuality it includes. This is the freedom both of God and of the creatures. For since the essence of God is compatible with any possible universe, we can be allowed some power of decision, as between possibilities, without infringing the absolute independence of God in his essential character or personality. And God's own freedom is likewise safe guarded, since freedom means a personal character with which alternative concrete experiences or states are compatible. True, the actual state of deity will be determined partly by the creatures; but this is simply the social character of the divine self-decision, and it is hard to know what to do with opponents who almost in one breath accuse one of an 'impersonal' idea of deity and yet object to the admission of social relativity, a basic aspect of personality, in the divine person.[85]

---

83. Hartshorne, *Divine Relativity*, 58–59.
84. Hartshorne, *Divine Relativity*, 90.
85. Hartshorne, *Divine Relativity*, 89.

For Hartshorne then, God is *both* supreme *and* indebted, *both* absolute *and* related to all, and these divine qualities assure us that God is entirely social. All things are connected uniquely through the intimate continuity of purpose and memory in the one divine life. Hartshorne sets God outside of any other class of event or occasion, while also noting that there is an infinite and continually increased class of previous, already actualized, divine experiences in God at each and any moment:[86]

> In this sense God, though not in a class, *is* a class, which is not member of any class of similar classes, and one every member of which enjoys dynamic, and not merely logical, connection with every other member. The divine attributes are the class character of this unique class, new members of which cannot fail to continue to become forevermore, and old members of which can never fade from the memory of new members, in which is the immortality of all our achievements of experienced quality, in ourselves and for whom we are concerned, and in every fragment of awareness actualized in time.[87]

Hartshorne argues that there are only three ways of understanding the divine nature, just three formally possible doctrines of God. First, it could be proposed that there is a being in all respects absolutely perfect and unsurpassable. Hartshorne called this *Theism of the first type*. He associates it with the absolutism inherent in classical models of God, especially that of St Thomas Aquinas and his five ways. Hartshorne also associates it with most European theology prior to 1880. Second, it could be proposed that there is no being in all respects absolutely perfect, but there is a being in some respects perfect, and in some respects not so; in some respects surpassable—either by self or others. Hartshorne called this *Theism of the second type*. He associates it with much contemporary Protestant theology. By making this association he acknowledges that many of the theological understandings of the twentieth century had already challenged and potentially moved beyond theism of the first type. The third proposal is that there is no being in any respect absolutely perfect. All beings are in all respects surpassable by something conceivable, by others or by themselves in another state. He associates this view with those who accept doctrines of a finite God, with some forms of polytheism, and with atheism.[88]

Religious experience, argues Hartshorne, is not compatible with theism of the first type. It seems, rather, to support the second type of theism,

86. Hartshorne, *Divine Relativity*, 157.
87. Hartshorne, *Divine Relativity*, 157–58.
88. Hartshorne, "Formally Possible Doctrines," 195.

as the God who enjoys absolute bliss in eternity does not have the capacity to be displeased with our sin, to sympathize with us in our suffering, or to be the one we serve and, in some way, contribute to overall. For God to have perfect power need not mean that other individuals have none, and perfect love cannot escape a share in the suffering of others.[89] For Hartshorne:

> The dilemma appears final: *either value is social,* and then its perfection cannot be wholly within the power of any one being, even God; *or it is not social at all,* and then the saying, 'God is love,' is an error.[90]

First type theism, synonymous with classical theism, also presents philosophical paradoxes, for in a being exempt from change in any substantial sense, time is not. Third type theism raises philosophical issues too, for if the highest possible being is surpassable in all respects there is no enduring being whose identity is assured even through change.[91] So the only one of the three possible doctrines of God that has a future for the Christian faith is the second one. Essentially, Hartshorne insisted that God really is the supreme power in existence, the causal influence superior to all others. He was equally sure, however, that superiority of power does not imply a one-way causal action, that is an action that does not react or interact.[92] Above all else, God responds to us and to the world with the different power of love:

> It will be seen that the God of second-type theism is not without qualification finite, or growing, or emergent; nor, without qualification, is he the contradictory of these. . . . The concepts which still function as absolute are the strictly religious and experiential ones of love and goodness. God is the Holy One, the ethical Absolute, the literally all-loving Father. In these affirmations second-type theism sees no exaggeration. . . . Whitehead and others have shown that it is precisely love which must be perfect in God.[93]

Hartshorne is very clear that any view which ascribes ethical perfection and yet the greatest possible power to God must face the problem of evil. He asserts that the minimum solution to the problem of evil is to affirm the requirement of a division of powers, and therefore of responsibilities, that are binding upon the highest power. He also acknowledges that giving

89. Long, *Western Philosophy of Religion*, 372.
90. Hartshorne, *Man's Vision of God*, 14.
91. Long, *Western Philosophy of Religion*, 374.
92. Hartshorne, "Formally Possible Doctrines," 203.
93. Hartshorne, "Formally Possible Doctrines," 213.

voice to this solution is usually seen to imply the passivity or weakness of the supreme power, which makes it unavailable to theists of the first type.[94] Hartshorne says:

> Those who think God cannot mean well toward us because he 'sends' us suffering can prove their point only by showing that there is a way to run the universe compatible with the existence of other real powers than just the supreme power, which would be more fully in accord with the totality of interests, or by showing that God sends us the suffering while himself remaining simply outside it, in the enjoyment of sheer bliss. Theologians themselves seem generally to have made a present of the latter notion to atheists; but the former view has its plausibility for all of us.[95]

In effect, Hartshorne finds that an adherence to theism of the first type is a gift given to atheistic humanists by many theologians. Such adherence is a gift to atheism because the inner logic of classical theism leads away from faith in the Christian God of love. Indeed, for Hartshorne, the motivation for getting the reasoning surrounding possible doctrines of God coherent and acceptable was his major concern that a sustainable, ongoing, and recognizably Christian faith be available to all thinking people.

According to Hartshorne, there are six mistakes about God which constitute theism of the first type, as outlined in *Omnipotence and Other Theological Mistakes*.[96] The first mistake is at the heart of the concerns of this thesis, and the one for which his book was named, the purported omnipotence of God. The idea of omnipotence, of God being perfect in power so that whatever happens is divinely made to happen, is rejected by Hartshorne. The suggestion that the highest conceivable form of power is the power to determine every detail of what occurs in the world is referred to by Hartshorne as the tyrant ideal of power. He notes that the standard solution to this divine tyranny is the notion that God *could* determine everything, but out of appreciation of the value of having free creatures God allows humans to make their own choices.[97] This response is deeply inadequate for Hartshorne, and indeed for many others, as the suggestion that when things go badly it is because humans have exercised their freedom of choice poorly does nothing at all to explain natural evil—disease and decay and disaster in the natural world through processes that are beyond human control. Hartshorne argues for a generalized freedom, pointing out that:

94. Hartshorne, "Formally Possible Doctrines," 204.
95. Hartshorne, "Formally Possible Doctrines," 205.
96. Hartshorne, *Omnipotence and Other Theological Mistakes*, 1–6.
97. Hartshorne, *Theological Mistakes*, 3.

> Our having at least some freedom is not an absolute exception to an otherwise total lack of freedom in nature, but a special, magnified form of a *general principle* pervasive of reality, down to the very *atoms and still further.*[98]

The recognition that it is a mistake to try and hold the notion of an omnipotent God, a "tyrant ideal of power,"[99] in tension with any understanding of the general freedom of nature, is key in Hartshorne's thinking and in process theology generally. It is the foundation of the agreement throughout the process movement that God exercises power in entirely persuasive and invitational ways, and that domination and control are not among the attributes of deity.

The second mistake is to seek to describe God as absolutely perfect and therefore unchangeable. Hartshorne notes that, in the ancient philosophy of Plato's *Republic,* which formed the foundation of classical theism, one finds this proposition: God, being perfect, cannot change. God cannot change for the better, as "perfect" means that there can be no better. God cannot change for the worse, since the ability to change for the worse, to decay, to degenerate, or become corrupt, is a weakness and an imperfection. Hartshorne notes in response that ordinary meanings of perfect do not entirely exclude change. He suggests that when the Bible speaks of God as perfect it does not exclude the possibility of change in every respect:[100]

> Where in the Bible God is . . . directly spoken of as strictly unchanging ('without a shadow of turning'), there is still a possibility of ambiguity. God might be absolutely unchangeable in righteousness (which is what the context indicates is the intended meaning), but changeable in ways compatible with, neutral to, *or even required by,* this unswerving constancy in righteousness. Thus, God would be in no degree, however slight, alterable in the respect in question (the divine steadfastness in good will) and yet alterable, not necessarily in spite of, but even because of, this steadfastness. If the creatures behave according to God's will, God will appreciate this behavior; if not, God will have a different response, equally appropriate and expressive of the divine goodness.[101]

---

98. Hartshorne, *Omnipotence and Other Theological Mistakes*, 13.

99. Hartshorne, *Omnipotence and Other Theological Mistakes*, 3.

100. Hartshorne, *Omnipotence and Other Theological Mistakes*, 2.

101. Hartshorne, *Omnipotence and Other Theological Mistakes*, 2. The example Hartshorne uses of reference to the unchanging nature of God in the bible comes from James 1:17.

The third and fourth mistakes, the omniscience of God and the notion of God's unsympathetic goodness, are both linked to the second mistake. The omniscience of God assumes unchangeable perfection in God and then goes on to assert on that basis that whatever happens is eternally known to God. It further asserts that everything is eternally present to God, so there is no open future. Hartshorne points out that a mistaken belief in the omniscience of God, like the belief that perfection cannot include change, denies freedom to people and the world, and also defies logic.[102] Hartshorne argues:

> With omniscience there is one difficulty: either knowing about the future differs essentially from knowing about the past, and hence even God knows our past decisions in one way and knows about the future of our decision making in another way, or else it is merely our human weakness that for us the future is partly indefinite, a matter of what may or may not be, whereas God, exalted altogether beyond such a 'limitation,' sees the future as completely definite. If God is to be thought in every respect immutable it is this second option that must be taken; but have we any other reason for rejecting the old Socinian proposition that even the highest conceivable form of knowledge is of the past-and-definite and of the future and partly indefinite *as* future and partly indefinite? Otherwise would not God be 'knowing' the future as what it is not, that is, knowing falsely? As we have seen, the arguments for the complete unchangeability of God are fallacious; hence the arguments for the growth of God's knowledge, as the creative process produces new realities to know, are sound.[103]

What Hartshorne denies in the fourth mistake (God's unsympathetic goodness) is the idea that God's love for us has no effect whatsoever on God. This is also linked to the ancient notion of perfection, for to be affected by love is to change. Hartshorne insists both that God loves and is changed by love, describing divine love in terms of divine sympathy: the

102. Hartshorne, *Omnipotence and Other Theological Mistakes*, 3. Hartshorne here does not argue against omniscience per se, but against what he describes as a *mistaken* omniscience grounded in the notion of a perfection in God that does not allow God to change. Hartshorne goes on to ask, "Is God all-knowing?" He answers his question, "Yes, in the Socinian sense. Never has a great intellectual discovery passed with less notice by the world than the Socinian discovery of the proper meaning of omniscience." Hartshorne, *Theological Mistakes*, 27. Socinianism developed in the Minor Reformed Church of Poland in the sixteenth and seventeenth centuries and denies the exhaustive foreknowledge of God. It is a position Hartshorne shares with Open Theists.

103. Hartshorne, *Omnipotence and Other Theological Mistakes*, 27.

feeling of other's feelings.[104] He suggests that Christian theology has argued to date from an insufficiently analyzed notion of God's perfection, and has demonstrated a preference for materialistic and prescientific ideas rather than spiritual ones.[105]

The fifth mistake is to see immortality as a career after death. Hartshorne describes both heaven and hell as myths. He notes that in the Old Testament generally, and particularly in the book of Job, with its focus on suffering in human life, individual immortality is not mentioned. He further notes that Judaism is very cautious about affirming immortality, that it very often denies it, and that Jesus in the New Testament says very little about it either.[106] For Hartshorne, the notion that we reap the benefits of God's goodness through our immortal souls seems almost to set human beings up as rivals to God. He does concede that there is a sense in which God would not destroy the object of God's love, and so human beings are in some way imperishable, but he does not see this necessarily requiring the idea of personal survival.[107] On Hartshorne's account:

> For God to love the earthly creatures which we are for our own sake is one thing; for Him to love us for our alleged capacity to be transformed into pseudo-angels is another thing. It begs the whole question to identify these two loves, or deduce the second from the first.[108]

For Hartshorne, God participates in the life of God's creatures and the creatures in him. Through this process every passing moment is understood to be taken up and cherished forever in God. It is in this way that we may be said to contribute to the life of God. Ultimately, in Hartshorne's schema, we do not live for ourselves, nor even for all of humanity, but for that hidden divine reality which embraces us all.[109]

The sixth mistake is to view revelation as infallible. Hartshorne had no problem with the idea of revelation per se, and certainly did not discount it all together. The question which concerned him was the extent to which, or in what circumstances, some individuals (or even a unique individual) are deemed to be worthy of trust in religious matters. This was particularly regarding religious leaders and those anointed by the Church. He always

---

104. Hartshorne, *Omnipotence and Other Theological Mistakes*, 31.
105. Hartshorne, *Omnipotence and Other Theological Mistakes*, 4.
106. Hartshorne, *Omnipotence and Other Theological Mistakes*, 4.
107. Long, *Western Philosophy of Religion*, 375.
108. Hartshorne, *Logic of Perfection*, 243.
109. Long, *Western Philosophy of Religion*, 375.

argued that no one is, or can be, infallible; that no one is divinely wise, indeed that we all make mistakes.[110]

The six common theological mistakes described above are intended by Hartshorne to be a summary of what went wrong in classical theism.[111] As a refutation of classical theism and an affirmation of a panentheistic vision of God as a Divine Relativity was essentially Hartshorne's life work, they also go a long way to summing up the process theology of Hartshorne. In Hartshorne's view, therefore, the traditional idea of divine perfection or infinity is hopelessly unclear and ambiguous. It breeds atheism as a natural reaction to its labyrinthine but flawed logic as neither contemporary science nor philosophy recognize the absolute worldly fixities assumed by the ancient Greeks: not the stars, not the species, not the atoms.[112] On Hartshorne's view, there are only two senses in which perfection (that is, perfection understood in terms of freedom from faults, defects, or objectionable features) may be applied theologically, and they are as follows. The divine, to be worthy of worship, must excel any conceivable being other than itself; it must be unsurpassable *by another*, exulted beyond all possible rivals. Hence all may worship God as in principle forever superior to any other being. On this basis, Hartshorne asserts that the tradition shared by both philosophy and theology captured only half the truth. He says that the neglected other truth is that an absolute best, unsurpassable by others and by the being itself, is conceivable only in certain *abstract* aspects of value or greatness, not in fully concrete value or greatness. And God, as Hartshorne so rightly insists, is no mere abstraction.[113]

This notion that God is less than God might be, while remaining more, in fact, than anything else can be, is a key feature of process thinking of all flavors. Hartshorne's life and academic endeavor was dedicated to engaging others in his quest to make a concerted attempt to worship the objective God rather than our forebears' doctrines about God. For him, neglecting the relativity of the divine other in favor of the absolutes of classical theism leads to otherworldliness, the worship of power, to asceticism, moralism, obscurantism, and to the confusion of deity and humanity. A last word on this from Hartshorne:

> Let us list some of the deficiencies of inherited religions.

110. Hartshorne, *Omnipotence and Other Theological Mistakes*, 4–6.

111. Hartshorne, *Omnipotence and Other Theological Mistakes*, 6.

112. Hartshorne, *Omnipotence and Other Theological Mistakes*, 8.

113. Hartshorne, *Omnipotence and Other Theological Mistakes*, 9.

Otherworldliness—the flight from the one task we surely face, that of human welfare on earth to a questionable one, the winning of a heavenly passport.

Power worship—the divorce of the notion of supreme influence from that of supreme sensitivity, in the concepts both of deity and of church and state authority.

Asceticism—the failure to genuinely synthesize 'physical' and 'spiritual' values, as shown above in the failure of practically all the churches to do justice to the meaning and problems of marriage.

Moralism—the notion that serving God is almost entirely a matter of avoiding theft and adultery and the like, together with dispensing charity, leaving noble-hearted courageous creative action in art, science, and statesmanship as religiously neutral or secondary.

Optimism—the denial that tragedy is fundamental in the nature of existence and God; an example being what one may call the pacifism of magical politics: let us (the pacifists) renounce force and there will be neither war nor any very terrible tyranny.

Obscurantism—the theory that we can best praise God by indulging in contradiction and semantical nonsense.

The confusion of deity and humanity in the theory of infallible revelation.[114]

THE SHAPERS OF PROCESS THOUGHT

Process thought in general, and the thinking of Whitehead and Hartshorne in particular, has some key interpreters and shapers. After World War II very few philosophers took great interest in Whitehead's metaphysics. The response was quite different among the students of theology and philosophy who studied with Hartshorne. As already noted, Hartshorne is the person most responsible for demonstrating the relevance of Whitehead's work for Christian theology, and for stimulating the process theology movement. In 1971 his effort led to a Journal called *Process Studies,* which was founded by John Cobb and Lewis Ford. Two years later the Center for Process Studies at Claremont was established by John Cobb and David Griffin.[115]

114. Hartshorne, *Divine Relativity*, 148–49.
115. Long, *Western Philosophy of Religion*, 375.

The most influential of the students of Hartshorne are two theologians who studied with him at the University of Chicago, John Cobb, and Schubert Ogden.[116] In reference to Whitehead and particularly to Hartshorne, in whose thought he specializes, Ogden writes:

> It is my belief that the conceptuality provided by this new philosophy enables us to conceive the reality of God so that we may respect all that is legitimate in modern secularity, while also fully respecting the distinctive claims of the Christian faith itself.[117]

John Cobb is well known as an interpreter of Whitehead, and for his efforts to develop a natural theology based upon Whiteheadian metaphysics. Cobb rejects the idea of natural theology that depends on reason alone on the grounds that it drives an unnecessary wedge between the God of philosophy and the God of religion. He defines theology in its broadest sense as, "any coherent statement about matters of ultimate concern that recognizes that the perspective by which it is governed is received from a community of faith."[118] Cobb therefore finds in a process understanding of the interrelatedness of all levels of reality, its rejection of dualism, and its understanding of God both affecting and being affected by the world, a model for talk of God that can take account of both a contemporary worldview and the experience of the Christian faith.[119]

Much has been written about the thinking of Whitehead and Hartshorne; about each thinker as an individual, and about the ideas they have in common, and it is possible to tease out their two somewhat different systems of thought stemming from a shared foundation. Although it has been suggested that Whitehead's metaphysical system is more empirical and Hartshorne's more rationalistic,[120] and, although both philosophers did refine and change their views over time, the differences in the overall thinking of Whitehead and Hartshorne are minor in comparison with their agreements. They hold a common position which can best be described as process philosophy and the theological movement influenced by their thought is process theology.[121] Bearing in mind this shared foundation, the two different systems, and the way they have been interpreted over the years, this study is most interested in those things that Whitehead and Hartshorne

---

116. Long, *Western Philosophy of Religion*, 376.

117. Ogden, *Reality of God*, 56–57.

118. Cobb, *Christian Natural Theology*, 252.

119. Long, *Western Philosophy of Religion*, 379.

120. Griffin, "Hartshorne's Differences from Whitehead," 47.

121. Cobb and Griffin, *Process Theology*, 7.

agreed upon. The conclusions they both drew about God and the world have never become mainstream and continue to challenge philosophers, but more particularly theologians, about the nature of reality, which, to their way of thinking, is also the nature of God. So, this study is less about contrasting the thinking of Hartshorne and Whitehead,[122] and more about finding ways of articulating the "big picture" of process theology in terms that are both Christian and trinitarian. There will, however, be a focus on the detail of some of Hartshorne's thinking, as he is the one who was observed to be "preoccupied with the problem of God, power and evil"[123] and those concerns are at the heart of this book.

Drawing upon the foundational thought of Whitehead and Hartshorne, shaped by some key contemporary process theologians, we now turn to some pivotal Christian doctrines. The insights of process theology into the foundational Christian notions of incarnation and resurrection, future hope in the eschaton, and ideals of God's love and justice, do give a somewhat altered vision of the faith of the Church. It is, however, a vision that does not damage the essential elements of Christianity.

KEY ISSUES FOR PROCESS THOUGHT

In process thought, the incarnation is described within a framework of there not being a time before the world when God existed independently of the world. Rather, God's life can only be thought of as in process with the world. The revelation of God in Jesus Christ is seen as an indication that the pattern of life in process is the path of self-giving love.[124] For Hartshorne, the Christian notion of a deity that can and does suffer, symbolized by the cross, along with the doctrine of the incarnation, is a legitimate indication of the "saving" quality in the process of all things, despite the existence of evil in the world.[125] While recognizing the important religious truths enshrined in the incarnation, Hartshorne was dubious about the traditional notion of the two natures of Jesus. He nevertheless allowed the legitimacy of language that spoke of Jesus as "in some sense" divine, as long as it was in the context of recognizing that to some degree every person could be said to

122. The two different systems represented by the thinking of Whitehead and Hartshorne are described by Clarke who points out that Whitehead's idea of God as an everlasting, single, actual entity, and Hartshorne's idea of God as a series of actual entities or a personally ordered society are distinctive. Clarke, "Two Process Views of God," 61–74. See also Griffin, "Hartshorne's Differences from Whitehead."

123. Lucas, "Whitehead: The Next Generation," xvi.

124. Loomer, "Christian Faith and Process Philosophy," 88.

125. Hartshorne, *Philosophers Speak of God*, 15.

be divine, due to the panentheistic nature of God.[126] The key to the person and work of Jesus for Hartshorne was that faith in Jesus as the Christ was to point logically to the truth of the existence of suffering in God. He notes that in the gospel record Jesus nowhere asserts, or even suggests, that God is immune to feeling pain. So, if Jesus is a disclosure in symbol of the divine, God as Jesus is revealed as one who shares in human anguish, even though this is not the last word.[127] Hartshorne made clear that he had no definitive christological formulation to offer, but nevertheless made what he termed a "simple suggestion":

> Jesus appears to be the supreme symbol furnished to us by history of the notion of a God genuinely and literally sympathetic (incomparably more literally than any man ever is), receiving into his own experience the suffering as well as the joys of the world.[128]

Similarly, Whitehead looked to a Christian formulation of God, and specifically to the person of Christ, to articulate what he referred to as a "new reformation" which would enable science, philosophy, and religion to make sense one to the other:

> The essence of Christianity is the appeal to the life of Christ as a revelation of the nature of God and of his agency in the world. The record is fragmentary, inconsistent and uncertain. . . . But there can be no doubt as to what elements in the record have evoked a response from all that is best in human nature. The Mother, the Child, and the bare manger: the lowly man, homeless and self-forgetful, with his message of peace, love

126. Hartshorne, *Reality as Social Progress*, 150–53. The title of this book is a reminder that Hartshorne understands all of reality, including God, as genuinely social. Hartshorne's diffidence about the "two natures," the traditional explication of the divinity and the humanity of Jesus, is thus due (at least in part) to his far bigger vision of sociality rather than simply duality (or even trinity). For him, God is "the super-creaturely individual of the inclusive creaturely society. Simply outside of this super-society and super individual, there is nothing." Hartshorne, *Omnipotence and Other Theological Mistakes*, 59. Hartshorne points out that his hesitation about the incarnation also comes down to general concerns about anthropomorphism and specific concerns about male supremacy. He says "one reason for my hesitation to accept any of the recent (or old) theories of the incarnation of God in Jesus of Nazareth . . . is that any such theory at least strongly suggests the idea of deity as highly spiritualized masculinity. It is a constant temptation to male chauvinism, and a temptation in historical fact not altogether resolutely resisted, to put it mildly." Hartshorne, *Omnipotence and Other Theological Mistakes*, 60.

127. Hartshorne, "Philosopher's Assessment," 175.

128. Hartshorne, "Philosopher's Assessment," 24.

and sympathy: the suffering, the agony, the tender words as life ebbed, the final despair: and the whole with the authority of supreme victory.[129]

Although the jury is still out as to whether by the end of his life Whitehead would have thought of himself as a Christian in the orthodox sense, he did believe that Jesus' life disclosed the nature of the Divine. Moreover, he was convinced that the agency of God in the world, the Divine Activity, is of the type demonstrated in the life of Jesus to which the New Testament bears witness. God, and all the workings of God, exercise persuasive rather than coercive power; God is the creative, dynamic, energizing love that was seen in the person of Jesus the Christ and in Jesus' own manner of being from birth to death to resurrection. Indeed, Whitehead asserted that Jesus was the "revelation in act"[130] of what others have discerned in theory. In other words, for Whitehead, Jesus was the concrete, historical occurrence of God among us.[131]

On a process view, Jesus is therefore not the entirely extraordinary "act of God"; he is the exemplary instance of self-disclosure by God. Likewise, God is not an exception to basic metaphysical principles, but rather their supreme exemplification.[132] So when it comes to the resurrection, process theology can talk in terms of the resurgence of the power of God in Jesus even when evil and death had seemingly triumphed. It can talk of evidence of the power of God and God's love over spiritual death; but it does not seek to provide evidence of God's control over physical death, as God is still subject to conditions that define the world.[133] So, for process thinkers, to believe in the crucial Christian miracle of the resurrection is in no way to challenge the method of science or to seek to suspend the warrants of responsible historical enquiry. Instead, it is to believe that the gift and demand which are re-presented to us in Jesus are none other than the very love of Godself, and a love which is even now the encompassing mystery in which all our lives are set.[134]

Process thought looks to *an experience of* the resurrection: to be confronted with the Lord's presence as an external reality. The earliest Christians did not believe in the resurrection primarily because they accepted the reports of the apostles, but because they *experienced* the Spirit of Christ

129. Whitehead, *Adventures of Ideas*, 214.

130. Whitehead, *Adventures of Ideas*, 214.

131. Pittenger, *Process-Thought*, 70–71.

132. Pittenger, *Process-Thought*, 73.

133. Loomer, "Christian Faith and Process Philosophy," 95.

134. Ogden, "Towards a New Theism," 183.

alive and active among them. The two facts of knowing Jesus and remembering Jesus constitute together the miracle of the resurrection. This unseen,
yet real, experience of Christ's directing activity in and through their lives
assured the early followers that Jesus was alive. As they also remembered
that he had died, so they could only infer that he was risen from the dead.
Although the resurrection appearances did confirm this conviction, these
visualizations were very likely understood as fuller manifestations of the
risen Christ bestowed on those few who were chosen to be leaders of the
Jesus movement. It was only when the sense of the immediate presence of
Christ among the early followers had faded over time that these reports
were reconceived and written as primary testimony to the resurrection.[135]

The resurrection, understood as a reality distinct from, yet part of the
reality of God, makes sense in a process framework. This is because, for
process thinkers, experience consists of discrete "buds" which each enjoy
their own subjectivity during their growing together into a unity. They then
perish as subjects, living on only in as much as their influence is felt by other
moments of experience, which makes each "bud" objectively immanent in-
itself.[136] Thus, the resurrection experience of knowing and remembering
Jesus was the activity of God mediated through the community. It can be
conceived as a bodily resurrection, as explained by Ford. On his view, the
body of Christ's resurrection is the body of Christ, which is the Church,
the emergent community of love guided by the dynamic activity of Christ's
spirit.[137]

Ford goes on to describe the Apostle Peter as the first person to form
the body whose mind is the risen Christ, thus giving effect to the bodily
resurrection. He says, "Peter is the rock or foundation for the building up of
the church, the cell to which all other cells are attached in the growth of that
body."[138] This speaks to a very human Church, one grounded in the reality of
human failings. For it was Peter who denied knowing the Christ three times
as Jesus journeyed to the cross, and Peter who was given the chance to rein-
state himself by declaring his love for the risen Christ—again, three times.
Rather than an idealized or divinized understanding of Church, Ford's
"emergent community of love"[139] guided by the spirit of the risen Christ is
an organic body of ordinary people who, however imperfectly, collectively
seek the aims of God for the good of the world. For Ford:

---

135. Ford, *Lure of God*, 73.

136. Hamilton, "Some Proposals," 376.

137. Ford, *Lure of God*, 78.

138. Ford, *Lure of God*, 79.

139. Ford, *Lure of God*, 79.

The resurrection is thus the incarnation of the divine Word addressed to the human situation. The incarnation is not located
solely or even primarily in the life of Jesus, although without
that life it could not have occurred then. The incarnation was the
total event of the emergence of the body of Christ. It required a
human life totally open to divine proposing, a life others could
completely trust as from God. Yet it also requires the emergence
of a new community knit together by the power of God. Initially
the continued identity of Jesus was objectively sustained in the
memory of his disciples. As these disciples responded to the
desires and aims of God as concentrated through this memory
by the interpenetration of their concerns for one another in
love, the organic life they knit together was able to support the
renewed subjectivity of the risen Christ, in the same way a living
body can support a living mind.[140]

It is the principle of immanence that explains the basic nature of all
experience in process thought, including the experience of the resurrection.
God is the chief exemplification of immanence—being "in" all things and
yet containing all things. In process thinking, the more we open ourselves
to God and deepen our agreement to God's call or lure, the more God becomes objectively immanent in us. This was supremely so in Jesus' case—as
he is the one who completely agreed with the lure of God and who therefore
carried more of God than any other person. So, existence is such that God
prehends or grasps at us, at everything, in each moment of our experience.
The more our thoughts and actions are compatible with God's loving purpose the more fully they will be incorporated as objectively immanent in
God's nature.[141]

An important aspect of process thought is the recognition that no
entity, including God, finally determines exactly how it will be prehended
by another entity. The ultimate decision always stays with the prehending
entity. On this view we think of God as both offering differentiated opportunities and a free response to those opportunities on the part of the recipient.
So, the call to Jesus was distinctive, and apart from that call Jesus could not
have been what he was. The initiative was God's, and the call did not compel
the response. Others may have been called this way before and since, but the
uniqueness of Jesus is located in his fullest response to the lure of God for
the good of the world. In a process framework, we can intelligibly and with
a level of historical justification affirm that God's presence in Jesus constituted Jesus' essential selfhood; the one God was uniquely present in him.

140. Ford, *Lure of God*, 79.
141. Hamilton, "Some Proposals," 377.

At the same time, Jesus was fully human, and no part of his humanity was displaced by God, making it a thoroughly human "I" that was constituted by God's presence in him.[142]

When it comes to the issue of personal resurrection and eternal life, it is fair to say that the proposals of process theology neither confirm nor deny the Christian doctrine that both Jesus and the "righteous" live on individually. They do, however, offer a meaningful interpretation of the resurrection of Jesus and of ourselves which does not *rely* on a belief in individual life after death. There is a place in contemporary theology for a general concept of resurrection that sees permanent meaning and value in our lives whether each individual lives on beyond their physical perishing.[143] Hartshorne can see no compelling philosophical arguments that would lead a person either to accept or reject the idea of individual immortality for humans, but he is more inclined to reject the idea, as previously discussed. Interestingly, he does this on the grounds that to wish for eternal life demonstrates a kind of selfishness which will not accept and rejoice in the accomplishments of goodness, truth or beauty unless "I" can have a share in the triumph—almost a "will to power" attitude.[144] For Hartshorne, because the basic drive through the entire created order is unselfish action towards a fuller good, this attitude is in contradiction to the purpose of creation. Any achievement of the good is for the greater glory of God—the one whose being is supreme and all-inclusive love. Anyone who sees this happen and delights in God's greater glory should be sufficiently satisfied.[145]

It is quite possible that Hartshorne was reacting to crudely individualistic "glory for me" ideals that are often associated with Christian sects, or the aforementioned "otherworldliness" he listed in the deficiencies he saw in inherited religion.[146] There is, nevertheless, room in this thinking for the much richer conception of "a communion of saints" in which there is a joy to be shared in widest commonality in and with God, and with a common rejoicing in the growing good that becomes further occasions of delight for Godself and for other subjects of experience. For, as Pittenger quite rightly points out, there is not now, there never has been, and there never will be a strictly logical explanation of what a Christian is talking about when they speak, not so much of immortality, but of eternal life, and above all when they speak of resurrection. In the face of the impossibility

---

142. Cobb, "Whiteheadian Christology," 394.

143. Hamilton, "Some Proposals," 379.

144. Pittenger, *Process-Thought*, 80.

145. Pittenger, *Process-Thought*, 81.

146. Hartshorne, *Divine Relativity*, 148.

of logically explaining miracles in the physical world, process thought has made a useful contribution by indicating that, in one sense at least, there will never be any lost good, because God accepts into the divine nature, distils the worth from, and is able to use for good every actual occasion in the created world. God participates intimately in the world and the world makes its contribution to God. It is this double movement that delivers the creation from frustration and futility.[147]

To speak of "end times" in the context of process thinking is almost a contradiction in terms. As it is the nature of God to be creative and as it is in the nature of the world to offer a creative possibility for the Divine Activity, we could conclude that for process thinkers to speak of an end in the chronological sense would be a denial of the presuppositions from which they start. To say that God is God, whatever the particular divine activity in whatever place or time, is to say that God is always active, living, reaching out to express the nature of Godself, and rejoicing in every expression of it; tenderly and compassionately entering into relationship with every finite occasion to give it a similar joy in actualizing all that might possibly be available for it, and accepting into Godself all that is achieved in the world.[148] Process theology in and of itself does imply that the creative process that is God and all things continues as both necessary and contingent. The concept of an expected future eschaton gives way to the satisfactions of particular occasions before an immediate vision of God.[149] This immediate vision of the divine, however, if it is applied to an eventual consummation of the world, points in process thought to the ultimate victory of God's reign over the forces of evil being attained by the manner of all God's activity in the world—that of persuasive and suffering love.[150] Hope thus lies in the general cosmic process Hartshorne described, after the words of Whitehead, when he wrote about God as cosmic adventure: "God is the cosmic 'adventure' (Whitehead) integrating all real adventures as they occur, without ever failing in readiness to realize new states out of the divine potency."[151]

When it comes to theodicy in the light of a process conception of God, there are three main things to say about evil in the world. The first is that in an evolving world where novelty is present and the future is open, there will inevitably be deviations from God's lure. If we maintain the idea of the world as either a static entity, or controlled in every manner from the outside, such

147. Pittenger, *Process-Thought*, 82.
148. Pittenger, *Process-Thought*, 83.
149. James, "Process Cosmology and Theological Particularity," 376.
150. Griffin, "Naturalistic Trinity," 26.
151. James, "Process Cosmology and Theological Particularity," 407.

erring would be impossible to understand. In a dynamic, processive world to err is not only possible, but also highly likely. There is clear risk, and the likelihood of "backwaters," where recalcitrance, negativity, and the refusal to move forward for the good of the whole congregate and take effect. As the world and individuals in it have such radical freedom to choose there can be times when resistance against taking up the invitational lure of God towards the good is so marked that it becomes an elected refusal to move.[152]

Secondly, it is a characteristic of God in God's consequent aspect to take into Godself all that has ever occurred, whether it be good or bad. Occurrences that are directed to further prospective fulfilment and occurrences that deny that end, whether they be adjustments or maladjustments, are all accepted by God and can in some way be appropriated into the divine life. Nonetheless, God always remains *God*, meaning that the divine is constantly working towards the most widely shared good. This is a mysterious but genuine aspect of divine agency in the world: the way in which error, refusal to move forward, maladjustment (the "evil" in the world) can become through divine love and concern the occasion for new possibilities of good. God makes the best from everything, even that which we can only describe as evil. Out of the free choice of the world, God can distil the good.[153]

The third thing to say about evil is that, in the tangible world of experience, and especially in human relationships, it may provide the opportunity for deepening love and for widening participation in the good. This is a dangerous claim, a little like the Christian understanding of the redemptive nature of suffering.[154] In both cases, however, the ground of the claim is found in the nature of God and in the idea that God's being is essentially love. It is of the nature of love to pour itself out for others, as Jesus did on the cross. It is of the nature of love to take into itself all that is made available to it; to absorb the evil which is there and out of it to distil something that is good, and to do all of this not for self-aggrandizement, but for the benefit of the entire relationship in its broadest and richest sense. God is love because God is infinitely related; God is love because God enters and participates in creation; God is love, supremely, because God will even absorb errors and maladjustments and then bring about genuine and novel occasions of goodness through the use of material that seems unpromising or hopeless.[155]

152. Pittenger, *Process-Thought*, 31.

153. Pittenger, *Process-Thought*, 32.

154. This is a link made also by Moltmann, most particularly in *The Crucified God*. In this book Moltmann asserts nothing less than the presence of God in all the suffering of human life, thus aligning himself with process theology in some respects. That God suffers with us remains open to debate in some theological quarters.

155. Pittenger, *Process-Thought*, 33.

Process theologians do not make light of the presence of evil and sin in the world but do claim that it can be transformed in the love of God. That sin and evil bring about real loss in individual lives is acknowledged, as is the possibility that some evil may not be "redeemable."[156] In a process view of human sin, at any stage of development, a person in community and the community of persons who are moving towards "civilization," may be deflected from following the main "aim" of God. By so doing they may become either a backwater in the ongoing movement or be sufferers of maladjustment so serious that damage is done, not only to the whole dynamic process, but also to smaller organisms or societies, including humanity itself as such an organic entity. The results can be tragic and terrible. Anti-social choices and anti-social patterns of behavior, choices, and patterns harmful to human community and to each human in their own integration, have occurred and do occur. Through these choices, and by acceptances of these patterns, each person can harm themselves as well as others. A person can (and observably often does) elect to live in self-contained ways, denying the drive towards fulfilment in personhood, failing to share in rich community with others, seeking satisfactions which are so partial, limited, and defective that they impede and damage the basic drive of a total personal organism which is on the way to realisation of its richest and widest possibilities.[157]

Regarding reparation for sin and wrongdoing, process theology rejects punitive justice and retribution, referring to restorative justice instead.[158] On a process view, even though the past is complete and cannot be changed, past occasions of experience can nevertheless be transformed in the immediacy of God's redemptive experience. This is a matter of grace rather than creaturely creativity or effort,[159] and it is based on the nature of God in process thought as love first and foremost. When love is understood as having a central role in the world and as an essential part in a human response to that love, we can better see the deeper implications of the truth that God desires and works for people to become fully human and in freedom to choose to

156. Pittenger, *Process-Thought*, 64.

157. Pittenger, *Process-Thought*, 63.

158. Hartshorne insists that it is meaningless to ask what we could do if God punished us rather than helping and restoring us, indeed that God is always restorative. He extends his understanding of the entirely restorative nature of the operation of God to the natural world, arguing for a universal "psychialism." In this way love will relate God not only to human beings but to all creatures. It will apply to the soul-to-bodily-cells relationship and, in its ultimate generality, to all relationships of creature to creature, creature to Creator, Creator to creature. Hartshorne, *Divine Relativity*, 146 and Hartshorne, *Theological Mistakes*, 63. For an explanation of Restorative Justice that does not rely on process theology see Broughton, *Restorative Christ*.

159. Epperly, *Process Theology*, 149.

live into their full potential. In reality, this means to become and act like God, who, in Godself, is love-in-action.[160] This continues eternally as we live on in God and experience ourselves as God experiences us, contributing to God's evolving realm of restoration and wholeness.[161] This process understanding of restoration and transformation into God's love models very closely my contention in this book that what we believe about God directs our action and our use of power.

The exploration of power and process thought in this chapter has included a consideration of the founding ideas of Whitehead and the translating of those ideas into theology by Hartshorne. In conversation with some of the shapers of process thinking, key issues of incarnation, resurrection, eschatology, and justice have been taken up in the light of the rethinking of divine power that I am proposing. In sum, process theology proposes that creativity belongs both to God and to finite beings, and that all entities therefore have the power of self-determination.[162] This, along with the key notion that the supreme power of the universe always works non-coercively, ensures a faith and/or a worldview where imitation of the divine does not lead to the domination and control of others. Imitation of the divine grounded in process thought leads instead to the edification and encouragement of others to realise their own freedom and creativity.[163]

While process theology can therefore be demonstrated to have much to contribute to a conversation on power, it is generally considered quite limited in its development of a trinitarian view of God. To be recognized as fully Christian, a theology of power will require a proper conception of the Trinity. With this in mind, the next chapter focuses on the triunity of the one God in the texts and traditions of the Christian Church. It will concentrate particularly on the development of the Social Trinity and the work of Jürgen Moltmann, drawing on the insights of other trinitarian theologians, to develop a trinitarian, process theology.

160. Pittenger, *Process-Thought*, 93.

161. Epperly, *Process Theology*, 149.

162. This idea can be traced directly to Whitehead, who speaks of the process, or concrescence, of any one actual entity involving the other actual entities among its components. He claims that this shared self-determination explains the obvious solidarity of the world, pointing out that "In all philosophic theory there is an ultimate which is actual in virtue of its accidents. It is only then capable of characterization through its accidental embodiments, and apart from these accidents is devoid of actuality. In the philosophy of organism this ultimate is termed 'creativity;' and God is its primordial, non-temporal accident." Whitehead goes on to criticize what he describes as "monistic philosophies" and "absolute idealism" where the ultimate is God. For, he says, "the ultimate is (then) illegitimately allowed a final, 'eminent' reality, beyond that ascribed to any of its accidents." Whitehead, *Process and Reality*, 7.

163. Long, *Western Philosophy of Religion*, 382.

3

POWER AND TRINITARIAN THEOLOGY

*What figure of us think you he will bear? For you must know we have with
special soul elected him our absence to supply, lent him our terror, dressed
him with our love, and given his deputation all the organs of our own power.
What think you of it?*

—William Shakespeare, *Measure for Measure*, Act 1, Scene 1

*The grace of the Lord Jesus Christ, the love of God, and the communion of the
Holy Spirit be with all of you.*

—2 Corinthians 13:13 (NRSV)

The conception of God as Holy Trinity, one God in three Persons, is
unique to Christianity and explicitly forms the foundation and heart
of the faith of the church. The formed doctrine of the Trinity is the work of
the church over time and describes the Christian understanding of salvation, "the experience of being saved by God through Christ in the power of
the Holy Spirit."[1] The Bible affirms from beginning to end that there is one
God, the Old and New Testaments alike sharing a clear monotheistic faith,
but the specific witness of the New Testament is that the one God is to be
understood and known in Jesus Christ and through the renewing Spirit.

---

1. LaCugna, *God for Us*, 3.

This chapter briefly traces the development of trinitarian theology in the early Christian centuries and highlights the key issues with which the founding thinkers of the church wrestled. It shows that, despite the church arriving at an accepted and orthodox conception of Trinity in the fourth century, the same issues have been and continue to be contentious whenever trinitarian theology is revisited or reassessed. Keeping this in mind, it considers what constitutes a "pro-Nicene"[2] foundation for contemporary theologies of Trinity before defining social trinitarianism as a useful line of trinitarian thinking that continues in the trajectory set by Nicaea. It then explores the egalitarian, power-sharing social model of Trinity developed by Jürgen Moltmann for its potential as an orthodox conception of the three-fold nature of God on which to build the rest of this book.

THE DEVELOPMENT OF TRINITARIAN THEOLOGY

Trinitarian theology began with the quest to find a way to speak of the "One" and the "Three" considering the person and work of Jesus Christ. This effort was based on the trinitarian references in the texts of the New Testament, the early focus very much on how the Father related to the Son. Over time the parameters were broadened to better articulate the Spirit as coequal and coeternal with the Father and the Son. A specific language was required to do this theological work. In the first four centuries, the nature of the One was referred to via a range of overlapping terms, including "being" (*ousia*), "essence" (*essentia*), and "substance" (*substantia*); the nature of the Three was referred to as "persons" (*personae*), "realities/subjects" (*hypostases*) or "modes." What precisely was meant by each of these terms depended on who was using it, the language they spoke, and the period in which they wrote.[3]

---

2. Ayres, *Nicaea and Its Legacy*, 236. A pro-Nicene theology of Trinity is one that accepts as foundational the agreed and orthodox formulations arrived at in the Nicene-Cosmopolitan credal statements.

3. As Ayers points out, specifically regarding the use of the terms *ousia* and *hypostasis* in the creed of Nicaea but applicable to other Trinitarian terminology developing concurrently, there is "a huge difference between deploying terms that appear to fulfil a technical clarifying function and understanding those terms clearly. There is . . . evidence that these terms had been the subject of debate and confusion since the mid-third century. Hence, it is important to attempt to understand what meaning was attributed to these terms at the time of Nicaea." Further, "that any attempt to define fourth-century theological terminologies by reference solely to their philological origins or to a history of non-Christian philosophical development runs the constant danger of resulting in an artificial clarity that is not reflected in actual theological usage. Rather, we need to be attentive to the histories of theological use of these terms prior to Nicaea." Ayres, *Nicaea and Its Legacy*, 62.

Due to this fluidity of interpretation, much of the contention, especially in the period between the Council of Nicaea (325) and the creed it developed, and the Council of Constantinople (381) and the credal modification that won the consensus of the early church, was about the language of the Trinity. This was particularly regarding the use of the terms *homoousios* "of the same substance" and *homoiousios* "of like substance." The import of finding the right word in this instance was deeply significant, no less than being able to affirm and describe the relationships between the persons within the Godhead as coequal and coeternal.

Understanding *how* the internal relationships of the divine being might function was every bit as contentious in the early Christian centuries and remains so. The orthodox line between the unacceptable extremes of tritheism or modalism, for example, is far from broad, and discussions about who is the "source," or "cause," of the three and from whom the Son is "begotten" and/or the Spirit "proceed" are as complex in contemporary trinitarian theology as they were in the third and fourth centuries. Further, the quality of the relations in the Godhead, indeed whether this can even be known or postulated in any respectful sense, is an ongoing discussion. For this reason, modern and contemporary trinitarian theology has focused primarily on the economy of salvation as the way God's triune being is known, leaving aside speculation about the inner life of God, abstracted from God's own self-revelation. The argument has been that doctrines of the Immanent Trinity are overly esoteric and speculative and have little to do with practical religion.[4] There are, however, theologians who hold the view that the communitarian inner life of God as Father, Son, and Spirit serves as a model for all relationships, human and non-human. This contention forms the heart of this study, particularly when it comes to the exercise of power in relationships.

It is the story of Jesus that discloses the trinitarian face of God. Jesus' relationship with the Father and his teaching about and gifting of the Spirit brought into human history an awareness of a threefold nature in the interpersonal life of God.[5] The earliest New Testament letters of the Apostle Paul display binitarian expressions of this new experience of God the Father

4. Hensley, "Trinity and Freedom," 83. The contention that exploring the immanent Trinity has nothing to contribute to practical theology is an overarching claim of Catherine Mowry LaCugna. For her, "theories about what God is apart from God's self-communication in salvation history remain unverifiable and ultimately untheological." LaCugna, *God for Us*, 231. In contrast, Paul Molnar argues for the value of a doctrine of the immanent Trinity. On his view, "theology must allow the unique nature of its object to determine what can and cannot be said about the triune God." Molnar, *Divine Freedom*, 1.

5. O'Collins, *Tripersonal God*, 35.

conveyed by the resurrection of Jesus from the dead.[6] As the implications of the involvement of the Spirit in the Father's raising of the Son from death were considered, more elaborate trinitarian language becomes evident. By the time the gospels had been written, the church had the triadic baptismal formula of Matthew 28, the prologue of John and the stories of the gift of the Spirit in John 19 and 20, the Pentecost scene of Acts 2, and was also reading the Old Testament in a christological and trinitarian fashion.[7]

The Christian writers of the first two centuries all talked of God in terms that resonated with the biblical texts. The focus of these early efforts to articulate the nature of the Christian God was on the relationship between Father and Son. Clement of Rome (c.96), for example, at the end of his first letter, prays to the "Creator of the universe" that he will "keep intact the precise number of his elect in the whole world through his beloved Child Jesus Christ." Although the Holy Spirit does gain a mention elsewhere in the letter, the Spirit is not included in the prayer.[8] Ignatius (d.110) describes Jesus as being "with the Father from eternity and appear(ing) at the end,"[9] repeatedly referring to God as the Father of Jesus Christ. Ignatius' constant emphasis is that the Son reveals the Father. He calls Jesus the "guileless mouth by which the Father has spoken truthfully,"[10] and refers to him as the "knowledge of God."[11] As the New Testament texts had already done, Ignatius describes Jesus in some places simply as God, and mentions the Holy Spirit in the same context. For instance, Ignatius affirms that "our God, Jesus the Christ, was conceived by Mary, in God's plan sprung from the seed of David and from the Holy Spirit."[12]

In the second century, Justin Martyr (d.165) defended his Christian faith against the backdrop of a hostile Roman Empire. He drew on the philosophies of Stoicism and Platonism, along with both Old and New Testament texts, to develop his Logos theology. His ideas informed the emerging understanding of a threefold Christian God, as for him the Logos is Jesus, God's Son.[13] Justin writes in his *First Apology*, "we have been taught that Christ is the First-born of God, and we have suggested above that he is the

6. O'Collins, *Tripersonal God*, 52.

7. O'Collins, *Tripersonal God*, 82.

8. 1 Clem. 59.2.

9. Ign. *Magn.* 6.1.

10. Ign. *Rom.* 8.2.

11. Ign. *Eph.* 17.2.

12. Ign. *Eph.* 18.2.

13. Emery and Levering, *Handbook of the Trinity*, 97.

logos of whom every race of men and women were partakers."[14] In Justin's thinking, it is the Logos who speaks and acts in the Old Testament, He is God immanent. The Father is God transcendent. Justin affirms the divinity of the Son but uses in places the rather difficult terminology of *another* God. His early explanation of how the Son might relate to the Father points readily to a full-blown polytheism or, at the very least, to subordinationism where the Son has less divinity than the Father and is therefore a secondary God. A sense of subordinationism surrounds Justin's thinking in general, which is hardly surprising as he thought and wrote well before the doctrine of an equality in communion shared by the three divine persons was firmly established.[15] Justin does confess the Holy Spirit, but third in rank after the Father and the Son,[16] based on the baptismal formula of the New Testament.[17]

Later thinkers like Origen (d. 254) continue the subordinationism of Justin by conceiving the Trinity in terms redolent of hierarchy.[18] Origen writes of the endless and measureless power of God conceived of as Father, before clarifying the apparently lesser power of Son and Spirit. He says, "to God there is nothing without end or without measure. For by his power he comprehends all things, and he himself is not comprehended . . . for that nature is known to itself alone."[19] Origen speaks also of a "diversity of participation in the Father and the Son and the Holy Spirit (which) is to be preserved."[20]

Just as the Son and the Spirit appear to be less than the Father, so, in Origen, the Spirit appears to be less than the Son. The sphere of the Spirit is limited to the saints, or holy ones. Origen explains: "the working of the power of God the Father and of the Son extended without distinction over every creature, but participation in the Holy Spirit is possessed, we find, only by the holy ones."[21] In a commentary he wrote on John, Origen suggested that the Spirit is the first in rank over all that came into existence by the Father through Christ, making the Spirit third in the hierarchy.[22] Origen's hierarchical Trinity has absolute control over the created order, it is the "blessed

---

14. Justin Martyr, 1 Apol. 46.

15. O'Collins, *Tripersonal God*, 90–91.

16. Justin Martyr, 1 Apol. 60.

17. Emery and Levering, *Handbook of the Trinity*, 97.

18. Emery and Levering, *Handbook of the Trinity*, 104.

19. Origin, *Princ.* 4.4.8.

20. Origin, *Princ.* 4.4.9.

21. Origin, *Princ.* 1.3.7.

22. Emery and Levering, *Handbook of the Trinity*, 104.

and sovereign power"[23] that exercises control of all things. Furthermore, as God *is* effectively his creative and beneficent power in Origen's thought, "it is both absurd and impious to suppose that these powers have been idle at any time even for a moment."[24] Origen concludes that creation always exists, or, at the very least, that creation is always present and prefigured in eternal Wisdom, who in his thought is personified in the Son. The problem with subordinationism and/or a hierarchical Trinity in Justin, Origin, or wherever else this thinking occurs, is that it undercuts the essential monotheism of Christianity. If both the Son and the Spirit are subordinate to the Father and yet all three are God, the logical conclusion to reach is that they are three detached beings, and therefore three Gods.[25]

The most famous voice of the fourth century is that of Arius, who was born shortly after Origen died. For Arius, the Father, the Son, and the Holy Spirit are three *hypostases,* or distinct subsistent realities, who share in the one divine nature, but who display a level of subordination, the Son and the Spirit both subordinate to the Father. Arius adopted an extreme take on what was a relatively common view,[26] illustrated by a section of his credal statement, the *Thalia:*

> God then himself is in essence ineffable to all.
> He alone has neither equal nor like, none comparable in glory;
> We call him Unbegotten because of the one in nature begotten;
> We raise hymns to him as Unbegun because of him who has beginning.
> We adore him as eternal because of the one born in time.
> The Unbegun appointed the Son to be Beginning of things begotten,
> and bore him as his own Son, in this case giving birth.
> He has nothing proper to God in his essential property,
> For neither is he equal not yet consubstantial with him . . .
> . . . there is a Trinity with glories not alike;
> Their existences are unmixable with each other;
> One is more glorious than another by an infinity of glories.[27]

Arius believed in the utter transcendence and uniqueness of God. He insisted that "God exists ineffable to the Son, for he is to himself what he is, that is, unutterable."[28] He was convinced that the Son cannot ever fully express God, "for it is impossible for him to explore the Father who exists

23. Origin, *Princ.* 1.4.3.

24. Origin, *Princ.* 1.4.3.

25. Emery and Levering, *Handbook of the Trinity*, 103–4.

26. O'Collins, *Tripersonal God*, 111.

27. Athanasius, *Syn.* 456–57.

28. Athanasius, *Syn.* 457.

by himself."[29] Arius adopted the slogan "there was when (the Son) was not," based on an encyclical letter of Alexander condemning his teachings.[30] This means that, in Arius' view, the Son was created; there was a time when he did not exist. The slogan became both a catch cry for those who held similar views to Arius and a jibe used against them. Essentially, for Arius and his followers, the Son, understood as either Logos or Word, was ontologically subordinate to the Father.[31] The One who became incarnate was neither truly divine nor truly and fully human, Arius teaching that the Logos took the place of the human soul in Christ.[32]

By the time of the conversion of Constantine and the official toleration of Christianity in 313, the intellectual center of gravity in the Church was fully focused on matters of doctrine. The most significant reflection on the triune God in this period occurs in polemic with other Christians, the Gnostics on one hand and the Monarchians on the other. There were many Gnostic sects in the early centuries of the church with a range of nuances of belief, but each interpreted the salvation history contained in the Old and New Testaments based on a foundational myth. The worldview of the myth was always dualistic, containing notions of contest between spirit and matter.[33] The shared focus of the Monarchians was the unity of God against what they understood to be the ditheistic Logos theology of thinkers like Justin Martyr. The two main forms of Monarchianism are modalism and adoptionism. In modalism the names Father, Son, and Holy Spirit do not refer to three individuals or three persons, but to three modes of acting of the one God. In adoptionism the Son is distinct from the Father but is simply a very virtuous human being. The Son becomes God's Son through adoption at his baptism. The thinking of the Monarchians and the Gnostics forms the context for much of the reflection on how to speak of the Three and the One of the Trinity throughout the third century.[34]

29. Athanasius, *Syn.* 457.

30. Socrates, *Eccl. hist.* 1.6.4.

31. Emery and Levering, *Handbook of the Trinity*, 110.

32. O'Collins, *Tripersonal God*, 113.

33. Williams, in his book about the teachings of Arius, points out that by the fourth century strongly apophatic statements about God were often associated with a type of Gnosticism, this being the case with the "non-existent" God idea championed by Basilides (117–138) in Alexandria. Williams notes that this association was also to be found in "neo-Arian circles" later in the century due to their "theological forebears" being those for whom Arius wrote the *Thalia*. He says that Basilides' Gnosticism was refuted by Hippolytus of Rome (170–236), among others, and points to Hippolytus, *Refutatio* VII.20, 195.24, 197.16 in which the non-existent God transcends even what is named due to being incapable of having *any* name. Williams, *Arius*, 107, 311.

34. Emery and Levering, *Handbook of the Trinity*, 99–100.

Irenaeus (d. 202) made it his mission to explain Christianity against Gnosticism, seeking unity in the church and in a Christian worldview. He took the step of attributing pre-existence to both the Son and the Spirit, describing them as the hands of God.[35] By itself, this analogy could simply imply parallel undertakings rather than a direct relationship between Son and Spirit, but Irenaeus also interprets human salvation through an assuredly trinitarian line. He starts from the Spirit to the Son, and then continues from the Son to the Father.[36] In his thinking, it is the Spirit that is Wisdom in whom God made all things.[37] The Spirit ministers to the Father along with the Son, with angels subject to them both,[38] and as the Spirit is poured forth in the Old Testament it is through his influence that the Father was revealed.[39] The trinitarian thinking of Irenaeus is sufficiently developed that the activity of the Spirit is both distinct yet inseparable from that of the Father and the Son.[40] He was able to reject both the tendency of the Marcionites to separate the Father God of the New Testament from the Old Testament Creator who made all things, and the Gnostic denial of the Son of God being made human flesh for the salvation of the world.[41]

With the writings of Tertullian (d. c.220) a language for the Trinity began to emerge. In his *Against Praxaeus*, Tertullian begins with the rule of faith which had been passed down to him:

> (We believe) in one only God, yet subject to this dispensation (which is our word for 'economy') that the one only God has also a Son, his Word who has proceeded from himself . . . (and) that thereafter he, according to his promise, sent from the Father the Holy Spirit, the Paraclete, the sanctifier of the faith of those who believe in Father and the Son and the Holy Spirit.[42]

Tertullian understood God to be alone before all things, although he had Reason with him "while he silently thought out and ordained with himself the things which he was shortly to say by the agency of Discourse."[43] Discourse is not a simple attribute of God but a substantive being, in fact,

---

35. O'Collins, *Tripersonal God*, 99.

36. O'Collins, *Tripersonal God*, 101.

37. Irenaeus, *Haer.* 4.20.1. This contrasts with Origin, for whom the figure of Wisdom is found in the Son.

38. Irenaeus, *Haer.* 4.7.4.

39. Irenaeus, *Haer.* 4.20.6.

40. Emery and Levering, *Handbook of the Trinity*, 101.

41. O'Collins, *Tripersonal God*, 103.

42. Tertullian, *Prax.* 2.

43. Tertullian, *Prax.* 5.

the Son, "alone begotten out of God in a true sense from the womb of his heart."[44] So also with the Spirit: "the close series of the Father in the Son and the Son in the Paraclete makes three who cohere, the one attached to the other. And these three are one thing, not one person . . . in respect of unity of substance, not singularity of number"[45] "The Spirit is God and the Word is God, because he is from God, yet is not God himself from whom he is."[46]

Tertullian worked out some significant distinctions in the Latin concepts and language behind Trinitarian thinking. Father, Son, and Holy Spirit are three persons (*personae*). They are three not in condition (*statu*) but in degree (*gradu*); not in substance (*substantia*) but in form (*forma*); not in power (*potestate*) but in aspect (*specie*). Yet they are all of one substance, and of one quality, and of one power.[47] By employing the terminology of one divine substance (*substantia*) in three persons, Tertullian became the first Christian writer to use the term person in theology. He was the first to apply Trinity (*Trinitas*) to God, and the first to develop the formulation itself: one substance in three persons. The Latin essence (*essentia*) dropped out of use for a time in favor of substance (*substantia*). When the Greeks wrote *ousia*, Tertullian used *substantia*, a word already applied to God by Seneca (d. 65). Where substance referred to the central reality shared by Father, Son, and Holy Spirit, Tertullian understood person to mean the principle of operative individuality. While the historical background of the Latin *persona* and the Greek *prosopon* can suggest that the terms describe only a mask or a manifestation, Tertullian avoided both the modalism and/ or the Monarchianism that would result from that interpretation when he wrote of the persons in God.[48] In seeking to illustrate his understanding of God as a differentiated Triune unity, Tertullian bequeathed the church some memorable images for the Trinity. He suggested that Father, Son and Holy Spirit are like root, shoot, and fruit; or spring, river, and stream; or sun, ray, and point of light.[49] Each picture emphasizes the distinction of the persons of the Trinity, without separating them.

The First Council of Nicaea in the middle of 325 was called in response to the crisis of doctrine initiated by Arius and his followers about the status

---

44. Tertullian, *Prax.* 7.
45. Tertullian, *Prax.* 25.
46. Tertullian, *Prax.* 26.
47. Tertullian, *Prax.* 2.
48. O'Collins, *Tripersonal God*, 105.
49. Tertullian, *Prax.* 8.

of the Son. The Council produced a creedal statement that denounced Arius' doctrine and confirmed that the Son is intrinsic to the being of the Father.[50]

> We believe in one God, the Father almighty, maker of all things, visible and invisible;
>
> And in one Lord Jesus Christ, the Son of God, begotten from the Father, only-begotten, that is, from the substance of the Father, God from God, light from light, true God from true God, begotten not made, of one substance with the Father, through Whom all things came into being, things in heaven and things on earth, Who because of us men and because of our salvation came down and became incarnate, becoming man, suffered and rose again on the third day, ascended to the heavens, and will come to judge the living and the dead:
>
> And in the Holy Spirit.
>
> But as for those who say, There was when He was not, and, Before being born He was not, and that he came into existence out of nothing, or who assert that the Son of God is from a different hypostasis or substance, or is created, or is subject to alteration or change—these the Catholic Church anathematizes.[51]

Against Arius' claim that the nature of the Father is unique, Nicaea stated that the Son was begotten from the substance of the Father and was therefore of the same being with the Father. Insisting that the Son was begotten rather than made differentiated the Son from the creatures and implied equal divinity with the Father, captured in the phrase 'true God from true God'. By repudiating Arius' catch cry about there being a time when the Son was not, Nicaea affirmed that the Father and the Son were co-eternal, a necessary corollary to consubstantiality, or being of the same essence or substance. The immediate consequence of the Council of Nicaea was that Arius was excommunicated and sent into exile.[52]

Nicaea stood clearly for the divinity of the Son, but three of the terms used continued to cause difficulties well after the conclusion of the Council. The terms were *ousia, homoousious,* and *hypostases. Ousia,* meaning variously: being, reality, essence, or substance, already had an ambiguous history in Gnosticism and Christianity before Nicaea. It had referred to a triple consubstantiality in Valentinian Gnosticism, where the human spirit is *homoousious* with God, the soul with the demiurge, and matter with the devil. This history made the term unpalatable to many. At issue was the

50. Emery and Levering, *Handbook of the Trinity,* 111.

51. Kelly, *Early Christian Doctrines,* 232.

52. Emery and Levering, *Handbook of the Trinity,* 111.

materialist implication of the Son being begotten from the *ousia* of the Father, as though the Son were somehow begotten by a just a portion of the Father's substance. Furthermore, although Nicaea used *homoousious* seeking to denote the unity of the Father and the Son, it did not qualify it in a manner that preserved the New Testament distinction between them. The failure to distinguish between Father and Son made the creed's use of *homoousious* appear to suggest that the Father and the Son were one and the same entity, which sounded decidedly modalist.[53]

The ongoing difficulty was that the same words were understood differently by various groups of thinkers. For example, the many meanings of *hypostases* can be gathered into two main definitions. The first is *hypostases* as the primordial essence, the second is *hypostases* as the individuating principle, subject, or subsistence. This ambiguity of definition made it possible to use the same term both to condemn those who divided one divine being into three *hypostases,* thus splitting the one divine essence into three divine essences and arriving at three gods, and also to speak of the triune God as three individual *hypostases* of the one principle subject. The language problem was compounded by the fact that Western Christians since the time of Tertullian understood the Greek *hypostases* to mean the same thing as their Latin term *substantia.* They understood *hypostases* in the first sense of the definitions above as primordial essence. So, when the Eastern, or Greek, Christians acknowledged the three *hypostases* of God those in the West understood them to be promulgating the idea of three separate divine substances, no less than tritheism. Conversely, Greek speakers could easily misunderstand Latin talk about the one divine *substantia* as leaning toward the modalist position of one *hypostases* in the sense of the second definition as an individuating principle, and thus as a denial of any personal distinctions in God. The outcome for Nicaea of this inherited ambiguity surrounding *hypostases* was that treating *ousia* and *hypostases* as synonyms made it likely that *homoousios* would be understood in a Sabellian way. The Sabellians treated the terms *ousia* and *hypostases* as equivalent words for an individual substance. Father and Son would then both be of the same *ousia* and the same *hypostases* in the second sense of the definition of *hypostases.* This would mean that there was no real distinction between Father and Son, and they could not be distinct, individual subjects.[54]

After Nicaea some bishops, although opposed to Arius, preferred the term *homoiousios* which had been discussed and rejected by the council. In reference to the Son, it means being of like substance with the Father.

53. O'Collins, *Tripersonal God,* 116–17.
54. O'Collins, *Tripersonal God,* 118.

There were also many bishops, and others, who were still not satisfied with
the term *homoousios* (of the same substance). Arius and his followers obviously rejected both terms, based on their belief that the Son was neither of
like substance nor of the same substance as the utterly transcendent God.[55]
Athanasius (d.373) eventually realized that those who were not satisfied by
homoousios, but who nevertheless supported Nicaea against the views of
Arian, were really allies, not adversaries. After all, they only disagreed on
one word. In his *De Synodis* of 359 Athanasius wrote:

> Those who deny the council (of Nicaea) altogether, are suf-
> ficiently exposed by these brief remarks; those, however, who
> accept everything else that was defined at Nicaea, and doubt
> only about the Co-essential, must not be treated as enemies; nor
> do we here attack them as Ariomaniacs, nor as opponents of the
> Fathers, but we discuss the matter with them as brothers with
> brothers, who mean what we mean and dispute only about the
> word. For, confessing that the Son is from the essence of the Fa-
> ther, and not from another subsistence, and that he is not a crea-
> ture nor work, but his genuine and natural offspring, and that
> he is eternally with the Father as being his Word and Wisdom,
> they are not far from accepting even the phrase Co-essential.[56]

Athanasius was keen to make clear that *homoousios* affirmed the Son's
full share in the Father's divine nature without in any way denying the distinction between the Father and the Son.[57] The fatherhood of God went on
to become the focus of sustained analysis for Athanasius. For later trinitarian thought, Athanasius developed the central principle that the Father-Son
relationship partially but necessarily defines the word "God," for to deny
the eternal existence of the Son, as Arius and others did, would be to deny
the eternal fatherhood of God. These considerations led Athanasius to also
reflect on the Holy Spirit, as he believed that a true doctrine of the Spirit
relied completely on a true doctrine of the Son and vice versa. For Athanasius, as a truly divine being, the Spirit "proceeds" from the Father and is
"given" by the Son. Athanasius held that, at the same time as deriving the
whole divine nature and existence from the Father, the Spirit is sent out by
the Son, making the Spirit "in the Son" as the Son is "in the Father." This way
of describing the inner relationship of God raised two problems, however.
The first was that it appeared to be necessary for the Spirit and the Word to
be brothers, and, if they were, the Word was not the only begotten of the

55. O'Collins, *Tripersonal God,* 120–21.

56. Athanasius, *Syn.* 472–73.

57. Emery and Levering, *Handbook of the Trinity,* 114.

Father. The second was the related idea that, should the Spirit be of the Son and the Son of the Father, then the Father becomes the grandfather of the Spirit. Athanasius' arguably less than helpful response was that God cannot be thought of in a human way and therefore such questions cannot be asked of God.[58]

Helpful or otherwise, Athanasius' response captures the view of the theologians past and present who find it impious to question too closely the inner nature of God. This indicates that the tension in trinitarian theology around what can genuinely and reverently be known of the Immanent Trinity has a long history. The associated question of whether whatever might be able to be known or postulated about God's inner nature is then applicable to human life and community, or whether it remains the unique domain of the Triune God, is a significant one in more contemporary trinitarian theology. This is particularly so for social trinitarians, who assert genuine personhood in the Trinity and understand that what is modelled in God is applicable to human life. Drawing on philosophy, psychology, and sociology, they point out that personhood requires social interaction, and further, that the One God is a social being of Three Persons. The social trinitarian whose work underpins this book is Jürgen Moltmann.

It was one of the Cappadocian writers, Gregory of Nazianzus, who defended an orthodox trinitarian faith in response to the objections raised with Athanasius. It is worth noting here that social trinitarians generally, and Jürgen Moltmann specifically, trace their community model of Trinity to the work of the Cappadocian thinkers. The Cappadocians are well known for developing an understanding of Nicaea that both maintained the unity of God which was necessary for affirming the full divinity of the Son and confirmed a distinction between the persons which earlier critics had seen to be absent.[59] Gregory insisted on the uniqueness of the Son as *only* begotten and thus without a brother. The Spirit is not a second Son, nor is the Son a father to the Spirit, for then the Spirit would be a type of divine grandson. To suppose this would be to assert within the divine being two "fathers" and hence two "gods." Only the "unbegotten" Father has the distinctive characteristic of being the principle or cause of the divine life that is in the Son and the Spirit.[60] Gregory of Nyssa says of the persons of the Trinity:

> For one is directly from the first Cause, and another through that which is directly from the first Cause; so that the attribute of being only-begotten abides without doubt in the Son and does

58. O'Collins, *Tripersonal God*, 128.

59. Emery and Levering, *Handbook of the Trinity*, 116.

60. O'Collins, *Tripersonal God*, 129.

not call into dispute that the Spirit is from the Father; and the interposition of the Son, while it guards his attribute of being only-begotten, does not shut out the Spirit from his relation by way of nature to the Father.[61]

Athanasius was an older contemporary of Gregory of Nazianzus and the other key Cappadocian writers, Basil and Gregory of Nyssa. Their combined work helped establish the view that Christians cannot know or say anything about the Son apart from the relationship with the Father and the Spirit, and that what applies to the Son is true also of the Father and the Holy Spirit.[62] Like Athanasius, the Cappadocians maintained that the Holy Spirit "proceeds from" but is not "begotten by" the Father, thus answering the objection that trinitarian faith makes the Spirit a second Son. The Cappadocians further validated orthodox doctrine by appealing to the trinitarian confession of faith at baptism. Their most significant contribution to speaking of God as Trinity, however, was in their development of the language of three coequal and coeternal *hypostases* (persons/subjects) sharing the one divine *ousia* (essence/being/substance). The Cappadocians perceived at the heart of God an interpersonal communion that was the function of all three divine persons rather than only of the Holy Spirit. In their interpersonal model of Trinity, the inner being of God is relational.[63]

The Cappadocians believed that it was possible to argue based on scripture that the divine persons were of the same substance or essence based on their power revealed in their energy or action. Some saw God's creative power as that of imperial authority which commands its ministers to do as is willed, and the Son as the perfect minister who carries out the will of the Father. Gregory of Nyssa disagreed, insisting that the Father and the Son do not have different powers but one and the same power. He argued in his *Catechetical Oration 5* that Logos is the power of God to create, sustain, and foresee the future. Gregory of Nyssa insists that the Son is equal to the Father who is the source of his being and power. Since the Son and the Spirit are of the same substance as the Father, they naturally possess the Father's infinite goodness and power. As there is no deficiency or limit to their power that would make them ontologically inferior to the Father, the Son and the Spirit are therefore equal in divinity with the Father.[64]

While affirming the unity and equality of Father, Son and Spirit, the Cappadocians avoided the charge of modalism that had accompanied

61. Gregory of Nyssa, "On 'Not Three Gods,'" 331–36.

62. O'Collins, *Tripersonal God*, 130.

63. O'Collins, *Tripersonal God*, 132.

64. Emery and Levering, *Handbook of the Trinity*, 115–16.

homoousios by maintaining clear distinctions between the persons. In their thought, each person is eternal, distinct, and subsistent. Each is a mode of God's being and is distinguished from the other by origin: the Father is unbegotten, the Son is begotten, the Spirit proceeds. The Cappadocians used the term "mode" to describe the relationship between the persons rather than to denote different essences. Their usage was significantly different to the Sabellian idea of different modes of the self-revelation of God. For the modalist, the persons are the way the one God reveals Godself in history without being real and eternal distinctions in the Godhead. In contrast, for the Cappadocians, the persons are real distinctions in God. There is no sense of God appearing as three persons only in the economy of salvation, as an Economic Trinity; God is triune from all eternity.

> We must, therefore, confess the faith by adding the particular to the common. The Godhead is common; the fatherhood particular. We must therefore combine the two and say, 'I believe in God the Father.' The like course must be pursued in the confession of the Son; we must combine the particular with the common and say, 'I believe in God the Son.' So in the case of the Holy Ghost we must make our utterance conform to the appellation and say, 'I believe also in the divine Holy Spirit.' Hence it results that there is satisfactory preservation of the unity by the confession of the one Godhead, while in the distinction of the individual properties regarded in each other there is the confession of the peculiar properties of the Persons.[65]

The work of the Cappadocian thinkers, Athanasius, and others ensured that towards the end of the fourth century the church had what would be understood henceforth as an orthodox Holy Trinity. The canons of the Council of Constantinople 381 reaffirmed the Nicene Creed, adding to the former simple declaration of belief in the Spirit a declaration of the divinity of the Spirit as the one who proceeds from the Father and who is worshipped together with the Father and the Son:

> (We believe) in the Holy Spirit, the Lord and life-giver, Who proceeds from the Father, Who with the Father and the Son is together worshipped and together glorified, Who spoke through the prophets; in one holy Catholic and apostolic Church. We confess one baptism to the remission of sins; we look forward to the resurrection of the dead and the life of the world to come. Amen.[66]

65. Basil, *Letter* 236.6.
66. *Creed of Constantinople*, 297–98.

The Council of Constantinople in 381 went on to anathematize the teaching of Arius, his followers, and other dissenting groups, with the formula that God is one Being in three Persons. This effectively ended the theological disputes over the Trinity regarding Nicaea's language of *homoousios*.[67] The resulting Nicene-Constantinopolitan Creed holds out the agreed view of the church about the nature of the Christian God, well summarized by Gerald O'Collins:

> That credal confession presents a divine communication in creation and salvation history that presupposes an eternal communion within God: the Father, the only begotten Son, and the 'proceeding' Holy Spirit. In particular, God's self-communication *ad extra* through the missions of the Son (who 'came down from heaven' and 'became man') and the Spirit (who 'spoke through the prophets' and effected the incarnation) in the history or 'economy' of salvation presupposes and reflects the self-communication *ad intra*: the eternal generation of the Son and procession of the Spirit. Thus the 'economic' Trinity or Trinity in creation and history on which the Creed largely focuses reveals the immanent Trinity and is identical with it.[68]

TRINITY EAST AND WEST AND THE HOLY SPIRIT

The consistent teaching of the Eastern (or Greek) Church is that the Holy Spirit proceeds from the Father through the Son. The trinitarian thinking of the Cappadocians ensures this explanation does not insinuate subordinationism because it is grounded in a full recognition of the *homoosious* of the Spirit, that the Holy Spirit is of exactly the same substance as the Father and the Son. The core of the doctrine of the Cappadocian thinkers is that the one Godhead exists concurrently in three modes of being, or *hypostases*. Here we have the notion of co-inheritance, or "*perichoresis*" as it later became known, of the divine three, where the Godhead exists undivided in three persons.[69] It is from this understanding that the image of the dance of God springs, the singular yet plural movement of the divine in perfect harmony and mutual deference. Essentially, for the Eastern Church, the *ousia*, or being, of Godhead is not an abstract principle but a concrete reality.[70]

67. Emery and Levering, *Handbook of the Trinity*, 116–17.

68. O'Collins, *Tripersonal God*, 126.

69. Kelly, *Doctrines*, 263–64.

70. Kelly, *Doctrines*, 268.

Augustine (d. 430) was a significant shaper of the theology of the Western (or Latin) Church. The overarching aim of his writing about the Trinity was to distinguish Christian teaching from myth, and to align it with the best insights of the philosophical culture of his day. In this he sought to show that Christianity cannot be derived from the teaching of the pagan philosophers but required revised philosophical thinking.[71] He understood the distinction of the Persons of the Trinity to be solely grounded in their mutual relations in the Godhead. A little differently to the Cappadocian teaching that shaped the East, Augustine taught the doctrine of the double procession of the Holy Spirit from the Father *and* the Son. He said that the Son is from the Father, the Spirit is from the Father; the former is begotten, the latter proceeds. The idea is that, as the Father has given all he has to the Son, he has given the Son power to bestow the Spirit. The action of the Father and the Son in bestowing the Spirit is mutual, as is the action of all three persons in creation. Despite this double procession, the Father remains the primordial source, in the sense that it is from him that the Son derives his capacity to bestow the Spirit.[72] This idea is reflected in one of Augustine's explanations of the Trinity in *City of God:*

> What is begotten of the simple good is likewise simple and is what the Begetter is. These two we call the Father and the Son and, together with their Spirit, are one God. This Spirit of the Father and of the Son is called in Sacred Scripture, in a very special sense, the Holy Spirit. The Spirit is other than the Father and the Son because he is neither the Father nor the Son. I say 'other than,' not 'different from,' because, equally with them, He is the simple, unchangeable, co-eternal Good. This Trinity is one God. And . . . it is true that the Father *has* a Son, yet he *is* not the Son. And the Son *has* a Father, yet *is* not the Father. Therefore, as regards himself, without reference to His relation with the others, the Father is what He has.[73]

In *On the Trinity,* Augustine discusses "the three things which are found in love" to create an analogy for the Trinity:

> When I, who make this enquiry, love anything, there are three things concerned—myself, and that which I love, and love itself. For I do not love love, except I love a lover; for there is no love where nothing is loved. Therefore there are three things—he who loves, and that which is loved, and love. . . . And if love is a

71. Cavadini, "Trinity and Apologetics in St Augustine," 240.

72. Kelly, *Doctrines,* 272–76.

73. Augustine, *Civ.* 11.10.

substance, it is certainly not body, but spirit; and the mind also is not body, but spirit. Yet love and mind are not two spirits, but one spirit; nor yet two essences, but one: and yet here are two things that are one, he that loves and love; or, if you like so to put it, that which is loved and love.[74]

In Augustine's trinitarian imagery, the Father is the Lover, the Son the Beloved, and the Holy Spirit the mutual Love that passes between Father and Son. The Eastern Church has criticized Augustine's analogy for depersonalizing the Holy Spirit, the point being that the I-Thou relationship, the gift of love that two persons share mutually, is neither a third person nor does it emerge as an activity that describes a person distinct from the I and the Thou.[75]

At the time Augustine wrote, the Western Church had not yet added the *Filioque* clause to the Nicene-Constantinopolitan Creed. The clause expressed the double procession of the Holy Spirit from the Father and the Son against heresies that tended towards the denial of true personal distinctions within the Godhead.[76] As already noted above, in Augustine's view the Spirit did proceed from the Father through the Son, with the Son being considered the agent of the Father in the procession by equally producing the divine Spirit. For Augustine, what the Son does in this he does through the gift of the Father rather than through independent action, for the divinity of the Son is derived from the Father. Importantly, acting and being in this derivative way does not exclude the Son being equal in divinity and in the production of the Spirit. The theologians of the Eastern Church did not in general find any difficulty in saying that the Spirit proceeds *from* the Father through the Son, the Son being considered the agent of the Father. It always remained clear that the *Father alone* is the ultimate source of deity and that both the Son and the Spirit stem from him, the Son by generation and the Spirit by procession. The *Filioque,* however, suggested to Eastern thinkers a profoundly different view of the Son being equal in the production of the Spirit. So, they rejected the Augustinian idea of the Son and the Father together forming a co-principle for the procession of the Spirit, for, in their view, such a double origin for the Spirit contradicts the divine unity.[77]

Beyond the less than extensive parameters of difference discussed above, the notion that there was a clear-cut separation between the Western/Latin, and the Eastern/Greek churches in regard to Trinitarian belief is

74. Augustine, *Trin.* 9.2.

75. O'Collins, *Tripersonal God,* 136.

76. O'Collins, *Tripersonal God,* 138.

77. O'Collins, *Tripersonal God,* 139–40.

now regarded by many scholars as untenable.[78] As our brief tracing of the historical developments of the early Christian centuries has shown, there were a variety of positions in regard to the Trinity that had adherents in both the Eastern and Western churches. It is therefore the group of late-fourth-century theologians, often referred to as the "pro-Nicenes" from both East and West, who provide the most assistance in coming to terms with Trinitarian doctrine, ancient and modern. The combined thinking of the pro-Nicene theologians presents what the Christian Church has come to accept as the orthodox doctrine of the Trinity. At one level it is quite a minimalistic explanation; at another, it synthesizes and summarizes a wide range of scriptural and creedal data and is therefore a basis for understanding revelation and redemption.[79]

There are three necessary elements in any contemporary trinitarian theology that would render it pro-Nicene. The first is a clearly articulated form of the distinction between person and nature in the Godhead, involving the principle that whatever is predicated of the divine nature is predicated of the three persons equally and understood to be one. The second makes clear that the eternal generation of the Son occurs within the unitary and incomparable divine being. The third expresses unambiguously the doctrine that the persons of the Trinity work inseparably.[80] So, contemporary reflections on the pro-Nicene account of Trinity, like those of the ancients, continue to be all about how the nature of the unity and diversity in the Trinity can be appropriately understood.

SOCIAL TRINITARIANISM

A perennial question surrounding the nature of this unity and diversity in the Trinity is what is meant when the term "person" is used. Stemming from that, the question of how we understand the oneness of the being or essence that is ascribed to the Trinitarian persons continues to be crucial. Augustine once wrote: "When the question is asked, 'What Three?' . . . the answer is given 'Three Persons,' not that it might be spoken, but that it might not be left unspoken."[81] Even if an answer to the question about the meaning of "person" (*persona*) in the doctrine of the Trinity was best left unarticulated in the fifth century, this is no longer the case. An answer to Augustine's

78. Hasker, *Metaphysics and the Tri-Personal God*, 14. See also an extensive bibliographic list in Coakley, *God, Sexuality, and the Self*, 92.

79. Hasker, *Metaphysics and the Tri-Personal God*, 15.

80. Ayres, *Nicaea and Its Legacy*, 236.

81. Augustine, *Trin.* 5.9.

question has become essential for twenty-first-century thinkers, and one has been provided by a relatively recent movement in trinitarian theology, social trinitarianism. At least in part, social trinitarianism can be seen as a reaction against widespread claims that the early terms *hypostases* and *persona* should not be viewed as the equivalent to the word "person" as we understand it now.[82] The following four propositions summarize the central contentions of social trinitarianism. Proposition one is that inter-personal unity is irreducibly social in nature. Proposition two is that the members of the Trinity are persons in the full, modern sense.[83] Proposition three is that, because the members of the Trinity are persons in the full, modern sense, the unity of the Trinity is genuinely social in nature. Proposition four is that the divine persons interpenetrate, co-inhere, and mutually indwell one another in *perichoresis*.[84]

Social trinitarianism draws on philosophy, psychology, and sociology to point out that genuine personhood more than permits, it requires, social interaction with other persons. In a similar manner to a human being, who, without relation to others cannot develop important aspects of their own personhood, so a unitarian image of God as a solitary person is singularly unattractive unless we view the created order as a necessary complement which provides an "other" to which to relate. A pro-Nicene historical precedent is claimed for social trinitarianism, particularly (but not exclusively) by appeal to the voices of the Cappadocians and the trinitarian tradition of the Eastern Church. While all adherents to the idea of a Social Trinity maintain that "person" in the doctrine of the Trinity is similar in a significant way to our modern conception of personhood, there are nevertheless substantial differences in understandings about how closely that similarity exists.[85] A helpful minimalist definition of social trinitarianism is provided by Cornelius Plantinga, one of the acknowledged leaders of the movement:

> By... Social Trinitarianism, I mean a theory that meets at least the following three conditions: (1) The theory must have Father, Son and Spirit as distinct centers of knowledge, will, love, and action. Since each of these capacities requires consciousness, it

82. Hasker, *Metaphysics and the Tri-Personal God*, 19.

83. This is in the sense of "person" as a distinct center of consciousness in relationship. It rules out notions of classic modern western individualism, as discussed further in this chapter.

84. Mosser, "Fully Social Trinitarianism," 133–34.

85. Hasker, *Metaphysics and the Tri-Personal God*, 20–21. It would not be correct to view Social Trinitarianism as a monolithic or cohesive movement. Some Social Trinitarians, for example, insist on the numerical identity of the divine essence, others do not. Hasker, *Metaphysics and the Tri-Personal God*, 23.

follows that, on this sort of theory, Father, Son and Spirit would be viewed as distinct centers of consciousness, or, in short, as *persons* in some full sense of the term. (2) Any accompanying sub-theory of divine simplicity must be modest enough to be consistent with condition (1), that is, with a real distinctness of trinitarian persons . . . (3) Father, Son, and Spirit must be regarded as tightly enough related to each other so as to render plausible the judgement that they constitute a particular social unit. In such social monotheism, it will be appropriate to use the designator *God* to refer to the whole Trinity, where the Trinity is understood to be one thing, even if it is a complex thing consisting of persons, essences, and relations.[86]

Of these three conditions, the first is the overall key to social trinitarianism: Father, Son and Holy Spirit are distinct centers of consciousness and therefore persons in the full sense of the term. As Moltmann points out, to fully be a person means "being-in-relationship." A person as a being in relationship will form part of a social network of intersubjectivity. To think of the trinitarian persons in this full sense enables "person," "relation," and "sociality" to be employed as complimentary terms.[87] The second condition is required for logical consistency; a doctrine of divine simplicity will affirm that God is without parts, but it must be articulated in such a way that it allows for a genuine distinction of the persons. The third condition, that the Trinity is understood to be one thing, is one that all social trinitarians claim to have satisfied in their theories. It is also the one that causes critics to dispute whether the Trinity understood this way can genuinely be described as only one God.[88] It gains this level of attention because the most usual charge against social trinitarianism as a movement, and against individual theologians who favor a social model of Trinity, is tritheism. The claim that the trinitarian thinking expressed by Moltmann, for example, *"verges on tritheism"* has certainly been made.[89] It is to Moltmann's social trinitarian framework we now turn, for if the notion of God as a social network of intersubjectivity—a Divine Sociality—can be defended, then it is important to the consideration of God's exercise of power that shapes this book.

Jürgen Moltmann was born in Germany in 1926 and is Professor Emeritus of Systematic Theology at the University of Tübingen. Over his long career as a theologian, he has contributed to many areas of Christian

86. Plantinga, "Social Trinity and Tritheism," 22.

87. Moltmann, *Spirit of Life*, 14.

88. Hasker, *Metaphysics and the Tri-Personal God*, 23.

89. O'Collins, *Tripersonal God*, 158.

thought, but it is his development of a social model of the Trinity which is immediately applicable to this study. As Moltmann has come to broadly embrace both a panentheistic understanding of God and a social notion of God, his trinitarian theology seems likely to be compatible with the process theology of Hartshorne, particularly regarding God's non-coercive exercise of power in the world. Moreover, Moltmann's theological views were deeply influenced by the problem of evil through his experiences during the Second World War. This also speaks to understandings of power, and of how the suffering of individuals and the world can be held in tension with belief in a good and loving God.[90] In an introductory essay to *The Crucified God*,[91] he refers to his experience as a prisoner of war and the impact it had on his theology:

> Shattered and broken, the survivors of my generation were then returning from camps and hospitals to the lecture room. A theology which did not speak of God in the sight of the one who was abandoned and crucified would have had nothing to say to us then.[92]

Moltmann is sure that if we are in any way to understand the humanity and the divinity of the One who was crucified, we can only think of God in trinitarian terms. Conversely, he insists that we can only think of God in trinitarian terms if we have the cross in mind. He sees the cross as a divine event involving Father, Son, and Spirit, and finds that viewing the cross in this trinitarian way rescues the doctrine of Trinity from the realms of esoteric speculation and places it firmly into a lived experience of liberation:

---

90. Moltmann was not a panentheist in his earliest works. His social trinitarianism can be traced to the publication of *Trinity and the Kingdom of God* (in German in 1980, translated into English in 1981). Müller-Fahrenholz points out some developments in the shaping of Moltmann's body of work in theology. He says, "Moltmann's early studies of Reformed covenant theology shaped his basic attitude to the theology of history, but it was substantially reinforced by the covenant theology of Old Testament exegetes like Gerhard von Rad and Ernst Bloch's philosophy of history." Müller-Fahrenholz goes on to point to "the resurrection of the crucified Christ" as the "decisive point of reference" for Moltmann, saying "the resurrection of Christ symbolizes a divine power which does not renew just one or the other *in* history, but puts history itself on a new footing. The flow of time is reversed. Time flows from God's future . . . (and) eschatology becomes the determining quality of history." Müller-Fahrenholz finds that the cross and the resurrection of Christ also form the substantive core of Moltmann's trinitarian theology, that it is "unfolded as one single great history of the love of God for his creation." Müller-Fahrenholz, *Kingdom and the Power*, 231.

91. Moltmann, *Crucified God*.

92. Moltmann, *Crucified God*, 1.

If the cross of Jesus is understood as a divine event, i.e. as an event between Jesus and his God and Father, it is necessary to speak in Trinitarian terms of the Son and the Father and the Spirit. In that case the doctrine of the Trinity is no longer an exorbitant and impractical speculation about God, but is nothing other than a shorter version of the passion narrative of Christ in its significance for the eschatological freedom of faith and the life of oppressed nature.[93]

He makes the point that the doctrine of the Trinity is what marks Christianity off from polytheism, pantheism, and the monotheism of Judaism and Islam, yet insists it has not been honored with any special significance in the history of Western theology. He does acknowledge the use of the trinitarian formula in the liturgies of the church, the three articles of the Apostles Creed, and the more recent tendency to refer to God in terms of Creator, Reconciler, and Redeemer. However, Moltmann maintains that in practice the religious conceptions of many Christians prove to be no more than a weakly Christianized monotheism. He further asserts that this generalized monotheism in theology and Christian belief not only creates a crisis of identity but is also a "permanent occasion for protest atheism, and rightly so."[94] For Moltmann:

> Even the doctrine of grace is monotheistic, and not trinitarian, in practice. Man shares in the grace of God or the divine nature. It is still said that we acquire this grace through Christ, but no trinitarian differentiation in God seems to be necessary. The same thing is true of the doctrine of creation. Faith in the one Creator God seems sufficient—as among Mohammedans. In eschatology, too, at best there is talk of the coming of God and his kingdom or of God as the absolute future. Understandably, Christ then fades away to become the prophet of this future, who fills this function as the representative of the now absent God and can go when God himself comes to occupy his place. Finally, Christian ethics establishes the obedience of man under the rule of God and Christ, and rarely goes beyond a moral monarchy.[95]

In this context, claims that Moltmann's social conception of Trinity leans toward tritheism are more easily understandable.[96] An enduring em-

93. Moltmann, *Crucified God*, 246.
94. Moltmann, *Crucified God*, 236.
95. Moltmann, *Crucified God*, 237.
96. O'Collins, *Tripersonal God*, 158.

phasis on the distinction of the persons as a counterbalance to a monotheistic and monarchical trend in Christian thinking could certainly be
construed as one-sided, especially over the course of a long theological career. Related to his charge of practical monotheism in much of the Christian
Church and his concomitant focus on the distinctiveness of Father, Son, and
Spirit in the Godhead, Moltmann is convinced that the doctrine of the Trinity became "isolated speculation and a mere decoration for dogmatics after
the Middle Ages." He finds the reason for this in the *Summa Theologica* of
Thomas Aquinas.[97] Moltmann suggests that, through the influence of Aquinas, a significant modification was made to the doctrine of God, and further
that this adjustment to Christian thinking has been taken for granted ever
since. Moltmann explains:

> Following Thomas, one began with the question 'Is there a God',
> and demonstrated with the help of the natural light of human
> reason and the cosmological arguments for the existence of
> God that there was a God and that God was one. Then, with the
> same method, conclusions were drawn as to the metaphysical,
> non-human properties of the divine nature. This knowledge was
> assigned to natural theology. Only then was a move made to
> describe the inner being of God with the aid of the supernatural
> light of grace, a move towards . . . the saving knowledge of God.[98]

The unhelpful modification to Christian thinking about God that
Moltmann ascribes to Aquinas is to make metaphysical speculation about
God and God's inner life a starting point, and only later and secondarily
considering God's relationship to us in salvation history. Moltmann calls on
the thinking of the Cappadocians as a favorable example of an understanding that all theology is essentially about the doctrine of the Trinity, and that
Trinity is the very nature of God. He notes that the Cappadocians did make
a distinction between the Immanent Trinity and the Economic Trinity as
a way of distinguishing between the inner life of God and God in salvation history, but insists that this points to the Cappadocian understanding
that God is beforehand in Godself everything that God reveals in Christ, in
other words, God is eternally trinitarian.[99] In considering the unity of God,
Moltmann points out:

> The early creeds, which set the trend for tradition, remain am-
> bivalent where the question of God's unity is concerned. The

97. Moltmann, *Crucified God*, 239.
98. Moltmann, *Crucified God*, 239.
99. Moltmann, *Crucified God*, 240.

Nicene Creed with its use of *homoousios* as keyword, suggests a unity of substance between Father, Son and Spirit. But the Athanasian Creed, with the thesis '*unus Deus*', maintains the identity of the one divine subject… In the first case the threeness of the Persons is in the foreground, while the unity of their substance is in the background. In the second case the unity of the absolute subject is in the foreground, and the three Persons recede into the background. The first case is obviously open to the charge of tritheism; the second case open to the reproach of modalism… . If the biblical testimony is chosen as point of departure, then we shall have to start from the three Persons of the history of Christ. If philosophical logic is made the starting point, then the enquirer proceeds from the One God.[100]

To Moltmann, it makes much more sense theologically to begin with the biblical history, thus making the unity of the three divine Persons the problem. The opposite method, favored by Aquinas, is of far less appeal to him, as previously discussed.[101] This is not to suggest that Moltmann fully approves of the Nicene doctrine of the one divine substance, rather he looks at the issue of divine unity quite differently:

The unity of the Father, the Son and the Spirit is then the eschatological question about the consummation of the trinitarian history of God. The unity of the three Persons of this history must consequently be understood as a *communicable* unity and as an *open, inviting unity, capable of integration*. The *homogeneity* of the one divine substance is hardly conceivable as communicable and open for anything else, because it would no longer be homogeneous. The *sameness* and the identity of absolute subject is not communicable either, let alone open for anything else, because it would then be charged with non-identity and difference. Both these concepts of unity … are exclusive, not inclusive. If we search for a concept of unity corresponding to the biblical testimony of the triune God, the God who unites others with himself, then we must dispense with both the concept of the one substance and the concept of the identical subject. All that remains is: the unitedness, the at-oneness of the three Persons with one another, or: the unitedness, the at-oneness of the triune God.[102]

100. Moltmann, *Trinity and the Kingdom*, 149.

101. Moltmann, *Trinity and the Kingdom*, 149.

102. Moltmann, *Trinity and the Kingdom*, 149–50.

Moltmann's notion of unity in the Trinity as open and communicable points to the idea that God's ultimate purpose is to unite human beings with God, hence the reference to eschatology. The strong suggestion is that the unity of Father, Son and Spirit will not be complete until the eschatological unity becomes a reality. Moltmann clearly states that there is no unity of substance in the Godhead, and a well-known and often quoted feature of his thought is that the unity of God is grounded in the doctrine of *perichoresis*. For Moltmann, divine unity "must be perceived in the *perichoresis* of the divine Persons. If the unity of God is not perceived in the at-oneness of the triune God, and therefore as a *perichoretic* unity, then Arianism and Sabellianism remain inescapable threats to Christian theology."[103]

What Moltmann is drawing on here is an idea that is already present in the Fathers of the early church and in the New Testament. The idea is that human beings are to be drawn into the relationship of love and communion that exists between the Father and the Son with the Trinity. Moltmann infers that the unity of Father, Son, and Holy Spirit cannot be anything that is not, in principle, open to human beings. Critics of Moltmann rightly ask whether this sort of unity is sufficient, just by itself, to constitute the unity of the Godhead? For if the human beings who will share in this eschatological *perichoresis* come (as they would) from all different sources and conditions of life, could not the same also be true or Father, Son and Spirit? And if the same is not true, why is it not?[104] In a later discussion of the Immanent Trinity, Moltmann offers additional explanation of his concept of *perichoresis*:

> John Damascene's profound doctrine of the eternal *perichoresis*
> or *circumincessio* of the Trinitarian Persons . . . grasps the cir-
> culatory character of the eternal divine life. An eternal process
> takes place in the triune God through the exchange of energies.
> The Father exists in the Son, the Son in the Father, and both of
> them in the Spirit, just as the Spirit exists in both the Father and
> the Son. By virtue of their eternal love they live in one another
> to such an extent, and dwell in one another to such an extent,
> that they are one. It is a process of most perfect and intense
> empathy.[105]

As Moltmann develops and explicates his view of the trinitarian nature of God it becomes clearer that *perichoresis*, vital as it is to his thinking, is not his sole descriptor of the unity of God. He refers to the eternal generation of the Son and the eternal procession of the Holy Spirit, demonstrating

103. Moltmann, *Trinity and the Kingdom*, 150.

104. Hasker, *Metaphysics and the Tri-Personal God*, 100.

105. Moltmann, *Trinity and the Kingdom*, 174–75.

a trajectory of thought that links him firmly to Nicaea and the accepted doctrines of the Church.

> In respect of the constitution of the Trinity the Father is the 'origin-without-origin' of the Godhead. According to the doctrine of the two processions, the Son and the Spirit take their divine hypostases from him . . . but in respect of the Trinity's inner life, the three persons themselves form their unity, by virtue of their relation to one another and in the eternal perichoresis of their love. They are concentrated in *the eternal Son*. This is the perichoretic unity of the Trinity. Finally, the mutual transfiguration and illumination of the Trinity into the eternal glory of the divine life is bound up with this. This uniting mutuality and community proceeds from *the Holy Spirit*. The unity of the Trinity is constituted by the Father, concentrated round the Son, and illuminated through the Holy Spirit.[106]

The "open" nature of the divine *perichoresis* in Moltmann does not mean that human beings and other creatures can be united with God in exactly the same way that the three persons are united with one another. It would be a misreading of Moltmann to suggest that he would consider it possible that any part of the created order could be eternally generated from God the Father. Moltmann therefore has a stronger concept of the divine unity than is often supposed.[107] For him, the one God is perfect community, and the perfect community of the *perichoretic* God can be depicted metaphorically as a round dance where the three persons are fully united in perfect movement. As Moltmann explains:

> The unity of the triune God is intensive liveliness, vibrant movement and perfect rest in movement. The unity of the triune God is not complacently shut in on itself, but is an open, inviting unity, as John 17:21 says: 'that they may also be in us', just as this eternal liveliness of the triune God in the communication of the Spirit is an attractive, life-giving life, and the eternal love which the triune God is in himself is the love which communicates itself to all the world in the surrender of the Son. The perichoretic concept of unity surmounts the 'dangers' of both 'tritheism' and 'modalism', since it combines threeness and oneness without reducing the threeness to oneness or the oneness to threeness.[108]

106. Moltmann, *Trinity and the Kingdom*, 177–78.
107. Hasker, *Metaphysics and the Tri-Personal God*, 101–2.
108. Moltmann, *History and the Triune God*, 132.

As far as Moltmann is concerned, "communion" and "fellowship" are terms that best describe the nature and purpose of God,[109] and he sees the biblical record as a testament to the history of this fellowship within the Trinity. As already noted, he is convinced that the fellowship of the Trinity is open to humanity and open to the world. So, he is working with a hermeneutic that invites us to think in terms of communities and relationships, setting aside what he describes as "the subjective thinking which cannot work without the separation and isolation of its objects."[110] For Moltmann:

> Thinking in relationships and communities is developed out of the doctrine of the Trinity, and is brought to bear on the relation of men and women to God, to other people and to mankind as a whole, as well as on their fellowship with the whole of creation. By taking up panentheistic ideas from the Jewish and the Christian traditions, we shall try and think *ecologically* about God, man and the world in their relationships and indwellings. In this way it is not merely the Christian *doctrine* of the Trinity that we are trying to work out anew; our aim is to develop and practise Trinitarian *thinking* as well.[111]

Like Hartshorne and much of the process movement, Moltmann is a keen panentheist. He affirms that the triune God is present in all things; conversely that all things are present in God. He always maintains, nevertheless, that God is more than the world. His focus on the relation of God to the world leads to what he describes as a pneumatological doctrine of creation. On his view, what is normative for all relationships in creation is the eternal *perichoresis* of the triunity rather than any structure of command and obedience within the Trinity. From this view there follows the ongoing presence of the Spirit in the fellowship of creation. There also follows a *perichoretic* doctrine of creation, that the essence of all things is found in the field of creation in which they live, move, and have their being. A fellowship of creation therefore replaces hierarchical notions of the order of creation. Indeed, order is not a dichotomy between super-ordination and subordination. It is instead mutual fellowship held in a fluid balance. As far as Moltmann is concerned, hierarchical parallels of Father-Son in the Trinity, God-world, heaven-earth, soul-body, man-woman must be dissolved and reanimated in terms of mutuality and *perichoresis*.[112]

---

109. Moltmann, *Trinity and the Kingdom*, xiii.
110. Moltmann, *Trinity and the Kingdom*, 19.
111. Moltmann, *Trinity and the Kingdom*, 19–20.
112. Moltmann, *Trinity and the Kingdom*, 127.

Moltmann's conception of a Social Trinity of reciprocal love and mutual empathy has much to contribute to a contemporary understanding of equal gender relationships. As his doctrine of God is deliberately non-hierarchical, it also challenges "patriarchal talk of God and the patriarchal oppression of women deposited in the centuries of historical Christianity."[113] Moltmann is keen that "masculine sexist language" about the Triune God be replaced with "Christian messianic language":[114]

> The difference between the Father God and Lord God of a patriarchal society and the Father of Jesus Christ was and is Jesus himself. Anyone who is oriented on him and with him cries 'Abba' has broken with the laws and the power-relationships of patriarchy. The domination of the father and the subordination of wife and children is replaced by the messianic community-in-solidarity of the female and male friends of Jesus, and in that community power is distributed fairly.[115]

Moltmann here focuses on the distribution of community power rather than individual power in his notion of messianic community-in-solidarity. This stems from his insistence that, in the Trinity, the divine persons do not first exist and then enter into relationship but are constituted and defined by their relationships.[116] Despite Moltmann's clear support for equality between the genders, this notion of mutuality over autonomy in community has been critiqued for its potential to disempower women. Karen Kilby, in surveying problems she associates with social trinitarianism, insists that:

> What women need is not to be urged towards mutuality and interrelatedness, but to learn to reclaim their own autonomy, to become aware of their own distinct desires and needs, to become aware of themselves as something other than wife, mother, sister. One might have thought, in other words, that it would be problematic to hold up for women an image of God as persons who are so utterly bound up in and defined by relationships that they lose even their numerical distinctness.[117]

The claim that imaging God as a Social Trinity is problematic for women, based on the experience of women's disempowerment through being defined by their relationships and the needs of others, is significantly

113. Moltmann, *History and the Triune God*, 16.
114. Moltmann, *History and the Triune God*, 16.
115. Moltmann, *History and the Triune God*, 17.
116. Moltmann, *Spirit of Life*, 221.
117. Kilby, "Perichoresis and Projection," 429.

weakened by a clearer understanding of Moltmann's social vision. For, as Joy Ann McDougall points out in a response to Kilby, although social relationships do equate to true personhood in Moltmann's trinitarian anthropology, this is not to suggest that the individual just disappears. Nor is it to suggest that the identity of any individual becomes a simple sum of his or her social relations. McDougall explains:

> Rather what Moltmann's Social Trinitarian anthropology prescribes is the inseparability of personal identity and sociality, so that self-relation and social relations come into existence together. Just as the unity among the trinitarian persons does not take precedence over the distinction among the three persons, so, too, the human community does not take priority over its individual members.[118]

In fact, Moltmann places significant responsibility on his own gender for the proper distribution of power in church and society. He declares that men will not become complete persons until they have overcome the distortions of patriarchalism,[119] and articulates his vision of the future as:

> A community of human solidarity, communication free of domination, an open society. This future is only betrayed in patriarchy and only hindered in a 'fatherless' bureaucratic society. Women and men, mothers and fathers, will only enter into a 'just, participatory and responsible' human society if first patriarchy and then also the fatherless society have been done away with. In principle that already happens in the motherly love which Jesus manifested in the Father and put into practise through his own behavior towards the poor, the sick and the sinners. This is the love which does not seek its own to confirm itself, but which seeks the other and the lost to save it. It is communicative and creative love, which makes the unjust just, the ugly beautiful, and the divided whole. It is the divine love which goes beyond the love of father and mother, by determining both. Matriarchy and patriarchy can find their limited meanings in history by helping to contribute to the formation of that messianic community of people in which this love permeates all things.[120]

This vision of messianic community is built on an understanding that the coequal and coeternal persons of the Holy Trinity form perfect

118. McDougall, "Moltmann on the Trinity," 192.

119. Moltmann, *History and the Triune God*, 17.

120. Moltmann, *History and the Triune God*, 17–18.

community within the Godhead that is One. It is not a patriarchal community, nor is it hierarchical. It is a community of equals who share one and the same power "with" each other and "for" the good of the world. For Moltmann, as for all proponents of a Social Trinity, this nature of God as genuine community provides a model for all human relationships, including those with the world and its ecosystems and creatures. It is impossible to countenance, in this context, one of the 'persons' of the Trinity overseeing the others, the persons of the Trinity being ranked in order of importance, or one of the persons of the Trinity being made less for any reason. This is because any person of the Trinity being more or less important, or independently powerful, than the others; any person of the Trinity exercising power "over" the other persons rather than "with" the other persons; any person of the Trinity being permanently lower on some kind of internal hierarchy, contradicts the very nature of God which is love and mutuality.

It is on this basis that Moltmann is deeply critical of the introduction of the *filioque* clause into the Nicene Creed; he finds that it interferes with the coequal status of the Spirit with the Father and the Son. The *filioque* affirmed that the Spirit proceeds from the Father *and* the Son and was a matter of intense debate within the medieval church. The East never accepted it.[121] Despite the clause becoming the official teaching of the medieval West, Moltmann unequivocally insists that it makes the Spirit a subordinate third:[122]

> For with the Filioque, the Holy Spirit is once and for all put in third place in the Trinity, and subordinated to the Son. But this makes it impossible to comprehend salvation history adequately. It is true that this order applies to the sending of the Spirit through Christ on the foundation of the resurrection, but it does not apply to Christ's own history in the Spirit. If Christ was conceived by the Holy Spirit, baptized with the Spirit, and ministered by virtue of the energies given him by the Spirit, then he presupposes the Spirit, and the Spirit precedes him. Christ comes from the Father in the Spirit.[123]

Moltmann identifies clericalism as a key factor that led to the *filioque* clause becoming part of the Nicene Creed. He argues that defining the operation of the Spirit through the Son has very little to do with theology. For him, it is instead about power and control; it is about holding the Spirit

---

121. Emery and Levering, *Trinity*, 405.

122. Moltmann, *Spirit of Life*, 293.

123. Moltmann, *Spirit of Life*, 293.

captive within the workings of a clerical hierarchy, resulting in congregations remaining submissive receivers of ministry of the Church:

> If God is represented by Christ, Christ by the Pope, and the
> Pope by the bishops and priests, then—by way of the Filioque
> in the primordial relationships—the Holy Spirit, with all his
> charismata and energies in salvation history, is tied down to the
> operative acts of the priesthood. The Holy Spirit is then nothing
> other than the operation of 'the spiritual pastors', their ministe-
> rial grace their proclamation, pastoral care and administration
> of the sacraments. The congregation turns into the passive re-
> cipient of the gifts of the Spirit mediated through the Church.
> But in this way the Spirit does not make Christians their own
> determining subjects, or the rulers of their own lives.[124]

Moltmann is therefore convinced that the way we understand the
interrelations of Father, Son, and Spirit in the Trinity impacts human relationships. This is certainly so in the Church, but also in the world, and
especially regarding power. On this basis, a change of mind-set about God,
specifically in the way we understand the triunity of God, really can inform
a convincingly different idea of the exercise of power. The key to this shift in
thinking about divine and human power is to acknowledge that God is not
described and named by theistic speculation or definition, but by the God
who *by the Spirit* comes to us as Christ.[125] A deep and abiding Spirit focus
is now required and long overdue, according to Moltmann, as the work of
the Spirit has been much neglected in trinitarian theology and the power of
the Spirit has been both resisted and confined by the Church.[126] This leads
him to take the risk of appearing to unsettle an appropriate coequal and
coeternal trinitarian balance in the Godhead, by describing the Holy Spirit
in terms of the new Maker, or Creator of all things; as that which is primary
to the life of God:

> Through the fellowship of the Spirit, the experience of God will
> reach out beyond experience of the self and the experience of
> sociality, and become the experience of nature too; for the Spirit
> is the Creator, the new Creator of all things. That is why bodily
> experiences, sensuous experiences and experiences of our fellow
> creatures in nature enjoy the same rank in experience of God as
> experience of self, or the social experience of love. These experi-
> ences of nature are inseparably bound up with experiences of

---

124. Moltmann, *Spirit of Life*, 294.

125. Inbody, *Many Faces of Christology*, 61.

126. Moltmann, *Spirit of Life*, 294.

self and experiences of sociality, and are a constitutive element in these experiences. Anyone who disparages this community of creation compared with a community of soul is quenching God's creative Spirit and denying him the fellowship he seeks with all created beings, so as to redeem them.[127]

In seeking to re-establish the place of the Spirit in the Trinity, and to challenge accepted descriptions of Father, Son, and Spirit, Moltmann reveals a dissatisfaction with the implicit patriarchalism and hierarchicalism of the power relations in the trinitarian models most often relied on in the Church. This dissatisfaction is not unique to Moltmann and proponents of a Social Trinity.[128] The possibilities opened by a sustained focus on the Holy Spirit will therefore be significant in reshaping trinitarian theology in a manner that is thoroughly pro-Nicene and takes us forward into a vision of God that models equal and mutually deferential relationships for both the Church and the world.

The early shaping of trinitarian theology, based on the startling New Testament witness of the life and work of Jesus, began with a binitarian focus on the relationship of the Father and the Son. From Clement of Rome in the first century, through Ignatius and Justin Martyr in the second, Origen in the third, up to and including Arius and his range of followers in the fourth century, discussions about the nature of God as Trinity were predominantly focused on two out of the three persons; the Holy Spirit was largely overlooked. Irenaeus and Tertullian, who both wrote in the third century, were somewhat more balanced in their trinitarian reflections, Tertullian being credited with laying the foundation of a language of Trinity. It was the fourth-century thinkers, Athanasius in the West, and the Cappadocians in the East, that were most influential in assisting the church to articulate a coequal, coeternal Trinity, one that, in official doctrine at least, fell neither into subordinationism (which leads to tritheism) nor into modalism.

All modern and contemporary thinking about the Trinity must, in one way or another, come to terms with the orthodox formulations agreed by the church in the fourth century. Perhaps less extensive than generally understood, such pro-Nicene theology rests on three necessities. First, a clear distinction between person and nature in the Godhead, that whatever is

127. Moltmann, *Spirit of Life*, 221.

128. Coakley, *God, Sexuality, and the Self*, 333. Although not sharing the social trinitarian view of Moltmann, nor finding the *filioque* clause particularly relevant, Coakley utterly resists any tendency to place the Spirit "third" in the Trinity. In a similar way to Moltmann, she calls instead for the Spirit to be in first place, and on this basis exhorts us to "submit to an adventure into God in which the Spirit *leads* by surprise, adventure, purgation, and conviction." Coakley, *God, Sexuality, and the Self*, 331.

grounded in the divine nature is held equally by each of the three persons
and understood to be one. Second, that the eternal generation of the Son
ensues from within the one divine being. Third, an unambiguous understanding that the three persons of the Trinity work inseparably.[129] Social
trinitarianism, which broadly maintains that "person" in the doctrine of
the Trinity is similar in a significant way to a contemporary conception
of personhood as a distinct center of consciousness in relationship, is, as
demonstrated in this chapter, a pro-Nicene theology.[130] So too is the trinitarian theology of Moltmann. His social theory of the Trinity understands
the cross as a divine event involving Father, Son, and Spirit, and, by this
understanding, seeks to release the doctrine of Trinity from esoteric speculation to place it decisively into a lived experience of liberation.[131] Moltmann
believes that the inner relations of the Immanent Trinity are a model for all
relationship, and that the *perichoretic* dance of the three persons of the one
triune God can and must set a pattern for the life of the world and all its
creatures and interconnections.

The next chapter considers how Moltmann's social trinitarianism can
connect with process theology and pursues a fully relational model of God
as a Social Trinity in process. What will be carried across to chapter 4 is an
understanding of the threefold nature of the one God that is thoroughly
pro-Nicene, as our tracing of the early history of the Trinity has shown. This
holds open the possibility of articulating a Social Trinity in process for the
present and the future that neither severs the cord of Christian orthodoxy,
nor does injury to a contemporary and scientific worldview.

129. Ayres, *Nicaea and Its Legacy*, 236.

130. Hasker, *Metaphysics and the Tri-Personal God*, 20–21.

131. Moltmann, *Crucified God*, 246.

4

RELATIONAL POWER

A Social Trinity in Process

Noble and young, when thy first griefs were but a mere conceit, ere thou had power of we had cause of fear, we sent to thee to give thy rages balm, to wipe our ingratitude with loves above their quality.

—William Shakespeare, *Timon of Athens,* Act 5, Scene 5

God is Spirit, and those who worship God must worship in spirit and in truth.

—John 4:24 (NRSV)

In the previous chapter I established that the trinitarian theology of Jürgen Moltmann is pro-Nicene by showing that his view connects with the orthodox formulations of Trinity agreed by the church in the fourth century. Any pro-Nicene theology of Trinity rests on a clear distinction between person and nature in the Godhead, which involves the principle that whatever is predicated of the one divine nature is predicated of the three persons equally. It holds that the eternal generation of the Son ensues from within that one divine being and is unambiguous in the understanding that the three persons of the Trinity work inseparably.[1] Moltmann's social trinitarianism affirms each of the three criteria that enable it to be traced back to, and grounded in, an orthodox vision of the Christian God.

1. Ayres, *Nicaea and Its Legacy,* 236.

As in chapter 3 I sought to explain social trinitarianism as a credible way of understanding God, in chapter 2 I presented process theology as a system of thought that has its own integrity and merit. From the outset, however, the idea behind this book has been to see to what extent the two different, but overlapping, conceptions of God could be integrated to form one. The questions behind my research asked: What model of God best explains God's exercise of power in the world, taking both metaphysics and the Christian tradition seriously? Can a synthesis of process theology and trinitarian theology through a mutual panentheistic understanding of God, offer such a model? If it does, what might it then contribute to a reconsideration of the theology of power and of suffering?

In response to these questions, in this chapter I draw together the accounts of Hartshorne's process understanding of the Divine Relativity and Moltmann's Social Trinity, beginning with a review of Hartshorne and Moltmann (as more fully considered in chapters 2 and 3) to demonstrate that both thinkers subscribe to a relational model of God. Having established that a fully relational understanding of God is a key link and point of crossover in the theologies of Hartshorne and Moltmann, I go on to explore other important ideas they share to begin to outline a potential Trinity in process. My development of a model of God in this chapter remains focused on the implications of such for understandings of God's exercise of power. As a thoroughly relational, panentheistic model where God is both characterized and constituted by social relations, in a Social Trinity in process God creatively and non-coercively invites choices for the good in human life and the life of the world.

A RELATIONAL GOD

In the introduction to *Trinity in Process: A Relational Theology of God,* Marjorie Hewitt Suchocki taps into the possibilities of what she describes as a "new relational paradigm" grounded in the thinking of Whitehead and the process movement. As she points out, if it does turn out that "relationality, far from being an inferior accident of finite existence, is indeed the *sine qua non* of all existence whatsoever, then the tension between God and the world is resolved."[2] What Suchocki calls "relational theology" is so closely connected to notions of a Social Trinity that the philosophical foundation of "relationality" in God can be used as a synonym for any social trinitarian model, and often is.[3] In the preface to his major work on the nature of God,

2. Bracken and Suchocki, *Trinity in Process,* viii.

3. As it is in Coutts, *Trinitarian Theology of Family,* 50, and in Bracken and Suchocki, *Trinity in Process,* x.

aptly subtitled *A Social Conception of God,* Hartshorne affirms God as one relational community:

> God is one who has social relations, really has them, and thus is constituted by relationships and hence is relative—in a sense not provided for by the traditional doctrine of a divine Substance wholly nonrelative toward the world, although allegedly containing loving relations between the 'persons' of the Trinity.[4]

For Hartshorne, the social/relational nature of God goes well beyond a fellowship between the three persons of the Trinity. The fellowship includes the entire world and all the creatures. Hartshorne promoted a cell theory of composite individuals where macroscopic objects are constructed as aggregates of sentient occasions of experience. On his view, rock and similar substances are not sentient, but the basic physical entities of which they are composed are sentient. Thus, everything has some degree of will, emotion, and perception, and the world is a vast system of organisms and non-organic societies of organisms. From microscopic physical events to God, every level of existence is constituted by social relationships. Hartshorne's social conception of God is in sharp contrast with more traditional views of the God/world relationship because we have tended to regard matter as too inferior to be social and God as too superior to be truly social.[5] Instead, for Hartshorne, reality is social at all levels and therefore so is the reality that is God. God alone, however, is directly related to all other creatures, both to influence them and be influenced by them.

Hartshorne's process understanding of God rests on the view that all of reality is temporal and creative, and that becoming is more fundamental than being. This challenges long established ways of understanding God's exercise of power and the extent to which God directs or controls events.[6] Hartshorne insists that adequate cosmic power is only the power to do for the cosmos, which he describes as the field of divine social relationships, all advantageous things that could be and need to be done by one universal/cosmic agent.[7] So, for Hartshorne, creativity belongs *both* to God *and* to finite beings, all entities therefore sharing power and together defining the future. This relational exercise of power, along with the underlying idea that the supreme power of the universe works non-coercively, ensures a vision of God in which there is no domination of others. Hartshorne's vision of God

---

4. Hartshorne, *Divine Relativity,* x.

5. Reeves and Brown, "Development of Process Theology," 29.

6. Brown et al., *Process Philosophy and Christian Thought,* v.

7. Hartshorne, *Divine Relativity,* 134.

includes instead the ongoing divine encouragement of others to realize their own freedom and creativity.[8]

The headings of the three main parts of Hartshorne's book *The Divine Relativity: A Social Conception of God,* as previously discussed in chapter 2, give an overview of his understanding of the social and relational nature of reality and thus God. Part one describes God as supreme yet indebted to all, part two describes God as absolute yet related to all, and part three articulates the attributes of God as types of social relationship.[9] In speaking of the balance between the supremacy and the indebtedness of God, Hartshorne suggests:

> A new era in religion may be predicted as soon as men grasp the idea that it is just as true that God is the supreme benefi-ciary or *recipient* of achievement, hence supremely relative to all achieved actualities, as that he is the supreme benefactor or *source* of achievement, and in so far nonrelative to its results. There has been a secret poison long working in religious thought and feeling, the poison of man's wanting to be an ultimate re-cipient of value. Religion then becomes man's self-service, not genuinely his service of God.[10]

Along with a balance between the supremacy and the indebtedness of God, Hartshorne also sought to articulate a balance between the transcendence and immanence of God. On his view, God is absolute and yet related to all. Hartshorne points out:

> It is worth noting . . . that if God (*qua* absolute) is abstract constituent of all things, then there is a clear meaning for the divine 'immanence.' What can more easily be in all things than something abstract? And the implication that the absolute is ob-ject for all subjects makes more sense than might appear at first thought. Here I wish to call attention to a little-noticed truth: to be known by all subjects is fully as distinctive a status as to know all objects. Take any individual other than God. It surely cannot be that this individual is known by all others. Ordinary individuals are known by their neighbors, by some few to whom they are significant; the greater the individual, the more widely will other individuals tend to take note of his existence. Only

---

8. Long, *Western Philosophy of Religion,* 382.

9. Hartshorne, *Divine Relativity,* 1–115.

10. Hartshorne, *Divine Relativity,* 58.

God can be so universally important that no subject can ever wholly fail or ever have failed to be aware of him.[11]

For Hartshorne then, God is *both* supreme *and* indebted, *both* absolute *and* related to all, and these divine qualities provide the assurance that God is entirely social. On this view, all things are connected uniquely through the intimate continuity of purpose and memory in the one divine life.[12] In his conviction about the relatedness of all things, Hartshorne agrees with the process movement in all its breadth.[13] As Moltmann also affirms that God is both social and relational, his notion of God as a Social Trinity which is "open" to the life of the world is a noteworthy connection and point of crossover between his trinitarian theology and Hartshorne's process view.[14] Although Moltmann's focus on God and the world begins with the trinitarian nature of the divine, while Hartshorne's focus is on the less specific nature of reality (which, for him, includes God), Moltmann seems on a similar trajectory as Hartshorne and his social/relational conception of God. He says:

> The salvation of creation consists in being accepted into the cycle of divine relationships and the mutual indwellings of the Father, the Son and the Spirit. Their mutual indwelling includes men and women: 'Whoever abides in love, abides in God and God in him' (I John 4:16). The indwelling is also the mystery of the new creation, 'That God may be all in all' (I Cor. 15:28). In this respect, the perichoretic unity of the triune God is an inviting and uniting unity, and is such a unity which is open to human beings and the world. . . . This is what I mean by my expression the 'open Trinity', which I have used as a contrast to the traditional figures of the circular or triangular Trinity. The Trinity is 'open' by virtue of its overflowing, gracious love. It is 'open' to its beloved creatures who are found and accepted.[15]

In *The Trinity and the Kingdom*, Moltmann discusses the transformations of the open Trinity in terms of a union within a union. Speaking of fellowship with God, and fellowship in God, he proposes that "the triunity is open in such a way that the whole creation can be united with it and can be one within it." Moreover, that "the union of the divine Trinity is open for the uniting of the whole creation with itself and in itself." This makes

11. Hartshorne, *Divine Relativity*, 70.

12. Hartshorne, *Divine Relativity*, 157.

13. Hartshorne, *Divine Relativity*, x; Epperly, *Process Theology*, 31.

14. Moltmann, *Spirit of Life*, 218–21.

15. Moltmann, *History and the Triune God*, 87.

"the unity of the Trinity . . . not merely a theological term; at heart it is a soteriological one as well."[16] The openness of God that Moltmann describes is closely related to *ekstasis*—God's going out of God's-self to others. In standard usage, *ekstasis* means a state of being "put out of place"[17] or being in a trance.[18] In a theological sense, referring to the characteristics of the Triune life of God, *ekstasis* means an openness of being or a movement towards communion.[19] Another social trinitarian, Miroslav Volf, describes this open characteristic in God as the voluntary outgoingness of each person of the Trinity in relationship. For him, the life of the Holy Trinity is one of constant self-donation. He describes this other-oriented *ekstasis* of the Trinity:

> The self gives something of itself, of its own space, so to speak, in a movement in which it contracts itself in order to be expanded by the other and in which at the same time enters the contracted other in order to increase the other's plenitude. This giving of the self which coalesces with receiving the other is nothing but the circular movement of eternal divine love—a form of exchange of gifts in which the other does not emerge as a debtor because she has already given by having joyfully received and because even before the gift has reached her she was already engaged in a movement of advanced reciprocation. If we adjusted the famous statement of John, 'We love because God first loved us' (1 John 4:19) to fit the cycle of exchange between perfect lovers, we would have to say that *each* always both loves first and loves because he is loved.[20]

Social trinitarianism therefore reinforces the idea that God, the Holy Trinity, desires to be in relationship with and to human beings. It does this by exhibiting an open characteristic in God, the *ekstasis* of the Trinity, that Moltmann describes as an "open Trinity"[21] and which Volf describes as the "self-donation" of God.[22] Furthermore, it is the clear teaching of the New Testament scriptures that the followers of Jesus are drawn into the loving relationships within the Trinity. They are enfolded in love between Father

---

16. Moltmann, *Trinity and the Kingdom*, 96.

17. Onions, *Oxford Dictionary of English Etymology*, 300.

18. Partridge, *Origins*, 661.

19. Coutts, *Trinitarian Theology of Family*, 337

20. Volf, "'Trinity Is Our Social Program,'" 412. Volf studied under Moltmann, gaining two advanced degrees in Theology under his supervision.

21. Moltmann, *History and the Triune God*, 87.

22. Volf, "'Trinity Is Our Social Program,'" 412.

and Son; at the very least, this is the implication of the words of Jesus in the gospel of John:[23]

> As you, Father, are in me and I am in you, may they also be in us, so that the world may believe that you have sent me. The glory that you have given me I have given them, so that they may be one, as we are one, I in them and you in me, that they may become completely one, so that the world may know that you have sent me and have loved them even as you have loved me.[24]

In process theology and social trinitarianism, and in the thinking of both Hartshorne and Moltmann, the best way of expressing the companionship within God and between God and the world is through the Johannine descriptor of God as love. Alongside his social conception of God, Hartshorne finds love a preferred way of metaphysically distinguishing God from all that exists. He says:

> When Charles Wesley, who must have known something of religious values wrote: 'Father, thou art all compassion, pure unbounded love thou art,' he was not distinguishing God by denying relativity or passivity to him . . . he was distinguishing God metaphysically. For all other beings limit their compassion at some point. They are sympathetic, passive, relative, in some directions, not in all. Their love is not pure, but mixed with indifference, hardness of heart, resistance to or incapacity for some relativities. We do not 'love' literally, but with qualifications, and metaphorically. Love, defined as social awareness, taken literally, is God.[25]

For Hartshorne, then, loving sociality is the key characteristic of God. Correspondingly, the process theologian David Griffin, who builds on the thinking of both Hartshorne and Whitehead, defines the three persons of the Trinity as one eternal society of creativity and love. He further suggests that Divine Creativity, Creative Love, and Responsive Love could function as appropriate terms through which to describe the persons of the Godhead.[26] In this Griffin affirms the open sociality of God that Hartshorne and Moltmann agree on by insisting that creative power is embodied, not by God alone, but by God and a universe of finite events. This sharing of

---

23. Hasker, *Metaphysics and the Tri-Personal God*, 211.

24. John 17:21b–23 (NRSV).

25. Hartshorne, *Divine Relativity*, 36.

26. Griffin, "Naturalistic Trinity," 37.

creative power means that God is not over against the world, but that God necessarily and consistently acts persuasively and lovingly.

Griffin points out that, if Jesus is understood not only as a special instance of God's saving activity, but also and thereby as a special revelation of God's manner of working at any and in all times, a focus on Jesus' message and example of non-retaliatory, suffering love is warranted. The message about loving enemies and about returning good for evil was lived out fully in Jesus' suffering on the cross and his prayer of forgiveness for those who tortured and finally killed him. Griffin is convinced that the early Christians understood themselves to be called to imitate Jesus in just one way, and that was to follow the way of the cross while proclaiming the love of God. In so doing, they relied on the persuasive power of preaching, and on their willingness to suffer and die after Jesus' example.[27] As Griffin explains, it was from this base of Jesus as both the revelation and exemplar of the true nature of God as persuasive-suffering love that the doctrine of the Trinity was formulated:

> One stimulus for the formulation of the doctrine of the trinity was the rejection of Marcionite and Gnostic dualisms, according to which the creator of heaven and earth, spoken of in the Jewish Scriptures, was not the God and Father of Jesus. Another stimulus was the rejection of Arianism, according to which the Divine Being itself was not incarnate in Jesus, because Jesus obviously suffered; whereas, the Divinity (Arius held) could not suffer. If these dualisms are rejected, so that the Holy One who created the universe also is held to have acted in an especially redemptive and self-revealing way in Jesus of Nazareth, then it seems that we should regard the world as having been created through the power of persuasive-suffering love. Furthermore, the application of this idea of divinity to the consummation of the world would have meant that the ultimate victory of God's reign over the forces of evil would be attained by the same method, that of persuasive and suffering love. . . . Whether we talk of God's activity in creating, sustaining, revealing, redeeming, sanctifying, or consummating, God always acts in one and the same way, a way that no more coercively violates the power or freedom of the creatures than Jesus' activity violated the freedom of his hearers.[28]

The argument Griffin makes about the action of God always being undertaken in one and the same way, as persuasive suffering love, grounded

27. Griffin, "Naturalistic Trinity," 25.
28. Griffin, "Naturalistic Trinity," 26.

in Jesus as the exemplar of the true nature of God, is in keeping with the trinitarian theology of Moltmann up to a point. In asking how theology can both respond to and articulate the love of God as revealed in Christ, Moltmann shares what appears to be a remarkably similar summation to Griffin and his process view. Moltmann speaks of the enactment of the love of God in the world and in human life this way:

> It cannot accept the conditions of lovelessness and the law . . . it cannot command love and counterlove. As its purpose is freedom, it is directed towards freedom. So it cannot prohibit slavery and enmity, but must suffer this contradiction, and can only take upon itself grief at the contradiction in men and does not angrily suppress this contradiction. God allows himself to be forced out. God suffers, God allows himself to be crucified and is crucified, and in this consummates his unconditional love that is so full of hope.[29]

The key point of difference between the suffering of God in Moltmann and the suffering of God understood through process thought is that, at least in *The Crucified God* (quoted above) Moltmann takes a *kenotic* position regarding God's power.[30] This involves God voluntary limiting divine power in order to participate vulnerably in the life of the world. In *Powers and Submissions: Spirituality, Philosophy and Gender*, Sarah Coakley notes that post war Christian thought, including that of Moltmann, tends toward the vulnerability of God and the associated admission of divine self-limitation and exposure in the face of human cruelty. She gives voice to the feminist implications of this idea, pointing out that "an abused God merely legitimates abuse."[31] In contrast, for process thinkers, God is constitutively open to suffering rather than accepting it voluntarily. The process vision of God thus provides a better response to the problem of evil and suffering and alleviates any tendency to divinize abusive relationships. On this basis, there is as much room for Moltmann to be drawn closer to process thought

---

29. Moltmann, *Crucified God*, 248.

30. Arguably, the kenotic position Moltmann demonstrates in *Crucified God* was held less strongly in his later work. Sidiris describes Moltmann as having much in common with process thinkers like Hartshorne and Whitehead, the latter being a frequent dialogue partner for Moltmann. Sideris, *Environmental Ethics*, 104.

31. Coakley, *Powers and Submissions*, xv. See also Feske, who argues that the idea of the "Crucified God," however radical in its identification of God with human suffering, contains an internal conflict which can allow it to work against those who have less power in human society, particularly women and people of color. Feske, "Christ and Suffering in Moltmann's Thought," 85–104.

as there is to draw Hartshorne's process vision in the direction of Nicene orthodoxy.

In Moltmann's more *kenotic* take on the enactment of God's suffering and unconditional love, all human history, despite it being determined by sin and death, is taken up into what he describes as the "history of God." Moltmann uses the term the "history of God" as a synonym for the Trinity. So, for him, all human events, including the Christ event, have been, are, and will be incorporated into the Triune God, who is known as, and indeed embodies, persuasive suffering love. Moltmann insists:

> There is no suffering which in this history of God is not God's suffering; no death which has not been God's death in the history on Golgotha. Therefore there is no life, no fortune and no joy which have not been integrated by his history into eternal life, the eternal joy of God. To think of 'God in history' always leads to theism and to atheism. To think of 'history in God' leads beyond that, into new creation and *hemopoiesis*.[32]

The way Moltmann describes our integration into the suffering love of God could not be any clearer in its symbolism. What is depicted is God's relationality and closeness at the deepest level. The word *hemopoiesis* is a medical term meaning the process of formation and development of blood cells in the living body, especially in the bone marrow.[33] In the use of this term Moltmann infers that we and all things are related to God at a cellular level. As blood cells are to a living body, as the live component of marrow is to the bone, Moltmann's vivid metaphor denotes the capacity of God to relate to and embrace all that is. Even more, it denotes a sociality in God that generates and maintains life into and beyond the new creation in Christ.

An important point of crossover and agreement between Moltmann and social trinitarians, and Hartshorne and process thinkers, is that those who relate to and worship this God who embodies constant self-donation and eternal suffering love, will seek to model themselves in some way on the divine. In process theology, creativity belongs *both* to God *and* to finite beings, and all entities therefore have the power of self-determination. This, along with the underlying idea that the supreme power of the universe works non-coercively, ensures a vision of God where imitation of the divine does not lead to the domination and control of others. For Hartshorne, imitation of the divine leads instead to the encouragement of others to realize their own freedom and creativity.[34] As Whitehead maintains in *Religion in the*

32. Moltmann, *Crucified God*, 246–47.

33. "Hemopoiesis," lines 1–2.

34. Long, *Western Philosophy of Religion*, 382.

Making, "in the long run your character and your conduct of life depend on your intimate convictions."[35] He believes this includes our intimate convictions about the nature and exercise of God's power, God's relationship with the world, the scope of salvation and the meaning of revelation. Whitehead describes rather starkly what he sees as a necessary shift from relating to God as an opposing force or "enemy," to relating to God as the loving companion whom we imitate:

> The... concept of the goodness of God replaces the older emphasis on the will of God. In a communal religion you study the will of God in order that he may preserve you; in a purified religion, rationalized under the influence of the world-concept, you study his goodness in order to be like him. It is the difference between the enemy you conciliate and the companion whom you imitate.[36]

The notion of God as a companion to be imitated, a model for human community, a view shared by both process theologians and social trinitarians, is contested. Mark Husbands is representative of the view that there is no theological legitimacy in human communities seeking to model themselves on the Triune God. In a response Husbands wrote to a paper in which Volf affirms that "the doctrine of the Trinity ought to shape our 'social vision.'"[37] He claims that social trinitarians like Volf are so focused on the imitation of God that they have little interest in God's creative and redemptive activity. Husbands says that "Volf offers us a doctrine of the triune God for which the immediate significance of the Trinity lies principally in being a model for us to imitate rather than being the constitutive ground of our reconciliation and promise of life."[38] While going to the heart of the contentions around the Social Trinity, Husbands is overstating his case. By portraying the Social Trinity as a crude imitation of God that overlooks the breadth of Christianity and the ongoing life of the kingdom, Husbands ignores the much more nuanced approach taken by various social trinitarians including Volf.[39] In fact, Volf is clear that it is only in the self-giving *ekstasis*

---

35. Whitehead, *Religion in the Making*, 15.

36. Whitehead, *Religion in the Making*, 40.

37. Volf, "'Trinity Is Our Social Program,'" 406.

38. Husbands, "Trinity Is *Not* Our Social Program," 126.

39. Coutts, *Trinitarian Theology of Family*, 314. Coutts asserts that Husband's dismissal of Volf and the social trinitarian movement based on its leading theological agenda being earthly social existence is unfair. Coutts suggests that Husbands somewhat misrepresents both Volf's intention, and the actual content of his paper.

of the Triune God, as previously discussed, that there can be any human approximation of the qualities inherent in the Trinity. He claims that:

> A plethora of proposals about the relation between the Trinity and human communities . . . are of limited value because they remain at the level of overly diffuse generalities, say about 'plurality-in-unity', the dialectic of 'one and many', or the balance between 'relationality and otherness'. In such proposals the doctrine of the Trinity serves more or less as the ore from which the presumed gold of abstract principles should be extracted and then used to construct images of human community or even of the whole reality. But this makes a misjudgment of what is in fact gold. Abstract principles are not pure gold; the narrative life of the Trinity, at whose heart lies the history of self-donation, is pure gold. The talk about . . . 'plurality in unity' and 'one and many' will be helpful only if they are 'gilded' by being dipped into the narrative of divine self-donation.[40]

Volf is of the view that the question is not whether the Trinity *should* serve as a model for human community per se. He is clear that the Trinity has already provided a model for people to follow, and continues to do so, based on the self-giving nature of God. For him, in the context of what he describes as "the narrative of divine self-donation,"[41] the question is much better framed in terms of *in which respects* and *to what extent* can human community helpfully be modelled on our understanding of the nature of the Holy Trinity.[42] He notes the very many times that trinitarian theology has been called upon to inform our understanding of what is socially just by pointing out that the doctrine of the Trinity has regularly been employed to pursue the project of re-arranging socio-economic structures.[43] He also affirms his social trinitarian view in his contention that "such projects are by no means misplaced." It is important to realize, however, that Volf genuinely and firmly acknowledges that "the road from the doctrine of the Trinity to proposals about global or national social arrangements is long, torturous, and fraught with danger."[44] In this it is quite apparent that Volf hasn't abandoned interest in the ongoing creative and redemptive activity of the Triune God in favor of a narrow and temporal social program.

40. Volf, "'Trinity Is Our Social Program,'" 412.

41. Volf, "'Trinity Is Our Social Program,'" 412.

42. Volf, "'Trinity Is Our Social Program,'" 405.

43. Examples of the crossover of Trinitarian theology with the re-arranging of socio-economic structures include, but are not limited to: Boff, *Trinity and Society* and a diverse range of Liberation Theologies from Feminist theology to Black theology.

44. Volf, "'Trinity Is Our Social Program,'" 406.

In an interesting offshoot to the question about to what extent we can helpfully model human life and community on the interpersonal relationships in the life of the Trinity, in *After Our Likeness: The Church as the Image of the Trinity*, Volf compares the ecclesiological doctrines of certain Roman Catholic, Orthodox and Protestant theologians. He then goes on very effectively to relate their doctrines of the Church to their respective view of the Trinitarian God. The entire modus operandi of his book supports my contention that the way we understand the nature of the Triune God affects the way we live and operate in the Church and the world.[45] Indeed, if God the Holy Trinity really is to be understood as a divine community, it stands to reason that we *would* ask what lessons for our lives and the life of our human communities might be learned from the life of God. This questioning is not at all merely a modern phenomenon. Gregory of Nazianzus made this very same connection between our lives and the trinitarian life of God very early on in Christian history:[46]

> In the *Second Oration on Peace*, (Gregory Nazianzen) encourages the discordant Christians in the capital to find harmony with one another by recognizing the internal harmony of the Trinity. All forms of peace and concord derive from the peace of the Trinity, he says, 'whose unity of nature and internal peace are its most salient characteristic.'[47]

Whether it is seen as valuable or dangerous, it appears that the modelling of ourselves and our relationships on our understanding of the nature of God in general, and on our understanding of the inner nature of the Trinity in particular, is an ongoing occurrence. This is recognized by both supporters of, and detractors from, a Social Trinity. Kathryn Tanner, a detractor, is concerned about the social and political dangers of seeking to apply what we believe about the trinitarian nature of God to human community. She points out that a theology of "strong communitarianism" and "fixed roles" within the Trinity can lead to subordinationism within the Trinity, and that this might then, by extension, be applied to human relationships, especially gendered relationships.[48] Kevin Giles, in his *Orthodox Doctrine of the Trinity*, gives an example of this very event. He notes how some contemporary evangelical Christians argue for maintaining a hierarchical understanding of the male-female relationship based on their interpretation of the nature of the Trinity:

45. Volf, *After Our Likeness*.
46. Hasker, *Metaphysics and the Tri-Personal God*, 211.
47. Beeley, *Gregory of Nazianzus on the Trinity*, 230.
48. Tanner, "Social Trinitarianism and Its Critics," 370–75.

'Complementarian' evangelicals argue that the equality texts speak of the eternal *ontological* equality of the Father and the Son, and the subordinating texts of the *eternal functional* or *role* subordination of the Son. We are told that men and women, like the divine Father and Son, are equal in *being*, yet have different *roles* that indelibly distinguish them. The Father has the role of commanding and sending, and the Son the role of obeying and going . . . the word *role* is given another meaning. It is used only to speak of who rules and who obeys in an unchanging and unchangeable hierarchy. In this usage, what indelibly differentiates men and women, and the Father and the Son, is that the Father is *eternally* set over the Son in authority as men are *permanently* set over women in the church and in the home.[49]

This leads Giles to assert that "we cannot define perfect, triadic, divine relations in terms of fallen dual human relationships."[50] Giles is correct about this in as much as it is more than possible for any of us to take our own ecclesiastical or socio-political convictions, wherever they come from, and read them back into a doctrine of the Trinity to then be used as a template for church or social structure. This possibility is one of the key criticisms of social trinitarianism. The criticism in a nutshell is that we will distort the doctrine of the Trinity by shaping it in favor of our preferred social program. Karen Kilby acerbically expresses it in terms of first projecting our best ideas about human community onto the Trinity, and then claiming to have discovered in the Trinity a new map for structuring human communities.[51] If, however, it turns out that the intrinsic relationality of God is the true pattern of all things; and if we see divine sociality as a broad vision to be embraced rather than as a narrow program to be enacted, the likelihood of reading our own agenda onto God significantly diminishes.[52]

It is at this point that process theology really begins to add value to social trinitarianism. Our inherited doctrines of God and conceptions of Trinity were founded and shaped in an ancient, pre-scientific worldview, while the thinking of Hartshorne and the trajectory of process thought is very much grounded in a contemporary and scientific worldview. Recognizing

49. Giles, "Orthodox Doctrine of the Trinity," 20.

50. Giles, "Orthodox Doctrine of the Trinity," 20. Giles is neither a Complementarian nor a Social Trinitarian.

51. Kilby, "Trinity, Tradition, and Politics," 75.

52. Although the title of Volf's paper included the quote "The Trinity Is Our Social Program," its contents argued that "the doctrine of the Trinity ought to shape our social vision" rather than being any kind of a detailed map or blueprint. Volf, "'Trinity Is Our Social Program,'" 406.

this credibly enables a respectful and careful informing of ancient ideas about God by new knowledge about the world and the nature of reality. This informing of ancient ideas is a broad and complex brief that includes seeking to appreciate more profoundly the Triune God in the context of our own lived experience in a physical world. It takes us well beyond simple attempts to enact narrow human social programs tentatively modelled on a God deemed beyond genuine relation. It takes us deep into a vision that seeks to recognize and advance the nature and being of God in relation to all things. That includes all things social, all things environmental, all things scientific or metaphysical. All things.

A vision of God in relation to all things takes us directly to the notion of panentheism. This model of God is shared, somewhat differently in detail but similarly in effect, by Hartshorne and later thinkers in the process movement, and Moltmann and a range of social trinitarians. In the thinking of Hartshorne, panentheism is best summed up by God's intimate relation to every moment of experience, giving and receiving love, touching, and being touched by the joys and sorrows of the world.[53] For Hartshorne:

> God orders the universe, according to panentheism, by taking into his own life all the currents of feeling in existence. He is the most irresistible of influences precisely because he is himself the most open to influence. In the depth of their hearts all creatures (even those able to 'rebel' against him) defer to God because they sense him as the one who alone is adequately moved by what moves them. He alone not only knows but feels (the only adequate knowledge, where feeling is concerned) how they feel, and he finds his own joy in sharing their lives, lived according to their own free decisions, not fully anticipated by any detailed plan of his own.[54]

Joseph A. Bracken pursues his "systems-oriented thought," very much a process view, in his approach to the key idea of panentheism.[55] For him, everything finite exists within God, but still works according to its own mode of operation. In this he takes a slightly different view of panentheism than does Hartshorne, as he believes that in Hartshorne's thinking God and the world are ultimately separable into two different kinds of reality.[56]

53. Epperly, *Process Theology*, 45.

54. Hartshorne, *Divine Relativity*, xvii.

55. Bracken, "Incarnation, Panentheism, and Bodily Resurrection." It is notable that in the very recent writing of Bracken he refers to process theology as "systems-oriented thinking."

56. Bracken, "Incarnation, Panentheism, and Bodily Resurrection," 37. Bracken

Bracken's view is notable in the light of the criticism of Hartshorne in particular, and process theology in general, that God and the world are aligned too closely in their thinking and that they therefore may leave themselves open to the charge of pantheism.[57] Bracken is sure that his somewhat differently articulated process/systems view of panentheism keeps an appropriate middle-ground, one that does not blur the line between the divine and the world or succumb to an unhelpful dualism between spirit and matter. He says:

> A systems-orientated panentheism guarantees that the persons and things of this world can exist within God and by the power of God and yet at every moment possess their own finite identity and distinctive mode of operation. Whereas pantheism tends either to collapse God into the world or the world into God, and whereas ontological dualism presupposes an unbridgeable difference between matter and spirit, the physical world and God, a systems-oriented panentheism keeps matter and spirit, the physical world and God, together as co-participants in an all-encompassing system corresponding to the fullness of the God-world relationship.[58]

Using the imagery of a Whiteheadian society as a structured field of activity Bracken sets forth an understanding of the God-world relationship that reflects a Social Trinity in process.[59] In his thinking, the three persons are one God and together preside over one and the same all comprehensive divine field of activity. At the same time, they each represent three different subjective foci or centers within that field of activity, and each divine person has an indispensable role in the maintenance of their common life.[60] He explains:

> If one claims with Alfred North Whitehead that the ultimate constituents of a 'society' (or, in my terminology, a system) are momentary self-constituting subjects of experience (actual entities), and if the society or system itself slowly evolves

---

includes McFague and her *Models of God* in the same kind of criticism. Both Hartshorne and McFague have proposed that the world is God's "body," and that God is the world's "soul." Bracken finds this problematic in that this line of thinking implies that God and the world are currently joined but could be separated into two kinds of reality. That is, God and the world affect each other while the world survives, but when the world ends, God survives, potentially to become the soul of another world.

57. By Gunton, for example. See *Becoming and Being*, 223.

58. Bracken, "Incarnation, Panentheism, and Bodily Resurrection," 41.

59. Bracken, "Panentheism from a Process Perspective," 100.

60. Bracken, "Panentheism from a Process Perspective," 101.

in its governing structure or 'common element of form' as a consequence of the interrelated activity of its constituent actual entities from moment to moment, then one has in hand an understanding of the reciprocal relation between matter and spirit within the world of nature.[61]

An answer to the complicated issue of the ontological relationship between spirit and matter in the world of nature is therefore found for Bracken in a panentheistic view of God. He looks to a principle of creative transformation in God, here disagreeing with Whitehead somewhat with his view of the relationship of creativity to God (or in God) by asserting that "creativity is... the ontological ground of the divine being and activity."[62] By linking in this way the life of God with creativity as practically one thing, Bracken can effectively explain God as a creative, Trinitarian society who works noncoercively. For him, God is "a tripersonal Being who gives direction and order to these creative processes without... controlling them rigidly."[63]

In his seminal text on the Holy Spirit, Moltmann grounds the creative, trinitarian society that is God firmly in the work of the Spirit. He insists that the distinctive work of the Spirit is much more than communicating between the persons of the Trinity, or between God and humankind, or between God and the world. For Moltmann, the Spirit is the fellowship extant in all relationships, the essence of the sociality of God, who is all in all:

> If it is characteristic of the divine Spirit not merely to communicate this or that particular thing, but actually to enter into fellowship with believing men and women—if indeed he becomes their fellowship—then 'fellowship' cannot merely be a 'gift' of the Spirit. It must be the eternal, essential nature of the Spirit himself. The Spirit does not merely bring about fellowship with himself. He himself issues from his fellowship with the Father and the Son, and is therefore a *trinitarian fellowship.* In the unity of the Father, the Son and the Holy Spirit, the triune God himself is an open, inviting fellowship in which the whole creation finds room: 'That they also may be *in us*', prays the Johannine Christ (John 17:21).[64]

The Holy Spirit in Moltmann's thought is therefore not a type of external bond that joins human nature with a divine essence. Spirit instead flows from the inner community of the threefold God, in all the richness

---

61. Bracken, "Incarnation, Panentheism, and Bodily Resurrection," 38–39.

62. Bracken, "Incarnation, Panentheism, and Bodily Resurrection," 105.

63. Bracken, "Incarnation, Panentheism, and Bodily Resurrection," 109.

64. Moltmann, *Spirit of Life,* 218–19.

of its relationships, and throws the divine community open in such a way that human beings are gathered into God, as indeed are all other created things. On Moltmann's view, this is the definition of eternal life. He insists that it follows that the fellowship of the Holy Spirit must be understood in trinitarian terms as a community of *persons*, rather than in unitarian terms as a community of essence.[65]

It is notable that, when speaking of God, Moltmann employs the term *persons* exclusively in a trinitarian sense. For him, the Christian conception of God can only ever be properly described as trinitarian. He eschews equally the terms monotheistic, polytheistic or tritheistic; none are sufficient. In speaking of the Holy Trinity, Moltmann claims that 'because of their eternal love, the divine persons exist so intimately with each other, for each other, and in each other that they themselves constitute a unique, incomparable, and complete unity.'[66] On this basis, it is true to say that for Moltmann, as much as for Hartshorne and the process movement, the nature of God is genuinely social. Furthermore, existence, the very nature of reality, is also social and relational. Moltmann explains the connection thus:

> The link between the Holy Spirit and community brings the experience of the Spirit into the community experienced by human beings and God's other creatures. The experience of sociality is the experience of life, for all life consists in the reciprocal exchange of foodstuffs and energy, and in mutual participation. There is no life without its specific social relationships. Isolated life without relation—that is, life that is literally individual and indivisible—is a contradiction in itself. It is incapable of life, and dies. Total lack of relationship is total death. So 'the fellowship of the Holy Spirit' is simply another way of describing 'the life-giving Spirit'. In fellowship with himself and through his creative energies, God the Spirit creates the network of social relationships in which life comes into being, blossoms and becomes fruitful.[67]

In articulating his social trinitarian view Moltmann points out that, whenever we talk of the Johannine potential for incorporation into the love of the Triune God, we find ourselves using the language of pneumatology.

65. Moltmann, *Spirit of Life*, 219.

66. Moltmann, "Unity of the Triune God," 166, and *Trinity and the Kingdom*, 175. The social trinitarian, Boff, takes an almost identical view to Moltmann, claiming that "it is the revelation of God as God is, as Father, Son and Holy Spirit in eternal correlation, interpenetration, love and communion, which make them one sole God." Boff, *Trinity and Society*.

67. Moltmann, *Spirit of Life*, 219.

This moves us from focusing on creation and God's works in history to recognizing how the Holy Spirit is poured out on all flesh and into our hearts; that it is out of the Holy Spirit that we are born again, and that the gifts of the Spirit are not created but rather spring from their source as divine energies. It moves us to recognize that the Spirit fills creation with life by descending on all things and indwelling them.[68] Moltmann explains:

> A different divine presence is revealed in the experience of the Holy Spirit . . . First of all men and women in their physical nature (1 Cor. 6.13–20), and then the new heavens and the new earth (Rev. 21), will become the 'temple' which God himself indwells. That is the eternal sabbath: God's rest, and rest in God. That is why the history of the Spirit points towards that consummation which Paul describes in the panentheistic-sounding formula: 'that God may be all in all' (1 Cor.15:28).[69]

The history of the Spirit within the doctrine of the Church, however, as previously discussed in chapter 3, has been relatively short since the early focus of the patristic thinkers was mainly on the relationship between Father and Son in the Trinity.[70] As a deeper doctrine of the Holy Spirit developed, the notion of procession came to the fore. The Church in the East understood the Spirit to proceed from the Father through the Son. Seeking to avoid subordinationism, Eastern thinkers duly acknowledged the *homoosious* of the Spirit, the idea that the Holy Spirit is of precisely the same substance as the Father and the Son.[71] Augustine, a major shaper of trinitarian thinking in the West, taught the somewhat different doctrine of the double procession of the Holy Spirit from the Father *and* the Son. He said that the Son is from the Father, the Spirit is from the Father; the former is begotten, the latter proceeds. On his view, the action of the Father and the Son in bestowing the Spirit is mutual, and the action of all three persons in creation is mutual, but the Father remains the primordial source.[72] Despite the Eastern affirmation that the Spirit is of the same substance as the Father and the Son and the Western support for the mutuality of the actions of Father, Son, and Spirit in creation, both of these attempts to articulate the operation of the Spirit in terms of procession have been criticized for implying a hierarchy within the Trinity.[73] This is significant because any inference of

68. Moltmann, *Spirit of Life*, 212.

69. Moltmann, *Spirit of Life*, 212.

70. O'Collins, *Tripersonal God*, 52.

71. Kelly, *Doctrines*, 263–64.

72. Kelly, *Doctrines*, 272–76.

73. As discussed in the previous chapter, the idea that there was a clear-cut

an internal hierarchical ordering within the traditional doctrines of Trinity has implications for theologies of power. A Trinity that is understood to be hierarchical, even mildly so, suggests quite a different view of God's exercise of power than does Moltmann's social vision of the Immanent Trinity as a fellowship of equals.[74]

In her book subtitled "An Essay on the Trinity," Sarah Coakley is convinced that we will only get powers and submissions right in God and in the world by appropriate and primary submission to the Holy Spirit.[75] She says that, should she be asked to comment on the notion of procession within the Godhead, she "can only start with the Spirit's invitation into that Godhead." Further, she starts "with the presumption of the Spirit's mutual infusion *in* Son and Father."[76] Coakley explains:

> There can be in God's Trinitarian ontology no Sonship which is not eternally 'sourced' by 'Father' *in the Spirit* (in such a way, in fact, as to query even the usual and exclusive meanings of Fatherly 'source' . . .). To argue this is to complete the purification from 'linear' subordinationism to which post-Nicene theologians constantly strove, though never with complete or unambiguous success. . . . Indeed, were we to speculate further about the 'processions' we would not only need to speak thus of the Son eternally coming forth from the Father 'in' or 'by' the Spirit (rather than the Spirit proceeding from the Father merely 'and', or 'through', the Son, as in classical 'Western' and 'Eastern' language); but, more daringly, we would also need to speak of the Father's own reception back of his status as 'source' from the other two 'persons', precisely via the Spirit's reflexive propulsion and the Son's creative effulgence. Here, in divinity, then, is a 'source' of love unlike any other, giving and receiving and ecstatically reflecting, ever and always.[77]

---

separation between the Western/Latin, and the Eastern/Greek churches regarding trinitarian belief before the Great Schism of 1054 is now viewed by many scholars as untenable. There were a variety of positions regarding the Trinity that had adherents in both the Eastern and Western churches. Nevertheless, on the matter of the processions, the standard understanding in the East has been that the Spirit proceeds from the Father through the Son, and in the West that the Spirit proceeds from the Father *and* the Son, after the teaching of Augustine.

74. Moltmann, *Spirit of Life*, 218.

75. Coakley, *God, Sexuality, and the Self*, 321–22. Coakley is herself neither a social trinitarian nor a process theologian. However, her writing informs my efforts to articulate a Social Trinity in process due to her view (shared with Moltmann) that in trinitarian theology, the Holy Spirit is primary.

76. Coakley, *God, Sexuality, and the Self*, 332.

77. Coakley, *God, Sexuality, and the Self*, 333.

What Coakley asserts here is that, although the post-Nicene theologians attempted to protect trinitarian theology from a linear subordination of Spirit, they fell somewhat short of the mark. Through her bold proposal that there has been an historical missing of the mark in the thinking of the Church about the Trinity, she seeks a more equivalent sense of procession within the persons of the Godhead whereby the Father is also sourced from Spirit and Son. By restating longstanding notions of trinitarian procession in this way, Coakley can go on to describe the Christian God as a unique source of love which eternally receives, gives, and reflects love. Her explanation of procession in the three persons of the Trinity exudes a strong sense of interdependence and relationality. In this, Coakley infers a level of sympathy both with Moltmann's notion of an "open" Trinity, in which there is room for all creation,[78] and Hartshorne's process vision of being "included in the ultimate purpose" of God as the essential nature of salvation.[79] It is noteworthy, however, that she fully subscribes neither to a Social Trinity nor to the process movement.

At the conclusion of her book, Coakley takes what could be construed as a further step in her restatement of procession within the persons of the Godhead. She summarizes her view of the primacy of the Spirit in the Trinity, a view woven throughout her writing, describing it in terms of Spirit being "first" rather than a problematic "third" in God. It is important to recognize that Coakley presents this primacy subtly and employs it only to address what she sees as an historical overlooking of the Holy Spirit of God as principal source of being. Coakley's closing words are:

> It has been the daring invitation of this book to make that problematic 'third' in God the 'first' in human encounter, not because the Spirit is thereby jostling *competitively* with the Father to be the primary ontological source, but because we humans have to cleanse our hearts and minds of any suggestion that the paternal divine 'source' could ever involve that sort of rivalry: 'source' here has become ecstatic goal as much as ecstatic origin, propelled inherently towards the transformative appearance of the God/Man. If, finally, we make this mind-shift, then everything changes.[80]

78. Moltmann, *History and the Triune God*, 87.

79. Hartshorne, *Divine Relativity*, 133.

80. Coakley, *God, Sexuality, and the Self*, 334. In this aspect of her thinking, Coakley is also very much in step with some of the thinking of process theologians such as Suchocki and Lee, who both see much scope for better annunciating the key role of Spirit in the Godhead. See Suchocki, "Spirit in and through the World," 173–90 and Lee, "'Other' Trinity," 191–14.

The idea of a primacy of the Spirit as source, goal, origin, and means of transformation is a significant theological response to any justification of a hierarchical ordering within the Godhead. It finds more than an echo in Moltmann's thought and that of some in the process movement. In fact, a broad acceptance of the notion of the Holy Spirit as the first in human encounter is really to acknowledge, with the writer of the gospel of John, that God IS Spirit.[81] As Moltmann points out, the possibility of encountering God in all things, and all things in God, finds its theological grounding in an understanding that God is Spirit, and that the Spirit is therefore the power of creation and the wellspring of life.[82] This understanding of God as Spirit based in the Johannine writings provides a significant foundation for any attempt to articulate God as a fully relational Social Trinity in process.

CONNECTING WITH NICAEA

Efforts to conceive the God who is Spirit as a fully relational Social Trinity in process cannot step away from the importance of maintaining an unambiguous connection with the foundations of Christianity, and specifically with orthodox trinitarian ideas. To be part of a proper Christian trajectory of thought, any model of the Holy Trinity must be shown to be pro-Nicene. As previously noted, there are three criteria that demonstrate support of the intent of the Council of Nicaea, the first being that the model of the Trinity must include a clear version of the person and nature distinction, involving the principle that whatever is predicated of the divine nature is predicated of the three persons equally who are understood to be one.[83] This first criteria is met for a Social Trinity in process in the description of God as Creative-Responsive Love initiated by David Griffin and John Cobb and developed by Griffin in his "A Naturalistic Trinity."[84] It affirms the one nature of God demonstrated in the three persons fully and equally. As this consideration of Trinity as Creative-Responsive Love is grounded in process thought, creativity is understood to be the ultimate reality of the universe. An ever-present reality rather than an actuality, creativity does not stand over against God in dualistic separation. It instead finds in God its primordial expression, and God gives creativity its primordial

81. John 4:24 (NRSV). Moltmann, *Spirit of Life*; Coakley, *God, Sexuality and the Self*; Suchocki, "Spirit in and through the World"; Lee, "'Other' Trinity."

82. Moltmann, *Spirit of Life*, 35.

83. Ayres, *Nicaea and Its Legacy*, 236.

84. Griffin, "Naturalistic Trinity," 37. This is a view and description Griffin shares with Cobb in their introduction to process theology: Cobb and Griffin, *Process Theology*.

characterization. In a Social Trinity in process, the creativity exemplified in God can be thought of as the first aspect of the threefold nature of God. God's manner of characterizing that creativity can provide the second and third aspects.[85] On the one hand, God's eternal purpose for the good of all creation characterizes Divine Creativity as Creative Love, the divine eros which initiates all movement. On the other hand, once creatures have been evoked into being, God responds to their experiences, feeling with them. This is the Responsive Love of God and can take the form of suffering or joy depending on the experience of the creature.[86]

In this model, the threeness immanent in God comprises Divine Creativity, Creative Love, and Responsive Love. The creativity embodied in God is always experiential and takes two modes. There is the creativity involved in self-determination, where a moment of experience creates itself by adopting influences it has received from the experience of others. In God, this is always characterized by Responsive Love, never by hate or even indifference. And, secondly, there is the creativity that influences a momentary actuality. Having self-created, that creativity is exerted on others and the one becomes incarnate in the many. It is an outgoing creativity with causal efficacy on others. Again, in God, this is always characterized by Creative Love; it is never destructive, hateful, or indifferent. God's outgoing creativity in every moment is informed by love both because it is based on God's eternal purpose of creating the best possible world, and because it is also based on God's Responsive Love to the previous state of creaturely experience and God's anticipation of "feeling with" creaturely experience in future moments. With this perfect sympathy an eternal feature of God's experience there can be no separation of God's good and the good of the creatures. In this way of thinking, God cannot be anything less than perfectly good, in the sense of both willing and seeking the good of the world as a whole and each creature with the world.[87] To understand Trinity this way is not to think monistically, as this view makes clear that there could never have been an alone God; a solitary one. This is due to a grounding in process thought where the very meaning of being one is to be a creative unification of the many. Furthermore, if the Divine unification really *is* Love as the Christian tradition has consistently claimed, it follows that reality is inherently social. Nor can this view be conceived of as tritheism, for Divine Creativity,

---

85. There is a potential connection here to God's "two hands": the Son and the Spirit, as in the early trinitarian thinking of Irenaeus. O'Collins, *Tripersonal God*, 99.

86. Griffin, "Naturalistic Trinity," 35.

87. Griffin, "Naturalistic Trinity," 36.

Creative Love and Responsive Love cannot and do not constitute three entirely separate beings.[88]

In this process model of Trinity, the distinction is effectively erased between the Immanent and the Economic Trinity.[89] The immanent trinitarian nature of God necessitates that creativity be embodied in the creatures as well as in the divine, so that the creatures have a level of self-efficacy and participate in creation. This ensures that the kinds of distinctions we make regarding God's action in the world (creation, redemption, revelation, for example) cannot involve incompatible types of operation on the part of God. The activity of God in the world cannot alternate between persuasion and coercion, nor can it be exclusively coercion, as the strongest form of theism has often inferred. In this way of thinking about the Trinity the creativity of the creatures is not able to be over-ridden or interrupted, either in its self-determining phase or in its phase of causal efficacy. Therefore, the Immanent Trinity provides the basis for a conception of the divine and its Economic Trinity that respects the creative freedom of the creatures.[90] This leads to the understanding that God's power is exercised "with" the world by invitation, lure, and persuasion, rather than "over" the world by coercion and force.

The second pro-Nicene criterion, that an understanding of the Trinity must give clear expression that the eternal generation of the Son occurs within the one unsurpassed divine being,[91] has sat less comfortably with process theology. In Hartshorne's thinking, Jesus is a disclosure in symbol of God, the one in whom God is revealed to share in the suffering of the world.[92] For Hartshorne, a Christian notion of a deity that can and does suffer, symbolized by the cross, alongside the doctrine of the incarnation, is a valid indicator of a saving or redeeming quality in the process of all things, notwithstanding the presence of evil in the world.[93] Hartshorne was not entirely comfortable about the concept of the two natures of Jesus.

---

88. Griffin, "Naturalistic Trinity," 37.

89. Ford quotes Lionel S. Thornton on the implications of this: "If the Trinity be understood in a purely economic sense, so that the distinctions correspond only to aspects of God manifested in His activities of creation, revelation, inspiration, or the like, then there are no eternal relations of self-giving in the divine life. . . . Thus the principle of self-giving in God . . . can find expression only . . . in relations with creation . . . this is to make creation necessary to God, in the sense that the full actuality of God's life is incomplete apart from creation." Ford, *Lure of God*, 68.

90. Griffin, "Naturalistic Trinity," 38.

91. Ayres, *Nicaea and Its Legacy*, 236.

92. Hartshorne, "Philosopher's Assessment," 175.

93. Hartshorne, *Philosophers Speak of God*, 15.

He certainly saw language about Jesus' divinity as valid, but this was in the context of recognizing every person, in some sense, as divine, given his conviction about the panentheistic nature of God.[94] Hartshorne never claimed any definitive christological formulation, instead contenting himself with a description of Jesus as "the supreme symbol" of a genuinely sympathetic God who receives into his own divine experience both the suffering and joy of the world.[95] Despite his minimalist and naturalistic christology,[96] it is the certainty in Hartshorne that God is in no way immutable but suffers with the world and exercises the power of redemption gently and persuasively, that a manner in which to affirm the eternal procession of the Son can be found. This is due to the intimate connection between questions about whether God suffers and how God exercises power, with understandings about the nature of an eternal relationship of the Son with the Father and the Spirit. To uphold the doctrine of the eternal procession of the Son, I shall broaden the naturalistic tendencies of Hartshorne, as a Social Trinity in process need not be entirely naturalistic.

Here I turn again to Bracken, who demonstrates in his *Incarnation, Panentheism, and Bodily Resurrection: A Systems-Oriented Approach*, that we don't have to eschew any sense of the supernatural to explain the nature of reality through a process lens.[97] He articulates the cosmic processes in terms of an evolutionary and open-ended system of entities in dynamic interrelation in very much the manner of Hartshorne and Griffin. Bracken then seeks what he describes as "a more socially oriented understanding" of three key Christian beliefs, including the incarnation of the second person of the Trinity, by taking the middle ground between the truth claims of natural science and theology.[98] Notably, Bracken nowhere claims that Christian theology is somehow dependent on contemporary science to rationalize traditional beliefs. He does claim, however, that good theology will incorporate contemporary science over time into its own mode of thinking as a matter of common sense.[99] He says:

94. Hartshorne, *Reality as Social Progress*, 150–53.

95. Hartshorne, "Philosopher's Assessment," 24.

96. Hartshorne's theology, along with his minimalist christology, is naturalistic as it deliberately avoids a reliance on the supernatural. Griffin operates in the same frame in his "Naturalistic Trinity." Griffin and Cobb are together known as interpreters of Hartshorne's naturalistic process view.

97. Bracken, "Incarnation, Panentheism, and Bodily Resurrection." 32.

98. Bracken, "Incarnation, Panentheism, and Bodily Resurrection," 32.

99. I take Bracken's use of the term contemporary science effectively to mean a scientific worldview. Both contemporary science and/or a scientific worldview are, by definition, based on ideas that can be tested with empirical observation, and it is widely

> I . . . have experimented with the thought of Alfred North White-
> head and other more process-oriented thinkers to come up with
> an alternative to Thomistic-Aristotelian metaphysics for the
> contemporary understanding and integration of Christian doc-
> trine. . . . I focus on this more consciously process—or systems
> oriented line of thought with respect to the relation between the
> natural and the supernatural within . . . key Christian beliefs.[100]

In Bracken's thought, the incarnation sets a pattern for an ongoing relationship between the natural and the supernatural in human life, in creation, and in Christ in his earthly life. He insists that the incarnation of the second person of the Trinity in Jesus is not to be understood as a one-off historical event but as the foundational moment in an ongoing process of divine self-communication to the world. This is significant, because thinking about the incarnation in this way affirms the doctrine of the eternal procession of the Son in the Trinity in process thought. It shows that, on a process view, God can be understood as trinitarian from all eternity, for Bracken sees the Big Bang as the primordial event through which the immaterial reality of the triune God is already incarnated. The reality of God is inherent in creation in a form that is intended over time to develop in scope and complexity through its own innate power of self-organization, guided by divine providence.

What Bracken proposes is that the new creation described in 2 Corinthians is the progressive incarnation of the divine into the whole of creation. This will happen until the end of the world when it reaches its consummation. Bracken understands it to be God's purpose for creatures to come into being, to achieve a distinct finite identity, and at their death to be integrated with that same identity into the communitarian life of the triune God.[101] In considering the natural and the supernatural at work specifically in the person of Jesus, Bracken turns to the doctrine of the incarnation that came from the Council of Chalcedon in 451:

> We confess one and the same Christ, the Son, the Lord, the
> Only-Begotten, in two natures unconfused, unchangeable, un-
> divided and inseparable. The differences of natures will never

---

recognized that religious ideas cannot (and should not) be tested by this means. In this context, Orr helpfully notes the difference between unscientific and non-scientific in any conversation between contemporary science and theology. He says: "the way out of this conundrum is to recognize that *non*scientific ideas, as distinct from *un*scientific ideas, are acceptable components of a scientific worldview, because they do not contradict science." Orr, "What Is a Scientific Worldview?," 435.

100. Bracken, "Incarnation, Panentheism, and Bodily Resurrection," 34.

101. Bracken, "Incarnation, Panentheism, and Bodily Resurrection," 34.

be abolished by their being united, but rather the properties of each remain unimpaired, both coming together in one person and substance, not parted or divided among two persons, but in one and the same only-begotten Son, the divine Word, the Lord Jesus Christ.[102]

Noting the difficulty in explaining how, in either Aristotelian metaphysics or human experience, the divine and human natures of Jesus could remain unchanged and yet distinct, Bracken turns to process thought. He points out that if the terms "process" or "system," which he uses as synonyms, are substituted for "nature" then the processes or systems could be combined to form a third more complex process. He uses as an example the multiple systems or processes at work in a human being as a highly complex life system. These bodily processes do not lose their distinctiveness due to being integrated into a higher order process, rather each continues to do its own work to sustain the life of the person each moment.[103] Bracken makes the point:

> If we then claim that Jesus as God incarnate is a higher-order process or system with divinity (the divine life system) and humanity (the human life system) as its sub-processes or sub-systems, then one has in principle a rationally plausible explanation for belief in the doctrine of the Incarnation. Jesus is, as the bishops at Chalcedon claimed, a divine person functioning equally well in two life systems: the one proper to his role within the divine community with the Father and the Spirit, and the other proper to his role within the human community and the ongoing process of creation.[104]

Bracken conjectures that, given the limitations of his self-awareness as a human being, Jesus might have only gradually become aware of all the implications of his unique interpersonal relationship with the Father and the Spirit during his human life. Moltmann takes a very similar trajectory of thought, finding in the operation of the Spirit, both chronologically and theologically, the qualification for Jesus of Nazareth both to recognize himself, and to be recognized by others, as the Christ. Moltmann says:

> We must suppose that at his baptism by or before John in the Jordan, Jesus had his special experience of the Spirit, and that through this he perceived his own calling and mission. 'The

102. Neuner et al., *Teaching of the Catholic Church*, 154.
103. Bracken, "Incarnation, Panentheism, and Bodily Resurrection," 35.
104. Bracken, "Incarnation, Panentheism, and Bodily Resurrection," 35.

Spirit descended upon him like a dove' (Mark 1:10). He hears a voice from God: 'Thou art my beloved Son; with thee I am well pleased' (Mark 1:11), and sees the heavens open. What is meant here is that this is the call to be the expected messiah of the End-time, on whom according to Isa. 61:1 the Spirit of God rests. It is in the special relationship to God in this Spirit that Jesus experiences himself as the messianic 'child' and experiences Israel's God as 'my beloved Father'. In the Spirit, Jesus prays 'Abba, dear Father'. In the Spirit he knows himself to be the beloved Son. So the Spirit is the real determining subject of this special relationship of Jesus' to God, and of God's to Jesus.[105]

This pondering of the relationship between the human and the divine within the person of Jesus also opens the question of the relationship between divine causality and creaturely causation within the rest of creation. It is notable that Bracken (unlike many process thinkers) leaves room for miracles in his worldview, wondering whether they can be explained as instances in which divine causality is more prominent than at other times.[106] Bracken suggests that:

Since every miracle is in itself an event taking place within the parameters of the space-time continuum of the cosmic process, the secondary causality of the creature must also be operative to make this miraculous event happen. At still other times, of course, the divine primary causality is conceivably operative only to bring into existence and sustain the existence and activity of the creature in one of the creature's own, customary modes of operation.[107]

It is this openness in the process thinking of Bracken to a level of supernaturalism and miracle, along with an underlining of divine primary causality, that makes it possible to affirm the second pro-Nicene criterion for a model of Trinity. This is especially regarding a doctrine of the incarnation and the two natures of Jesus that does not contradict the overarching process conception of God as non-coercive and invitational: God working with and through the world to shape an open future. Bracken unmistakably understands the Trinity to be more than a transcendent individual entity. For him, God exists as three divine persons, and yet one God, as an eternal corporate reality. He explains:

105. Moltmann, *Spirit of Life*, 61.
106. Bracken, "Incarnation, Panentheism, and Bodily Resurrection," 36.
107. Bracken, "Incarnation, Panentheism, and Bodily Resurrection," 37.

Each of the divine persons is a subsystem within the higher-order system of their communal existence as one God. Each of the divine Persons has 'his' own agency or mode of operation, and together they constitute the corporate agency of their conjoint existence as a divine community.[108]

Bracken's explanation of the corporate agency of three divine persons, one Holy Trinity in process from eternity, links the incarnation of the second person of the Trinity to the doctrine of the eternal procession of the Son. To see the incarnation as the foundational moment in an ongoing process of divine self-communication to the world, rather than as a later event in history, supports the central trinitarian ideal that the Son is eternally begotten of, and coeternal with, the Father. Clear expression can then be given to the key idea that the eternal generation of the Son occurs within the unitary and incomparable divine being, thus keeping a Social Trinity in process within a pro-Nicene framework.[109]

The third criterion for a pro-Nicene theory of the Holy Trinity is an unambiguous understanding that the three persons of the Trinity work inseparably.[110] Moltmann is well-known for his contribution to articulating the inseparable nature of the work of the three persons of the one God through the notion of *perichoresis*. *Perichoresis*, from the Greek language, and its Latin equivalent *circumincessio*, refers to the mutual indwelling or mutual interpenetration of the Trinity. The *perichoresis* of the Trinity begins with the unity of the persons and affirms a reciprocal interrelation. This affirmation of the inseparable work of the trinitarian persons makes *perichoresis* a necessary implication of orthodox trinitarian thought.[111] The concept of *perichoresis* is at the heart of Moltmann's social trinitarianism. For him:

> The divine persons exist not only in relationships to one another but also, as the Johannine formulations show, *in one another:* the Son *in* the Father, the Father *in* the Son, and the Father and the Son *in* the Holy Spirit. This intimate indwelling and complete interpenetration of the persons in one another is expressed by the doctrine of the trinitarian *perichoresis*. It denotes that Trinitarian unity which goes out beyond the doctrine of the persons and their relations: by virtue of their eternal love, the divine persons exist so intimately with one another, for one another and

108. Bracken, "Incarnation, Panentheism, and Bodily Resurrection," 37.
109. Ayres, *Nicaea and Its Legacy*, 236.
110. Ayres, *Nicaea and Its Legacy*, 236.
111. Smith, "Perichoresis," 843.

in one another that they constitute themselves in their unique, incomparable and complete unity.[112]

This intimate existence of Father and Son and Spirit, with, for, and in each other constituting an incomparable unity, enables the understanding that the three do work inseparably. This is so, as Moltmann was wont to say throughout his writing, because "the doctrine of *perichoresis* combines the threeness and the oneness without reducing the threeness to the oneness or the oneness to the threeness."[113] Moltmann explains:

> The perichoretic unity is to be thought of as being equally original for the divine persons and the divine relations. If the life within the Trinity is understood perichoretically, then the divine life is as little lived by one subject alone as is the Trinitarian history of the Father, the Son and the Spirit. It is the perichoretic concept of unity which is the Trinitarian concept of triunity.[114]

For Moltmann, this unity and triunity points unequivocally to a society of equals. There is, therefore, no hierarchical ordering within the Trinity, no permanent "leader" or "ruler" within the one community. In this, Moltmann's view is very much in sympathy with Coakley's daring call, previously discussed, to restate the notion of procession in the Godhead. Coakley's sense of the primacy of the Spirit, her insistence that "there can be in God's Trinitarian ontology no Sonship which is not eternally 'sourced' by 'Father' *in the Spirit*," and that we "need to speak of the Father's own reception back of his status as 'source' from the other two 'persons'"[115] exudes a similar sense of relationality inherent in Moltmann's vision of a fully interdependent Trinity.

Notions of the inseparable work of the three co-equal persons of the Trinity are also available through process theology. In this regard Bracken critiques what he describes as the "classical cause-effect relationship" of traditional theism, insisting that when such thinking is applied to the relations of the divine persons of the Trinity the result is the primacy of the Father *over* the Son and the Spirit.[116] To understand the Father over the Son and the Spirit is grounded in the idea that the Father is the one origin of the divine life which is then shared with the Son and the Spirit. In pointing out that this effectively denies the equality of the three persons as necessary

112. Moltmann, *History and the Triune God*, 85–86.

113. Moltmann, *History and the Triune God*, 86.

114. Moltmann, *History and the Triune God*, 86.

115. Coakley, *God, Sexuality, and the Self*, 333.

116. Bracken, *World in the Trinity*, 138.

co-participants in the divine communitarian life, Bracken shares the concerns of Coakley and Moltmann just discussed. Bracken calls for a new
approach to the Trinity based on a process/systems vision, rather than the
classical vision he critiques, in which the "Many" through interrelation-
ship co-produce the reality of the "One." Notably, in Bracken's trinitarian
thought, there is room for the "World in the Trinity."[117]

Bracken notes that constant checks and balances are required in all
potential models of Trinity to ensure that developing trinitarian theology is
pro-Nicene, thus remaining connected to the accepted trajectory of orthodox Christianity. He issues a reminder for thinkers about the Trinity that if
the central focus is on differentiating each divine person, and attempts are
then made to explain that together they are one God, there is a risk of tritheism. Whereas, if the focus is on the unity of the divine being, and from there
explanations are developed about how God is also three persons, modalism
may result.[118] Therefore, as I turn next to the sketching of a relational model
of God that is a Social Trinity in process, one that meets the three criteria
for a pro-Nicene theory of Trinity, these checks and balances remain very
much in play.

SOCIAL TRINITY IN PROCESS

A Social Trinity in process is effectively a relational model of God and the
God/world connection as it is grounded in an understanding of the importance of relationship and connection within and to all things. It views
relationality as "the *sine qua non* of all existence whatsoever,"[119] bound as it
is to Hartshorne's description of God as entirely social, and to Moltmann's
insistence that the immanent Trinity is a divine society open to the life of
the world. A Social Trinity in process operates according to *ekstasis*, the voluntary outgoingness of each person of the Trinity in relationship. The life of
the Trinity understood this way is one of constant self-donation where gifts
are exchanged between the persons in a movement of advanced reciproca-
tion, a "circular movement of eternal divine love."[120]

117. Bracken, *World in the Trinity*, 139. Although Bracken's process, or systems,
approach to the Trinity is grounded specifically in the thinking of Whitehead, this does
not put it at odds with process thought more generally.

118. Bracken, *World in the Trinity*, 140.

119. Bracken and Suchocki, *Trinity in Process*, viii.

120. Volf, "'Trinity Is Our Social Program,'" 412.

Divine Creativity, Creative Love, and Responsive Love are appropriate terms through which to describe the persons of a relational Trinity.[121] These descriptors both affirm the open sociality of God that Hartshorne and Moltmann agree on and support the idea that creative power is embodied, not by God alone, but by God and a universe of finite events. It is through this sharing of creative power that a Social Trinity in process is not over against the world, but consistently acts persuasively and lovingly with the world. This relational model looks to Jesus as a special revelation and exemplar of the persuasive suffering love that characterizes the nature of God's action in the world. It follows that, whether we are considering God's action in creation, revelation, redemption, sanctification, or consummation, the Triune God forever acts in one and the same way. The non-coercive manner of God's action in the world does not impinge on the power or freedom of the creatures any more than the activity of Jesus destroyed the freedom of those who heard his message.[122]

The solidarity that epitomizes a Social Trinity in process is evident in both immanent and economic ways of viewing the Trinity. The economic work of God flows both from and to the immanent God, for the economic work of God is everlastingly to offer creative lures to the world as initial aims. These aims are the means of God's immanence in the world, and the degree to which the initial aims are embraced by the world, God is incarnate in the world.[123] The vivid term *hemopoiesis*, as employed by Moltmann, implies that we and all things are related to God at a cellular level. As blood cells are to a living body, as the live component of marrow is to the bone, the notion of *hemopoiesis* represents both the capacity of God to relate to and embrace all that is, and a sociality in God that generates and maintains life into and beyond the new creation in Christ when all human history is taken up into the history of God.[124]

The close relationality between a Social Trinity in process and the world is best described by the term panentheism. This way of understanding God takes the middle ground between a too far distant theism and a non-differentiated pantheism. It is embracing of a reality in which God is intimately related to every moment of experience, giving, and receiving love; touching, and being touched by the joys and sorrows of the world.[125] A Social Trinity in process therefore influences the universe, according

---

121. Griffin, "Naturalistic Trinity," 37.

122. Griffin, "Naturalistic Trinity," 26.

123. Suchocki, "Spirit in and through the World," 185.

124. Moltmann, *Crucified God*, 246–47.

125. Epperly, *Process Theology*, 45.

to panentheism, by accepting into its own life each current of feeling that exists. God alone knows and feels each current of life, yet each life is free to make its own decisions rather than being directed by a detailed divine plan.[126] The nature of what Bracken calls "a systems-oriented" or process panentheism "guarantees that the persons and things of this world can exist within God and by the power of God and yet at every moment possess their own finite identity and distinctive mode of operation."[127] Through linking the divine life with creativity as the ontological ground of the divine being and activity, God can be explained as a creative, trinitarian society who works non-coercively;[128] as a Social Trinity in process.

In process theology generally and the thinking of Whitehead particularly, God is known as the companion we imitate. The idea of modelling ourselves and all our relationships on what we understand to be the nature of the Triune God is also very much at the heart of social trinitarianism. This shared ideal comes together naturally in a Social Trinity in process through agreement that the nature of God is a proper model for all of life. As process thought developed in the milieu of contemporary science it can make such claims based on knowledge about the workings of the natural world that were unavailable to the ancients, thus informing doctrines of Trinity that have their roots in antiquity. In fact, a respectful enhancing of pre-scientific thinking about God will consistently advance the idea of a relational God because the relationality of all things completely coheres with what we now know about the workings of the universe. Despite its grounding in a scientific worldview, however, a Social Trinity in process is not exclusively reliant on natural theology. While certainly seeking to be intelligible to scientists and philosophers as well as theologians, at no point need such a view of God discount the possibility of supernatural influences on the mechanisms of the universe, so long as it is understood that miracles are the exception rather than the rule in the workings of nature.[129]

To understand God as a Social Trinity in process therefore builds a substantial bridge between metaphysics and theology, particularly for the growing number of philosophical theologians who are convinced that God *necessarily* reveals Godself as Trinity.[130] The dualistic theory of God which has been associated with process thought can certainly be reconsidered, as

126. Hartshorne, *Divine Relativity*, xvii.

127. Bracken, "Incarnation, Panentheism, and Bodily Resurrection," 41.

128. Bracken, "Incarnation, Panentheism, and Bodily Resurrection," 109.

129. Bracken, "Incarnation, Panentheism, and Bodily Resurrection," 46.

130. Clayton. "Pluralism, Idealism, Romanticism," 137. See also Hasker, *Metaphysics and the Tri-Personal God*.

some third movement is required to mediate between infinite and finite, ground and consequent. It is on this basis that a Social Trinity in process, while being pro-Nicene and therefore fully Christian, looks to a deeper and fuller expression of the Holy Spirit in trinitarian theology.[131] The notion of the Spirit of God being the "first"[132] in God's encounter with the world is arguably the feature of a Social Trinity in process which challenges traditional theologies more than other key associated ideas such as the panentheistic nature of deity, and the sharing of power with the world. Nevertheless, the challenge of seeking the primacy of the Spirit in a Social Trinity in process is always in the context of the persuasive manner of being which marks each of the three Persons of the Trinity. All are equally divine and genuinely one.

Based on key points of crossover between the process thinking of Hartshorne and the social trinitarianism of Moltmann, this chapter has sketched a Social Trinity in process: a fully relational model of God. The aim has been to recalibrate theism, particularly regarding its understanding of the nature and exercise of divine power, and to demonstrate that ideas associated with traditional theism about an all-controlling and immutable God can well be reconsidered in the light of a contemporary worldview informed by a deeper understanding of the processes of the natural world. This reconsideration of the relationship between the Triune God and the world has been careful to demonstrate compatibility with the trinitarian formulations of Nicaea with a view to being recognized as thoroughly Christian. This chapter has demonstrated that panentheism is a helpful way of modelling God in relationship with the world, a valid middle ground between theism and pantheism. Panentheism addresses the exercise of God's power in consistent terms of "with" rather than "over" the world, for a panentheistic God is "God with us," by definition.

In a Social Trinity in process, the unity of the Trinity is grounded in the relationship between the divine persons who interpenetrate, co-inhere, and mutually indwell one another in *perichoresis*.[133] This loving, divine community is the exemplar for human community, both in the church and in the world. In shifting the focus from a monarchical, hierarchical conception of God to a divine unity and community of equality between the persons of the Trinity, a Social Trinity in process has both a theological function and a social function. Theologically, it critiques a falsely hierarchical idea of God where either by nature or role the persons are ranked based on perceptions

131. Lee, "'Other' Trinity," 60; Suchocki, "Spirit in and through the World," 186; Coakley, *God, Sexuality and the Self*, 334; Moltmann, *Spirit of Life*.

132. Coakley, *God, Sexuality, and the Self*, 334.

133. Mosser, "Fully Social Trinitarianism," 133–34.

of greater power or importance. Socially, it describes the Trinity as the proper paradigm for society.[134] This way of understanding the threefold nature of God in process both gives honor to the historical development of trinitarian theology within the church and accounts for a contemporary, scientific worldview for today's theologians. It addresses God's exercise of power in solidarity with the free choices of all creation. A Social Trinity in process, a fully relational God, creatively, actively, and lovingly invites choices for the good in human life and the life of the world without resort to coercion and force. The next chapter will explore the implications of understanding God in this relational manner for the life of the world and church.

134. McGrath, *Christian Theology*, 258.

5

DIVINE AND HUMAN POWER

Implications of a Relational God

My crown I am, but still my griefs are mine. You may my glories
and my state depose but not my griefs; still am I king of those.

—William Shakespeare, Richard II, Act 4, Scene 1

Jonah prayed to the Lord and said, 'O Lord! Is this not what I said while I was
in my own country? This is why I fled to Tarshish at the beginning; for I knew
that you are a gracious God and merciful, slow to anger and abounding in
steadfast love, and ready to relent from punishing.

—Jonah 4:2 (NRSV)

Throughout this book I have consistently argued in favor of understanding God's exercise of power as both invitational and shared with the
world. This understanding is based predominantly in Hartshorne's process
thought. I have argued equally for a social understanding of God based particularly in Moltmann's social theology of Trinity. The combination of these
two key ideas: the non-coercive power of God in solidarity with the free
choices of all creation, and the relationality of God as a foundational pattern
for all of life, was considered in chapter 4 through modeling God as a Social
Trinity in process. That chapter found that joining the already overlapping
theologies of Moltmann and Hartshorne—to describe the nature of God as

Trinity through a process framework—presents a helpful model of God for the twenty-first century. It is positive for our times because it both honors the historical development of trinitarian theology within the church and provides a logical progression of ideas for contemporary thinkers about the exercise of God's power in a suffering world.

In this final chapter I consider some of the implications of this panentheistic vision of God by focusing on the pivotal alliance between divine and human power when considering the nature of God as a Social Trinity in process. I first explore how changing understandings of God's omnipotence, alongside the relatively recent change of mindset about the immutability of God in theology, provides a compelling response to the problem of evil and suffering in the world. Then, focusing on a Social Trinity in process as a vision of a companion God whom we rightly imitate,[1] I demonstrate what such relationality offers to the nurture of healthy relationships within the Church, giving specific examples of the exercise of power as we image God in the ministry and pastoral care of the Church. Lastly, I summarize my findings and conclude.

POWER: THE MOVE FROM THEISM TO PANENTHEISM

Towards the end of the twentieth century some features of classical theism that had shaped Christian theology for centuries, such as the idea of the immutability of God, had begun to be set aside in theology. The work of Hartshorne[2] and Moltmann[3] features in this gradual movement towards an acceptance of the reality of suffering in the Godhead. This specific change in thinking represents one aspect of a broader movement away from the categories of traditional theism to an embracing of panentheism as a valid and helpful model of God. The Old Testament scholar, Terence E. Fretheim, whose writing about divine suffering echoes important, connecting ideas found in Moltmann and Hartshorne on the fully relational nature of God,[4] strongly critiques classical theism for its emphasis on divine atemporality, immutability, omniscience, and omnipotence.[5] Fretheim says:

> As one surveys the landscape of OT scholarship on the under-
> standing of God, the portrait of God which normally emerges

---

1. Whitehead, *Process and Reality*, 351.
2. Hartshorne, *Divine Relativity*.
3. Moltmann, *Theology of Hope* and *Crucified God*.
4. Fretheim, *Suffering of God* and *What Kind of God?*
5. Chan and Strawn, "Introducing Fretheim," 6.

bears a striking resemblance to the quite traditional Jewish or Christian understanding of God regnant in synagogue or church. Save for matters relating to historical development (e.g., for henotheism to monotheism) one can read back and forth between church dogmatics textbooks and most God-talk in OT studies without missing a beat. Thus, for example, God is understood in terms of traditional categories: freedom, immutability, omniscience, and omnipotence; if not explicitly stated, they are commonly assumed. I cannot ever recall a commentator on an OT text dealing with the future, suggesting that God's knowledge of the future is limited, and that consequently the text should be interpreted with that in mind.[6]

Fretheim demonstrates how these notions of immutability, and omnipotence, and other categories of traditional theism are simply not to be found in a range of Old Testament texts on which they are readily believed to depend. For example, in his commentary on the book of Jonah, Fretheim asks:

> What is involved in God's being moved to spare? The use of the verb '*moved* to spare' points us to the fact that God's action has its effect upon God himself. This verb has reference to suffering action, action executed with tears in the eyes. . . . And so 'to have pity' would mean action undertaken with 'tears flowing down the cheeks.' It is suffering action. Here God takes upon *himself* the evil of Nineveh.[7]

Further, about the book of Judges, Fretheim writes: '

> God's people, again and again, exhibit patterns of life which threaten their existence. God's response is remarkable in its variety and flexibility, in order to accomplish salutary purposes. A highly personal divine response is revealed, which values mercy above retribution; we see a God who chooses to experience suffering rather than visit the people with the finality of death; we are surprised by a God who finds ways of working in, with, and under very compromising situations in which people have placed themselves in order to bring about good.[8]

Important to Fretheim's argument from the bible against classical theism is his understanding of the relationship between God and metaphor. He

---

6. Fretheim, *Suffering of God*, 17.

7. Fretheim, *Message of Jonah*, 130.

8. Fretheim, *Deuteronomic History*, 98.

believes that the metaphors used for God essentially define God for us and that metaphor is therefore a crucial methodological and theoretical issue for both the life of faith and for theology.[9] As Fretheim points out:

> It is not enough to say that one believes in God. What is important finally is the kind of God in whom one believes. Or, to use different language: metaphors matter. The images used to speak of God not only decisively determine the way one thinks about God, they have a powerful impact on the shape of the life of the believer.[10]

Fretheim sees real danger in the possibility that Christians will remain content with a very limited fund of metaphors. He points to "the court of law metaphor,"[11] where God is envisioned as a judge with absolute sentencing power and describes it as having become unhelpfully predominant in the thinking of some parts of the Church, while other valid metaphors for God have been blocked out. The caring, rather than judging, metaphors are often overlooked—especially the mother images.[12] The eagle metaphor,[13] for example, where God is envisaged as a mother bird hovering over her nest of young, and bearing them up on her wings, is regularly seen as an anomaly rather than as a valid descriptor of the divine nature. As the biblical metaphors carry significant truths about the nature of God, it follows that the metaphors we favor in envisioning God, as much as the ones we leave out of the picture, will shape the way we relate to and understand God. Further, and as I have suggested throughout this book, the model or picture we have of God from the metaphors we have chosen, or inherited, or simply assume, will go toward shaping and validating the nature of all our relationships, both human and environmental.

Due to his view that metaphors are "reality depicting,"[14] alongside his relational understanding of God and the world, Fretheim interprets the biblical texts in which God "repents," "regrets," or "changes" God's own mind as literary windows into the nature of God and the world God has created. So,

---

9. Chan and Strawn, "Introducing Fretheim," 7. See also McFague, *Metaphorical Theology*.

10. Fretheim, *Suffering of God*, 1.

11. Fretheim, *Suffering of God*, 8.

12. Examples include Isaiah 49:15 which uses language that presents God as a nurse and a mother, Deuteronomy 32:18 which refers to God giving birth to Israel, and Hosea 11:1–4 which presents God loving her child and teaching him to walk, embracing her child with tender love, and feeding him. All these tasks taken on by God belonged to women in Israelite households.

13. Deuteronomy 32:11.

14. Fretheim, *Suffering of God*, 7.

rather than seeing metaphors as simple illustrations,[15] Fretheim finds that the semiotics of metaphor—the meaning metaphor produces—is deeply significant in communicating truth about the divine nature.[16] It is on this basis that he insists:

> God is not powerful and the creatures powerless; we need constantly to be reminded that the Godness of God cannot be bought at the expense of creaturely diminishment. In the very act of creating, God gives to that which is other than God a certain independence and freedom. God moves over, as it were, and makes room for others. There is an ordered freedom in the creation, a degree of openness and unpredictability wherein God leaves room for genuine decisions on the part of human beings as they exercise their God-given power. But, even more, God gives them powers and responsibilities in a way that *commits God* to a certain kind of relationship with them. . . . One implication of this is that the divine sovereignty in creation is understood, not in terms of absolute divine control, but as sovereignty that gives power over to the created for the sake of a relationship of integrity. This is a risky move, for it entails the possibility that the creatures will misuse the power they have been given, which is in fact what occurs.[17]

This concept of a divine sharing of power in relationship, and the associated idea of a potential misuse of power by the creatures, in no way contradicts Hartshorne's view of God having the maximum power *possible*. The important point made is that, while God does have the greatest conceivable power, that greatest conceivable power is not the same as the concept of omnipotence that we have inherited from classical theism. Hartshorne explains:

15. Hartshorne agrees that the metaphors we use for God are not just word pictures that can be taken lightly, describing the God as judge or as monarch metaphors as highly dangerous. Hartshorne, *Divine Relativity*, 38.

16. The truth about the nature of God conveyed by metaphor in religious and theological language is always symbolic and analogic rather than literal. On this point, Long suggests that the metaphysical significance of metaphor is best found through understanding the relationship between language about God and Godself. He says that, when we are clear that God is always to be understood as holy being, an *analogia entis* or analogy of being is possible, but it is one consistent with a panentheistic understanding of God as both transcendent and immanent. Long, *Western Philosophy of Religion*, 332.

17. Fretheim, "Creator, Creature, and Co-Creation," 204–5. It is important to note here that, although both critics and supporters of Fretheim sometimes associate him with the process movement, he is more nearly an Open Theist. This category of thinker affirms panentheism and power sharing between God and the world but operates on the basis that God has freely chosen self-limitation and relationship.

The notion of a cosmic power that determines all decisions fails to make sense. For its decisions could refer to nothing except themselves. They could result in no world; for a world must consist of local agents making their own decisions. Instead of saying that God's power is limited, suggesting that it is less than some conceivable power, we should rather say: his power is absolutely maximal, the greatest possible, but even the greatest possible power is still one among others, is not the only power. God can do everything that a God can do, everything that could be done by 'a being with no possible superior.'[18]

This line of argument has much to say in response to claims that models of God grounded in process theology need somehow to justify that they conceive of an "adequate" God.[19] It is still common to insist that, unless God is understood to have unilateral power (whether God chooses to exercise it)[20] then God is not truly worthy of worship. The assumption seems to remain that non-coercive or shared power in God is somehow synonymous with a crippling weakness, yet to make this kind of correlation is to completely overlook the subversive message of the kingdom of God inherent in the person and work of Christ:

> We proclaim Christ crucified, a stumbling block to Jews and foolishness to the Gentiles, but to those who are the called, both Jews and Greeks, Christ the power of God and the wisdom of God. For God's foolishness is wiser than human wisdom, and God's weakness is stronger than human strength.[21]

Finding a way to ease the tensions between the monarchical and almighty descriptions of God in the Old Testament, and vulnerable Christic power in the New Testament, alongside the Johannine descriptions of God as love, is to begin to come to terms with qualitative power rather than quantitative power. It is the qualitative strength of God's weakness and love that both Hartshorne and Moltmann, process theology and social trinitarianism, hone into as primarily important. It is true to say that this focus is taken for different reasons, although each is grounded in a theology of

---

18. Hartshorne, *Divine Relativity*, 138.

19. This dialogue centers around the "alleged inadequacies of process theism" and charges of "a restriction in divine power." Cobb and Pinnock, *Searching for an Adequate God*, 247, 256.

20. This critique is also relevant to Fretheim's view, reflective of the position known as Open Theism, of God permanently and irrevocably giving up a monopoly on power for the sake of relationship with the world. Fretheim, *Suffering of God*, 72.

21. 1 Corinthians 1:23–25 (NRSV)

experience. For Hartshorne and process theology the focus is principally, though not exclusively, on ensuring that the notion of God makes logical sense in an evolving world that can be investigated by science, and this includes some manner of theodicy to account for the existence of natural evil. In Moltmann, it is about ensuring that an understanding of the Triune God makes at least some sense of the human experience of suffering that so marked the twentieth century.

Taking Fretheim into account, alongside a range of protest theologians from the middle of the twentieth century on, it could be argued that notions of God's power as dominance and absolute control have well and truly been questioned from the context of the life and experience of marginalized groups in society, and from those who suffer. Even with this questioning, despite Moltmann and his suffering God,[22] Gutierrez and Boff and the liberation theologians of South America,[23] feminist and gay theologians,[24] and the process movement as more fully discussed in this study, the idea of God as a sovereign monarch in total control of the world continues to have remarkable tenacity, particularly in popular theology.[25] Notwithstanding this, with the notable exception of Tanner who represents a differing metaphysical view in regard to power,[26] the theologians canvassed for this study were unanimous that a different way of understanding God's power *must* be found. Divine power exercised as domination and control was considered unacceptable theologically and logically, both within and without the process camp.[27]

22. Moltmann, *Theology of Hope* and *Crucified God*.

23. Gutierrez, *Theology of Liberation*; Boff, *Church, Charism and Power*.

24. Reuther, *Sexism and God-Talk*; Heyward, *Redemption of God* and *Staying Power*.

25. An example of this is to be found in Warren's *Purpose Driven Life* and associated publications coming out of Orange County, California. This best-selling brand of American evangelical theology affirms God's full control of everything from the molecules in each human body to the future of the planet, following the traditional integration of omniscience and omnipotence. In the words of Warren, "God's plan for your life involves all that happens to you—including your mistakes, your sins, and your hurts. This includes illness, debt, disasters, divorce, and death of loved ones." Warren, *Purpose Driven Life*, 195–96. Armstrong, in her survey of belief and religion, affirms that this less than sophisticated view of God is relatively widespread. She points out that "despite our scientific and technological brilliance, our religious thinking is sometimes remarkably undeveloped, even primitive. In some ways the modern God resembles the High God of remote antiquity, a theology that was unanimously jettisoned or radically reinterpreted because it was found to be inept." Armstrong, *Case for God*, 1.

26. Tanner, *God and Creation*, 163–68.

27. Case-Winters, *God's Power*, 10. Case-Winters' thesis is that the underlying meaning of power that the classical view of omnipotence presupposes is the crux of the problem. Migliore agrees that God's power must be understood "differently" to

A core reason that divine power exercised as domination and control is untenable is because this way of understanding God and power has little to say in response to the problem of evil. In the history of philosophy and religion, consideration of this problem was at its height in the seventeenth century. At this time philosophers and theologians grappled with ways of reconciling the obvious fact that the world is full of sin and suffering with what was, for them, "the non-negotiable belief that the universe was created by an infinitely good, wise, all-powerful, and all-knowing God."[28] The problem of evil, thus defined, is not merely an historical or philosophical dilemma, it is a recurring scene in the ongoing production of seeking for a proper conception of God. The question of how God acts in the world, with what abilities and capacities and power God is endowed, to what extent God's manner of operation is open to rational understanding, and whether the ways of God can be explained or justified, are matters of keen ongoing interest in theology and the philosophy of religion.[29]

The incompatibility of evil with the existence of an omniscient, omnibenevolent, and omnipotent God has been considered both logically and evidentially. The logical consideration of the problem leads to the view that the mere existence of evil contradicts the existence of such a God. Considered evidentially, it can be conceded that the existence of evil is logically compatible with the existence of God as traditionally understood, but that the extent of evil in the world provides significant evidence against the existence of such a God, so much so that the presence of an all-powerful, all-loving, all-knowing God is likely to be false.[30] Alfred Lord Tennyson's *In Memoriam A. H. H.*, 1850. Canto 56. captures well the evidential problem of evil. He describes humankind:

> Who trusted God was love indeed
> And love Creation's final law
> Tho' Nature, red in tooth and claw
> With ravine, shriek'd against his creed

Tennyson poetically summarizes the reality that evidence garnered from our experience of the processes of the natural world contradicts the

---

domination and control. He describes it as "the power of self-giving, liberating, renewing, and reconciling love." Migliore, *Power of God*, 35. Sykes finds no necessary connection between power and force. Sykes, *Power and Christian Theology*, 103. Coakley wants the "standard binary" of "power" and "submission" to be rethought wherever it occurs. Coakley, *Powers and Submissions*, x.

28. Nadler, *Best of All Possible Worlds*, xi.

29. Nadler, *Best of All Possible Worlds*, xi.

30. Goetz, "Argument from Evil," 449.

idea of God as a benevolent divine force in direct control of all the workings of a harmonious creation. This is due to the observable fact that natural disasters stemming from seismic events and calamitous weather patterns are part of the normal cycles of the world. Predation, disease, malformation, and death are inherent aspects of natural selection and the evolutionary processes and systems of all life on earth. Evil and suffering are naturally occurring phenomena and part of the standard functioning of world processes. Furthermore, contemporary knowledge of natural science underlines that suffering and conflict are both characteristic of, and necessary to, healthy and well-functioning biotic systems.[31] On this basis, those who focus on the logical problem of evil would be inclined to say that the cruel processes of nature make it impossible to believe in God as traditionally described by Christianity. Responses to evidential and logical arguments from evil against the existence of a Christian conception of God continue to be developed by theists, however, for the problem of evil is predicated firmly on a theistic understanding of God which describes God as omnipotent, omnibenevolent, and omniscient.

Beyond formal theological or philosophical considerations of the theodicy question, in the many times "when bad things happen to good people," questions about the way God acts and uses power are asked differently and with far greater intensity.[32] People who are suffering due to disease, death, despair, or disaster, place little value on an academic pondering of logical notions of God grounded in the problem of evil. For those who find themselves in the midst of suffering, the theodicy question becomes a heartfelt cry for help and understanding, a cry surrounded by anguish and doubt.

Similarly, for people whose lives and livelihoods are at immediate risk from climate change and environmental disaster, and people who are appalled and distressed by the suffering inherent in nature and the natural processes of the world, academic considerations of theodicy are far removed from their daily experience of suffering. In *Ask the Beasts: Darwin and the God of Love*, Elizabeth A. Johnson's stated goal is to underline that the love, celebration, and protection of the natural world is an essential part of the Christian faith, to *practical* effect.[33] In seeking a model of interaction be-

---

31. Sideris, *Environmental Ethics*, 6. Although not necessarily agreeing with what she describes as their "ecological theology," Sideris (interestingly for this study) includes Moltmann with the process thinkers Charles Birch and John Cobb, describing their collective approach to theology as one that is committed to articulating the role of God in natural processes. Sideris, *Environmental Ethics*, 92.

32. Kushner, *When Bad Things Happen*.

33. Johnson, *Ask the Beasts*, xviii.

tween Christianity and the cruel processes of the natural world, Johnson is effectively seeking tools for a response to the problem of evil and suffering. In this she acknowledges the insights of process thought for the task, saying:

> One example would be process philosophy and theology, an inclusive metaphysical position shaped by fundamental insights from both evolutionary science and Christian religious thought. Its insight that God is the source of novelty, immanent in the processes of the world and operating with persuasive rather than dominating power, has been widely influential, though not without critics.[34]

Through a method of "practical co-operation" Johnson looks to create a dialogue between Darwin's *Origin of the Species* and the creeds of the Christian Church.[35] She describes Darwin's magnum opus as an extended argument that species are constantly in motion, coming into being from prior species by a process that can be explained naturally, without any need to appeal to a supernatural cause.[36] Johnson nevertheless points out that Darwin was not content to view "this wonderful universe and especially the nature of man, and to conclude that everything is the result of brute force."[37] Importantly, this is despite his recognition of the cruelty inherent in nature. Darwin saw such things as the instinct of cuckoo chicks, who destroy the young of other bird species into whose nests they hatch as impostors, and wasps that lay their eggs in caterpillars as a future source of food, as "small consequences of one general law." The general law, colloquially referred to as the survival of the fittest, was, in Darwin's terminology, "let the strongest live and let the weakest die."[38] Johnson points out that it is a "relief to think of this law of nature as a secondary cause" rather than seeking to make an attempt to attribute these instincts to the "direct plan of a loving God."[39] She rightly acknowledges that, particularly for communities of faith which believe that the living world is God's good creation, the theory of evolution is "theologically consequential."[40] She further affirms that the Christian

---

34. Johnson, *Ask the Beasts*, 10–11.

35. Johnson, *Ask the Beasts*, 11–17. Johnson focuses on "God is love" (as in 1 John 4:16 NRSV) as a summary of the Creeds of the Christian Church and as a guide for her project.

36. Johnson, *Ask the Beasts*, 27.

37. Johnson, *Ask the Beasts*, 39. Cited in Costa, *Annotated Origin of Species*, 492.

38. Darwin in Johnson, *Ask the Beasts*, 72.

39. Johnson, *Ask the Beasts*, 72.

40. Johnson, *Ask the Beasts*, 121.

story can still be good news in this changed context of a world understood to change and develop:

> For all Christian theology, the gospel is good news. The love of God is a saving, healing, restoring power that benefits human beings. A significant stream of theological interpretation parses this to mean that divine love ultimately enhances the powers of the human person rather (than) being a zero sum game in which one protagonist's gain is the other's loss.[41]

It is notable that Johnson's affirmation of the goodness of God in the face of the change and suffering inherent in the natural world, her theodicy or defense,[42] comes down to power. Johnson insists that the power of God is not the exercise of control. Instead she describes divine power as "sovereign cruciform love that empowers others,"[43] and further clarifies that "divine love unfailingly manifests itself not as coercive 'power over' but as 'power with' that energizes others."[44] Her declaration that the nature of God's exercise of power is not represented in the zero-sum terms of winner takes all explicitly taps into the terminology of game theory.[45] This use of the language of game theory by Johnson, and more broadly by contemporary environmental and scientific theologians,[46] informs an understanding of the prevalence of mechanisms of cooperation in the natural world and an evolving universe—including the idea of divine cooperation and collaboration. This connects game theory, specifically the non-zero-sum metaphor it encompasses, to aspects of theologies of power which focus on the quality, or type, of God's power rather than solely on its quantity. On this basis,

---

41. Johnson, *Ask the Beasts*, 157.

42. Goetz, "Argument from Evil," 454. Responses to the problem of evil can be described as either a "defense" or a "theodicy." A defense is a statement outlining what God's justification for permitting evil *might* be. Those who merely defend God in the face of evil generally believe that, due to our limited epistemic powers, we cannot know the "why" of such things. A theodicy is more robust in that it is a defense presented, not as possibility, but as God's *actual* justification for the existence of evil.

43. Johnson, *Ask the Beasts*, 158.

44. Johnson, *Ask the Beasts*, 159.

45. The terms "zero-sum and non-zero-sum" in Game Theory, as discussed in chapter 1, work as metaphors for different aspects of power relationships. The zero-sum metaphor is one in which an individual or sector achieves its will in the face of opposition by exercising power "over" the other and garnering all power through competition. The non-zero-sum metaphor is more collaborative. It is a power "with" model which focuses on the possibility of attracting consent and support and thus achieving collective objectives and sharing power. Mennell, *Sociological Theory*, 108.

46. See Nowak and Coakley, *Evolution, Games, and God*.

when it comes to natural evil, Johnson reaches a conclusion about the power of God that resonates strongly with a Social Trinity in process:

> The living God acts by divine power in and through the acts of finite agents which have genuine causal efficiency in their own right. The wonderful word *concursus*, meaning flowing or running together, comes into play to express this idea. Far from being merely a tool, instrument, or puppet in divine hands, the world acts with its own free integrity to shape its own becoming. It is empowered to do so by the transcendent mystery of the Spirit of God, who pervades the world, quickening it to life and acting in and through its finite agency.[47]

Johnson is clear that the operation of power in God is unfailingly non-coercive. She also affirms that God's exercise of power cannot be omnipotence as it is usually understood, a view she shares with a majority of the theologians of power canvassed for this study, as previously discussed in chapter 2.[48] In this, Johnson steps beyond theism into panentheism, defining God, power, and the world in a manner consistent with Moltmann and Hartshorne and their relational models of God.[49] She therefore supports their joint view that the only potentially realistic response to the problem of evil and suffering involves describing God in terms other than through the standard categories of theism.

A realistic theodicy thus involves a reconceiving of the power of God from the dominance and control that is associated with the traditional idea of omnipotence. It will also involve the key understanding that suffering includes not only human beings, but God. A retrospective looking back to the story of Israel, grounded in the rabbinic and kabbalistic notion of a God who shares in the suffering of God's people, provides a reminder that this

47. Johnson, *Ask the Beasts*, 165.

48. Case-Winters, *God's Power*, 10; Migliore, *Power of God*, 35; Sykes, *Power and Christian Theology*, 103; Coakley, *Powers and Submissions*, x; Pasewark, *Theology of Power*, 3.

49. Johnson finds value in a range of theories that eschew omnipotence as it is traditionally understood which lean toward panentheism. These include the *kenotic* position, which sees God voluntary limiting divine power so to participate vulnerably in the life of the world, strongly resonant of Moltmann in *Crucified God*. Also, the process thought of Hartshorne, in which God is a creative participant in the cosmic community acting persuasively in all events. She also lists single action theory, top-down causality, the "causal-joint" theory, and the organic model as having merit. Johnson points out that they each "in different ways . . . seek to make intelligible the idea that the creating God as ground, sustaining power, and goal of the evolving world acts by empowering the process from within." The theory she finds the most productive of all is that of primary-secondary causality. Johnson, *Ask the Beasts*, 162–63.

view has a valid history.[50] Indeed, the same idea is paralleled in the Christian story of the passion of Jesus Christ where the pain of the love of God is manifested to all who suffer, through the cross. Expressed through Moltmann's concept of Trinity, this means that the Father follows his beloved Son to the cross and the suffering of the Son becomes Divine suffering: a suffering in solidarity, a redemptive suffering.[51]

A Social Trinity in process brings together the key thinking behind Moltmann's social trinitarianism and Hartshorne's process view of God and the world. This amalgamation provides a helpful model for the abovementioned theological paradigm shift from theism to panentheism. Such a movement from understanding God as a separate omnipotence to understanding God as a fully relational Trinity who suffers with us, is both logical and orthodox. As Moltmann reasons:

> If we can follow Whitehead in describing theism in moral, political and philosophical respects as idolatry, it follows conversely, that theism removes man from his humanity and alienates him from his freedom, his joy and his true being. . . . A God who is conceived of in his omnipotence, perfection and infinity at man's expense cannot be the God who is love in the cross of Jesus, who makes a human encounter in order to restore their lost humanity to unhappy and proud divinities.[52]

Moltmann further critiques theism by making a link between traditional theism and atheism, a link dating back to the Enlightenment.[53] In the Enlightenment period, questions of evil and suffering were asked in terms of natural theology, the general governance of the world, much as they are being asked today. The answers at the time of the Enlightenment were that God allows evil without approving of it; that God directs evil in such a way that it must benefit believers; that God sets limits to evil and will completely overcome it at the end of the world in the final fulfilment of the kingdom of God. From this foundation, the German logician, mathematician, and natural philosopher, Gottfried Wilhelm (von) Leibniz (1646–1716) famously

---

50. Moltmann, *History and the Triune God*, 28.

51. Moltmann, *History and the Triune God*, 28. Fretheim says, "It can reasonably be claimed that the idea of a God who suffered with his people had its roots in the Exodus and in the subsequent reflections on the significance of that event." Fretheim, *Suffering of God*, 127.

52. Moltmann, *Crucified God*, 250.

53. Moltmann, *Crucified God*, 247.

formulated his confident understanding of the world we inhabit as the best of all possible worlds.[54]

Leibniz asserted that God allows moral evil for the sake of maintaining human free will, and that God uses physical evil as a punishment to educate and sanctify human beings. This trust in the gracious providence of an Almighty God, indeed in the entire optimistic Enlightenment view of the world, collapsed as an explanation in just one night in 1755 when ten thousand people died in an earthquake in Lisbon, the capital city of Portugal. As Moltmann correctly points out, no reasonable claim could be made that any theological significance was associated with such a terrible event. The catastrophic natural disaster consequently became a catalyst for the end of eighteenth-century confidence in God as the kind and loving ruler of a harmonious world. Moltmann further explains that, in place of the previously confident theism, the Nietzschean announcement of the death of God became from that point the persuasive symbol of a far-reaching theological collapse and for European protest atheism.[55]

Hartshorne too specifically links theism with atheism. In fact, he describes the theistic notion of a God who controls and directs the course of the world and sends suffering, as a kind of "present" to atheists.[56] Theism and its view of the omnipotence of God is a gift to convinced non-believers because many, not least Hartshorne, find that the inner logic of a theistic way of conceiving God leads away from, rather than toward, faith in the loving God described by Christianity. Certainly, for Hartshorne, whenever the implications of traditional theism are really thought through, and when there is no alternate model for belief, atheism will be the inevitable result.[57]

54. Nadler, *Best of All Possible Worlds*, 200.

55. Moltmann, *History and the Triune God*, 28. Friedrich Nietzsche's announcement of the death of God first appeared in *Gay Science* (also translated as *Joyful Pursuit of Knowledge and Understanding*) which was first published in 1882 and appeared again in *Thus Spoke Zarathustra: A Book for All and None* which was first published between 1883 and 1891. Protest Atheism emerged during the time of the Enlightenment based on the view that the coexistence of finite and infinite beings was impossible. It "maintained that the affirmation of God as infinite being necessarily implies the devaluation of finite being, and, in particular, the dehumanizing of man." Masterton, *Atheism and Alienation*, 1. The thinkers who most clearly exemplify this protest against an oppressive God in the name of humanity are Feuerbach, Marx, Nietzsche, and Sartre. Macquarrie, *In Search of Deity*, 49.

56. Hartshorne, "Formally Possible Doctrines," 205.

57. Hartshorne describes the God of traditional theism as a "supreme autocrat." In contrast, the God of panentheism, his alternate model for belief, he describes as "a universal agent of persuasion." Hartshorne, *Divine Relativity*, xvii. Throughout his writing career Hartshorne maintains there is a causal link between traditional theism and atheism. Hartshorne, "Formally Possible Doctrines," 205. See also Tillich, *Courage to Be*, 177–78, as discussed in chapter 1. Tillich also makes a clear link between theism and atheism.

After what he describes as "the unspeakable crime and unutterable suffering"[58] of the Second World War, Moltmann sees in Auschwitz and Hiroshima the end of any attempt to describe God in the theistic terms that see all events as part of the plan or will of God. Moltmann sought a viable alternative to atheism through a panentheistic vision of God that was credible in the face of the evil and suffering of his experience of the twentieth century. No less could be said of Hartshorne, who, in his 1948 preface to the first edition of *The Divine Relativity* (less than three years after the end of the Second World War) wrote:

> In this vision of a deity who is not a supreme autocrat, but a universal agent of 'persuasion,' whose 'power is the worship he inspires' (Whitehead), that is, flows from the intrinsic appeal of his infinitely sensitive and tolerant relativity, by which all things are kept moving in orderly togetherness, we may find help in facing our task of today, the task of contributing to the democratic self-ordering of a world whose members not even the supreme orderer reduces to mere subjects with the sole function of obedience.[59]

Ongoing Jewish and Christian theological discussion, including Hartshorne's process vision above, informed the development of Moltmann's social trinitarian conception of God in the decades after World War II. Three key ideas from this time have particular relevance to a Social Trinity in process, very much a panentheistic model of God. The first is that any justification of God by a just world cannot be answered in a history of injustice and violence, nor yet can such an ideal be given up—for it is identical with the very question of God.[60] From his social and political milieu in the middle of the twentieth century, Moltmann was well aware that the question of God is always to be asked in the light of our experience of the world. It was on the same basis that the process movement deliberated about the justice of God and concluded that such an ideal can only be realistically defended if our understanding of God and the God-world relation, particularly regarding power, changed. As Whitehead contemplated the potential of religion post World War I, just a handful of years after the death of his son Eric in air combat in the last year of that war, he described the religious vision as "our one ground for optimism."[61] Aside from the potential of the goodness

58. Moltmann, *History and the Triune God*, 29.

59. Hartshorne, *Divine Relativity*, xvii.

60. Moltmann, *History and the Triune God*, 29.

61. Whitehead, *Science and the Modern World*, 238.

of God, Whitehead said, "human life is a flash of occasional enjoyments lighting up a mass of pain and misery, a bagatelle of transient experience."[62]

Secondly, it is important to recognize that there can be no theology done *after* a terrible event, such as a natural disaster or a war, which does not take up the theology *within* that terrible event. Hence, any attempt to theologize about the goodness or otherwise of God after Auschwitz, for example, without reference to the theology (the prayers and cries of the victims) *in* that place of evil and suffering, will be fruitless.[63] On this basis, Moltmann maintains:

> God was present where the Shema of Israel and the Lord's Prayer were prayed. As a companion in suffering God gave comfort where humanly there was nothing to hope for in that hell. The inexpressible sufferings in Auschwitz were also the sufferings of God himself.[64]

It is notable that Moltmann's two most celebrated works are those most deeply influenced by the tragedy of the Holocaust: *Theology of Hope* in 1964, and *The Crucified God* in 1972. *The Crucified God is* profoundly incarnational, feeding into notions of God being both with us, and for us. The echo in Moltmann of some of the terminology of process theology, along with the incarnational focus in his earlier works and his development of a doctrine of the Social Trinity, all keenly resonate with Whitehead's early-twentieth-century description of God as "the fellow sufferer who understands."[65]

Very much related to this view of a God who suffers with us, a view shared between process theology and Moltmann, is a third key idea. It is that the question of God which arises out of our suffering can be answered neither theoretically, nor philosophically. The question of God can only be answered personally and experientially. As did Job in the Old Testament, each innocent sufferer in any time, place, or circumstance will rightly and indignantly reject any explanation of why he or she must suffer. The only possible response to the pain of innocent suffering is that God is bound to us in our grief. This response rings true alongside Hartshorne's conception of God as Love, and that love expressed as Divine Sympathy: the feeling of other's feelings.[66] In Moltmann's words:

62. Whitehead, *Science and the Modern World*, 238.

63. Moltmann, *History and the Triune God*, 29.

64. Moltmann, *History and the Triune God*, 29.

65. Whitehead, *Process and Reality*, 351.

66. Hartshorne, *Omnipotence and Other Theological Mistakes*, 31.

> Our true suffering is also his suffering, our sorrow is also his
> sorrow, our pains are also the pains of his love. Only a God in
> whose perfect being there is room for pain can comfort us and
> gain our respect. In our pain we would have to despise an im-
> passible and indifferent being.[67]

A Social Trinity in process, based on Hartshorne's process thought and
Moltmann's view of the Trinity, therefore offers a theodicy grounded in a
movement away from the classical doctrine of the impassibility of God, a
movement particularly evident in theology from the middle of the twentieth century. It embraces the notion of God as the One who suffers with us.
The overall focus of this study provides the rest of the answer, which is that
the only viable response to the problem of evil and suffering in our current
context is intrinsically related to power. A shift in the traditional focus on
the quantity of God's power to the quality of God's power takes us closer to
a solution.

The gift of Hartshorne and the process movement to a workable theodicy is a logical explanation of how it is that God is not omnipotent in the
classical sense, without that explanation being an admission of passivity,
indifference, or feebleness in God. As previously discussed, the usual criticism of process thought is that, in denying that God is all-powerful, it offers
the Christian tradition a weak, irrelevant God. This is far from the case,
as Hartshorne's aforementioned point about God having the maximum
possible power, that which is adequate for cosmic need, makes abundantly
clear. Hartshorne states:

> To say . . . that omnipotence is the power to do anything that
> could be done is to equivocate or talk nonsense. There *could
> not* be a power to 'do anything that could be done.' Some things
> could only be done by local powers; some only by cosmic power.
> The cosmic status of the latter cannot consist in its ability to
> 'do anything.' What then is this cosmic status? Is it power to get
> local agents to do anything they could do, power to make or
> cause them to do it? No, for in spite of what Thomists say, it
> is impossible that our act should be both free and yet a logical
> consequence of a divine action which 'infallibly' produces its
> effect. Power to cause someone to perform by his own choice an
> act precisely defined by the cause is meaningless.[68]

Understanding God as a Social Trinity in process therefore provides
an answer to the theodicy question on very traditional terms. The answer is

---

67. Moltmann, *History and the Triune God*, 29.

68. Hartshorne, *Divine Relativity*, 134–35.

that God is indeed good, but not all-powerful in the classic sense. God does not, in fact God *cannot,* unilaterally will, plan or enact disease, misery, or disaster on individual lives or the life of the world. God, rather, suffers with us in love and solidarity, and seeks to lure us and the world to actualize the good God wills in our free choices.

Here I note again the strong alignment that theologians like Fretheim have with the case I seek to make. In rejecting the classical attribute of omnipotence in God, however, Fretheim and others who hold the position known as Open Theism contend that God has "limited" power, and specifically that God has limited God's *own* power. This point of difference is an important one, for a theodicy based on a limitation of the power of God, whether or not that limitation comes about through divine choice,[69] is much less satisfactory than one built on the understanding of power found in process theology. Firstly, it can be argued that, if God ever did have the power to prevent, subvert, or change the unfolding of evil and suffering in individual lives and the life of the world and chose not to do so, then God's goodness is in serious doubt.[70] Secondly, the idea in Open Theism of God being omnipotent and yet deciding to limit that power, keeps the focus firmly and unhelpfully on the *quantity* of power exercised by God rather than on the *quality* of power exercised.

In contrast, to suggest via process theology that God is not omnipotent is not the same as saying that God has "limited" power, in whatever way that supposed limitation has come about. Hartshorne makes it very clear that God's power is "the kind and degree of power that the world needs as its supreme ordering influence."[71] As discussed in chapter 3, in process thought the power that God exercises is qualitatively different from human power and therefore cannot be properly understood in quantitative terms alone. This is illustrated particularly through the life, death, and resurrection of Jesus who, as both the revelation and exemplar of the true nature of God, exercised power as non-retaliatory, persuasive-suffering love.[72] The

69. Fretheim maintains that the choice to limit power, once made by God, is an irreversible commitment. Fretheim, "Creator, Creature, and Co-Creation," 204–5.

70. This is effectively the argument of Ivan Karamazov to his brother Alyosha in Dostoyevsky's late-nineteenth-century philosophical novel, *Brothers Karamazov.* This famous novel, published as a serial in "The Russian Messenger" from the beginning of 1879 to the end of 1880, joins the ethical debates about God, free will, and morality that were a feature of the late nineteenth century. A key character in the novel, Ivan Karamazov, finds his answer to the problem of evil in protest atheism. Dostoyevsky, *Brothers Karamazov.* It is notable that Whitehead, born in 1861, enters those ethical debates through process philosophy.

71. Hartshorne, *Divine Relativity,* 134.

72. Griffin, "Naturalistic Trinity," 25.

different nature of God's power is both beyond human capacity and has a particular gracious, forgiving, luring quality.

IMAGING GOD IN THE WORLD AND THE CHURCH

In his study of the changing way God has been modelled over the Christian centuries, Jeremy Campbell, alongside social trinitarians and others, supports the contention that the way we image God in relation to the world has and does set a pattern for human behavior.[73] This is particularly so in the exercise of power, and in this context Campbell articulates the consequences of understanding God's relationship to the world as one in which divine power is exercised through domination and control. He says:

> (The) intense monotheism of the kind promoted by Newton, stressing absolute transcendence, and the divine 'difference' helped to secularize the world, with the consequence that the human individual, God's image on earth, sets up as a godlike ruler of his environment, a sure prescription for ecological crisis and much else besides.[74]

Campbell makes a twofold point. Firstly, that the focus of traditional theism on God as the transcendent "other," entirely different from the world, creates a gulf between the sacred and the profane, creator and creation, spirit and matter. This gulf is arguably further emphasized in the deism that emerged in the Enlightenment period of the late seventeenth and eighteenth centuries, influenced by Newton's thought. Both theism and deism set God omnipotently "over" the world directing and controlling everything. Secondly, Campbell highlights how the notion of humans made in the image of God in the first creation account in Genesis provides an invitation, subliminal if not overt, to form our relationships with each other and the natural world based on how we understand God and God's operation in the world. The dire consequences of the acceptance of this invitation by a humanity keen to dominate and control "the other," founded on the perception that this is the nature of God's exercise of power, have readily been identified and critiqued in a range of protest theologies.[75] Environ-

73. Campbell, *Many Faces of God*. Social Trinitarians mentioned in this study include, but are not confined to: Mosser, "Fully Social Trinitarianism"; Hasker, *Metaphysics and the Tri-Personal God*; Plantinga, "Social Trinity and Tritheism"; Moltmann, *Trinity and the Kingdom*.

74. Campbell, *Many Faces of God*, 46.

75. Including, for example, the liberation theology of Gutierrez, *Theology of Liberation*, the feminist theology of Rosemary Reuther, *Sexism and God-Talk*, and the black liberation theology of Cone, *Black Theology and Black Power*, among many others.

mental theologians have roundly criticized our historical interpretation of the Genesis text about the sending forth of the first humans to oversee God's good creation. They point out that we have subjugated and dominated the natural world founded on either theism or deism as a concept of God, rather than exercising the stewardship with and for nature that a relational and panentheistic model of God could invite.[76]

For many, including Moltmann and Hartshorne, the ecological destruction that has been the consequence of humanity setting up as "godlike ruler"[77] over the environment, alongside the application of similar strategies of dominance and control in interpersonal relations, can be directly traced back to monarchical models of God informing the human exercise of power in relationships.[78] To look instead to a Social Trinity in process as a model of God to inform how we use our power is to find that the nature of God is relational, and that "the ultimate power of the universe, which we as religious beings seek to imitate and which we can trust, achieves its purposes through exclusively peaceable means"[79] Understanding the divine as a peaceable and persuasive communion markedly changes conceptions of what it is to operate in the image of God. It provides an entirely different pattern for the exercise of individual and collective power in the world, and in the Church.

As classical theism is the conventional view of God in the history of philosophy and religion and has therefore been a significant shaper of the Christian vision of God, it stands to reason that the leadership, governance style, and order of the Church has been founded on its conventions. These

---

76. McFague, *Models of God* and *Life Abundant*; Moltmann, *God in Creation*. McFague and Moltmann both connect the reality of human damage to the natural environment to the reading of Genesis 1:26–28 that images God as the dominant ruler over all things and calling those in his image to do likewise. The notion of omnipotent control in God has been critiqued by these environmental theologians, and others, for if God is in absolute control of directing world events, then environmental damage and natural disasters that are the result of climate change (for example) become the will of God. If environmental destruction is the will of God, there is no reason or mandate to protect the earth. This view is closely connected with apocalyptic ideas of a personal/anthropomorphic salvation in Christ which takes place in a heavenly afterlife separate from the world of nature.

77. Campbell, *Many Faces of God*, 46.

78. Moltmann points out that theological understandings of humanity "under the rule of God" rarely goes beyond an unhelpful "moral monarchy." Moltmann, *Crucified God*, 237. Hartshorne finds that humans worship power and describes this in terms of "the divorce of the notion of supreme influence from that of supreme sensitivity." He sees this desire for power modelled "in the concepts both of deity and of church and state authority." Hartshorne, *Divine Relativity*, 148.

79. Griffin, "Naturalistic Trinity," 39.

conventions include the divine attributes of omniscience, omnipotence, and omnibenevolence as a minimum. As Moltmann avers, if the doctrine of the Trinity has genuinely had an impact on the shaping of order and authority in the Church, it has been based on a monarchical model of the threefold nature of God with its internal hierarchical overtones. On Moltmann's view, a monarchical model of God as Trinity denies the reality of three co-equal, co-eternal persons. It "puts the divine lordship before the Trinity and uses the 'doctrine of the Trinity' to secure and interpret the divine subjectivity in that lordship." This makes for a trinitarian hierarchy where a divine person can be understood to be subject to, or less than, another.[80]

Denominations that have a priesthood and an episcopacy, as do the Orthodox, the Roman Catholic, and the Anglican Church, are undeniably "wedded to a strong hierarchical pattern of authority and ministry."[81] It is nevertheless true that the word "hierarchy" refers more to "order" than to anything else. As there is a required order in the governance of human affairs in both the secular and the religious domain, a simplistic and dismissive critique of the tiered ordering to which "hierarchy" refers is unwarranted. Ideas of sweeping away entirely negative hierarchies in favor of an entirely positive utopian equality, for example, promotes an uncritical and unhelpful dichotomy that does not honor ongoing efforts in the church to find cooperative ways of ministering together.[82] Moltmann has been accused of feeding this kind of gulf between notions of tiered order and egalitarianism in church and society due to his insistence that the hierarchical parallels of Father-Son in the Trinity, God-world, heaven-earth, soul-body, man-woman must be dissolved and reanimated in terms of mutuality and perichoresis.[83] Likewise, Hartshorne's social conception of God has been criticized for

80. Moltmann, *Trinity and the Kingdom*, 143–44.

81. Pickard, *Theological Foundations*, 226.

82. Pickard, in reference to Romans 12 and 1 Corinthians 1:12, suggests that most of Paul's letters attempt to smooth conflict in the official ministry structures of the early churches. He questions whether the apostle would have written at length to the church at Rome about shared ministry and the diversity of gifts for ministry and mission unless there was a problem in the body of Christ regarding collaboration and teamwork in undertaking the shared work of the gospel. Pickard is quite clear that "the Church has always aspired to a truly collaborative approach to its mission and its best theology has undergirded it. But the painful reality has been that teamwork has been a matter we have struggled with. Grace and forgiveness seem to be the essential prerequisites. And a good dose of longsuffering and occasional bouts of prophetic activity." Pickard, *Theological Foundations*, 227.

83. Moltmann, *Trinity and the Kingdom*, 127. Coakley is of the view that Moltmann is unnecessarily wary of notions of hierarchy. She is unconvinced that all meanings of the word are incompatible with the modern feminist agenda and so where hierarchy refers to order in an organizational sense, Coakley sees no problem. In her view the

eschewing the monarchical hierarchy that has informed traditional theistic models of God in favor of panentheism. For him, as previously discussed, the attributes of God are types of social relationship in which God is both supreme yet indebted to all, absolute yet related to all.[84] Hartshorne certainly speaks to the relationality of all things, but not necessarily to the simple, non-ordered equivalence of all things.

Grounded as it is in the thinking of Moltmann and Hartshorne, a Social Trinity in process can accurately be described as a non-hierarchical model of God, but there is no promotion of a superficial or uncritical equality in church or society based on that model. Inherent in the model, however, is a challenge to what Moltmann calls "patriarchal talk of God and the patriarchal oppression of women deposited in the centuries of historical Christianity."[85] This leads to an active quieting of the "masculine sexist language" that assumes Father first, Son second, Spirit third in an hierarchical Trinity, in favor of giving voice to the "Christian messianic language" of mutual deference and profound equality that is found between people living as the image of a Triune God.[86] A Social Trinity in process can therefore readily be viewed as a protest theology that seeks to liberate the ministry of the church from its patterning over centuries by a masculine pyramid type understanding of God.[87] Hartshorne finds that continued adherence to such monarchical and male-dominated models of ministry in the church is evidence of an "unwarranted . . . metaphysical snobbery toward relativity" in God.[88] He makes his point thus:

---

problem begins with worldly gendered subordination. Despite her defense of hierarchy as an idea that can make sense in the human realm, Coakley stridently resists the notion of hierarchy in the Godhead. She insists that when humans come into authentic relationship with the God in Trinity through the Holy Spirit their ideas and orders of hierarchy change. She does not believe that humans are imitating God in this, nor is she in favor of Social Trinitarianism. On her view, it is rather that humans are being transformed by ecstatic participation in the Spirit. She believes this works against human versions of hierarchy that justify themselves with an incorrect patriarchal trinitarian theology in the world or in the church. In recognizing this, however, Coakley tacitly acknowledges that understandings of the relation of three persons of God the Holy Trinity, whether they are correct or not, can and do influence human social behavior, indeed that people model themselves and their relationships on their notion of the highest power. Coakley, *God, Sexuality, and the Self*, 319–21.

84. Hartshorne, *Divine Relativity*, 1–115.

85. Moltmann, *History and the Triune God*, 16.

86. Moltmann, *History and the Triune God*, 16.

87. This is what Coakley refers to as the "three men" analogy. Coakley, *Powers and Submissions*, 129.

88. Hartshorne, *Divine Relativity*, 50.

This almost slavish (doubtless it would be too much to say knavish) worship of mere absoluteness, independence, and one-sided activity or power, this transcendentalized admiration of politico-ecclesiastical tyranny, the ideal of which is to act on all while avoiding reaction from them, this spiritual blindness and false report upon experience is . . . the chief source of the metaphysical paradoxes of which so much has been heard. Just as the loyal Roman Catholic (and, according to official statements, everyone in an overwhelmingly Catholic State), unless high in the hierarchy, can have little hope either of influencing or of evading papal decrees, so, and in a more strict sense, there is, according to the old theology, no hope either of influencing or of evading divine decrees. The politically, and I am confident, theologically, sounder principle is rather this, that he who is most adequately influenced by all may most appropriately exert influence upon all. The best ruler is an intermediary in the universal interaction, able to moderate and harmonize action because all that is done is done also to him, whose reaction to this action absorbs and transmutes all influences into a counterinfluence, integrative and harmonizing in tendency, discouraging excessive factors and encouraging insufficient ones.[89]

The potential pattern for ecclesiology that Hartshorne lays out is based in an understanding that God rules as a mediator for the interactions of the universe; an understanding that God is influenced by all and so is able then to exert influence upon all; an understanding that God works to integrate and harmonize rather than to isolate and regularize. This is the understanding that underpins the notion of God as Social Trinity in process as described in chapter 4. If, as I contend in that chapter and throughout this book, our relationships in world and church have been based in the way we have understood God over the centuries, to change our thinking about God's manner of existence in accord with Hartshorne and Moltmann and a fully relational model of God will call for an associated change to our way of being in the church.

The social trinitarian, John D. Zizioulas, affirms both the reality and desirability of individual and church seeking to become an image of the way in which God exists. In his *Being as Communion,* he says:

The Church is not simply an institution. She is a 'mode of existence,' *a way of being...* In the first place, ecclesial being is bound to the very being of God. From the fact that a human being is a member of the Church, he becomes an 'image of God,' he exists

89. Hartshorne, *Divine Relativity*, 50.

as God himself exists, he takes on God's 'way of being.' This way of being is not a moral attainment, something that man *accomplishes*. It is a way of *relationship* with the world, with other people and with God, an event of *communion*. . . . However, for the Church to present this way of existence, she must herself be an image of the way in which God exists. Her entire structure, her ministries etc. must express this way of existence.[90]

In keeping with his relational understanding of God, when it comes to order in the church, Zizioulas finds that the church is hierarchical only in as much as the Holy Trinity is hierarchical. He makes this claim based on the notion of specificity of relationship in the Trinity that was first suggested by Gregory of Nazianzus in the fourth century. This idea of Trinitarian specificity ensures that the Son has everything in common with the Father and the Spirit except being Father or Spirit and the Spirit possesses everything the Father and the Son possess except being Father or Son.[91] Furthermore, Zizioulas points out, if the church is to be a genuine reflection of the love of God in the world, then ideally its internal order and authority is born out of relationship rather than power.[92] This helps with the realization that when hierarchical leadership or governance structures in the church do become unhealthy and reflect negative structural relations more than positive ones, it is due to forgetting the demands of relationship and becoming caught up in a competition for power.

The threefold order of ministry in the Anglican Church, that of bishops, priests, and deacons, was always intended to be grounded in relationship rather than focused on power. Bishops have long been referred to as "the first among equals," denoting their formal equality with other members of the clergy while recognizing that bishops hold more responsibility and power.[93] Despite a formal equality between those in holy orders, and between those in holy orders and the laity, the outworking of this ideal over centuries has been markedly inequitable. This is particularly true of the experience of many lay people who find they have neither the power nor prestige of the ordained within the church.[94] Stephen Pickard, in *Theological*

90. Zizioulas, *Being as Communion*, 15. Zizioulas is generally understood to be a social trinitarian alongside Moltmann.

91. Zizioulas, *Being as Communion*, 223.

92. Zizioulas, *Being as Communion*, 224.

93. "First among Equals," lines 1–3.

94. From her long experience as a leading lay person involved in the governance of the Anglican Church, Porter claims: "Lay people and ordinary clergy are too often dominated by those in power over them. This domination can be as simple as a minister deciding arbitrarily to change the worship pattern or music in his/her congregation, or

Foundations for Collaborative Ministry, is clear that this disparity is due in no small way to the language that surrounds ordination. For Pickard:

> The language of 'removal from', 'set apart' and 'distance' has never been far away from the traditional construals of those in orders. It generates a false dichotomy between those who inhabit orders and the people of God. To be in orders is to be in a particular place within the ecclesia; to be related to others in a particular and quite specific way.[95]

Pickard suggests that the false dichotomy in the church between those who are ordained and those who are lay can be avoided by a proper focus on baptism. He says that baptism is the "fundamental ordering,"[96] joining Zizioulas in the view that there is no such thing as "non-ordained" people in the church, for the act of baptism confers both membership and forms a specific order in the eucharistic community.[97] Pickard finds in this wider context of the order of the laity an understanding of ordination that establishes a new set of relationships within the body of Christ. As far as Pickard is concerned, ordination therefore has "unmistakable ontological weight."[98] He says:

> Those in orders are different people after ordination by virtue of the new ways in which they will be called to exercise responsibilities and function in relation to the wider body of Christ. Ontology and function are both relevant but only in the context of the community as well as the individual admitted to orders. This discussion points to what may be termed a relational ontology of orders.[99]

Pickard claims that a relational ontology of orders ought to be well established in the church due to the development of both Trinitarian theology and the science of emergence during the twentieth century. He makes a clear distinction between a hierarchy based on power exercised over lower levels, and an emergent hierarchy, in which leadership comes from lower

---

a bishop blocking a priest from securing a particular appointment. Bishops and clergy continue to exercise enormous power, much of it in ways that defy accountability and in what would appear to outsiders as trivial parochial matters. To insiders who experience this power as a form of oppression, these issues are symbolically very important." Porter, *Sex, Power and the Clergy,* 8–9.

95. Pickard, *Theological Foundations,* 161.

96. Pickard, *Theological Foundations,* 161.

97. Pickard, *Theological Foundations,* 161; Zizioulas, *Being as Communion,* 216.

98. Pickard, *Theological Foundations,* 161.

99. Pickard, *Theological Foundations,* 161.

levels, belongs to them, and does not set itself apart from them. In this Pickard indicates how compatible is his thinking with an understanding of God as a Social Trinity in process, at once fully trinitarian and cognizant of the scientific implication of an emerging universe—a relational model of God. He points to the "important work on ministry in relation to the doctrine of the Trinity and an evident concern to redevelop a theology of ministry and break the prevailing non-relational, excessively hierarchical patterns of ministry."[100] Pickard finds, however, that a robust trinitarianism embedded in an emergent worldview has not yet fully borne fruit in the orders of the Christian Church.[101]

In this regard, the current impossibility in the Roman Catholic Church and the Orthodox Church of women being ordained into holy orders, the relative recency with which ordained women have become part of the structures of other denominations, and the ambiguity about the place of homosexual or gender diverse clergy, with or without partners, in a range of denominations, speaks volumes. It is a reality that paints a clear picture of the unevenness of the distribution of power within the contemporary church. Muriel Porter, an Australian lay Anglican, notes that Christian denominations seldom acknowledge the difficulties and inconsistencies of their internal power dynamics, claiming that each institution remains "hierarchical," "profoundly patriarchal," and "built on almost feudal power structures." She further maintains that "power, its use and abuse, is a major theological issue in the formal ministry structures of all the churches."[102] As Porter explains:

> Hierarchical power is enshrined most obviously in the Catholic Church, under the worldwide control of one man, the Pope, and the Vatican bureaucracy. But the Anglican Church, despite its broader, nationally based representative governance structure of elected synods, is more subject to control by bishops and clergy than even most Anglicans realise. The Uniting Church, though it has no bishops and its governance by elected committees seems perfectly democratic, nevertheless has a subtle

---

100. Pickard, *Theological Foundations*, 162. Pickard notes that Zizioulas helpfully forged a new frontier regarding ministry with his *Being as Communion*, recovering the Trinitarian ontology as the basis for personhood; but that the downside of his work was a reinforcing of a traditional hierarchical notion of holy orders populated by men. He sees Robin Greenwood's *Transforming Priesthood* as a determined effort to follow the implications of Trinitarian theology into ministry.

101. Pickard, *Theological Foundations*, 162.

102. Porter, *Sex, Power, Clergy*, 8.

power structure than can be manipulated to suppress dissent and complaint.[103]

Unfettered clerical power and a lack of accountability is, according to Porter, a key factor in the pervasive sexual abuse and cover-up that has come to light in the worldwide church in recent decades. Porter insists that the overtly hierarchical and patriarchal nature of churches, especially the episcopally led Anglican and Catholic Churches, readily attracts people to the ministry who need to create for themselves a substantial identity. This need includes the use of power and control over others to achieve their goal. She suggests that clergy who bully their congregations are more common than most people imagine, and that there are few institutions where power is as unrestrained and unaccountable as the church.[104] Citing the American Jesuit theologian James F. Keenan, Porter agrees with his claims that abusive church power has supported a sexual abuse crisis. He describes certain actions of bishops, including moving offending priests from parish to parish, denouncing parents who made accusations of abuse against priests, and blaming the media for a frenzied bias against the church, as "acts of power." Porter points to Keenan's 11 May 2002 piece in *The Tablet*, noting his view that the great task that the church must address is neither sexual morality nor chastity, but power:

> We need to know that we have more power than we realize and that, as some of us move up the hierarchical ladder, we grow exponentially in power. And as we grow in power we grow in the capacity to abuse power. . . . We in the priesthood, from seminarians to the Pope himself, need to learn more about power, about sharing power and about accountability in the exercise of power.[105]

The systems of the institutional church have led to significant abuses of power over a long period of time. In Australia this is sadly borne witness to in the Royal Commission into Institutional Responses to Child Sexual Abuse.[106] The Commission has exposed some of the power structures which

103. Porter, *Sex, Power, Clergy*, 8.

104. Porter, *Sex, Power, Clergy*, 118.

105. Keenan in Porter, *Sex, Power, Clergy*, 118.

106. The Royal Commission into Institutional Responses to Child Sexual Abuse was established in 2013 by the Australian government to inquire into and report upon responses by institutions to instances and allegations of child sexual abuse in Australia, in accordance with the Royal Commissions Act 1902. The commission examined the history of abuse in educational and state institutions, sporting and youth organizations, and religious groups. The final report of the Commission was made public on 15 December 2017.

have enabled individuals to commodify children for their sexual gratification and allowed other individuals and church organizations to cover up the extent and circumstances of much of the abuse. Where the focus has been on the church and its schools, orphanages and hospitals, the power granted to priests and bishops, in particular, has been under scrutiny. The potential of unaccountable power to support and enable negligence in duty of care at best, and at worst to encourage flagrant and active abuses against the vulnerable, has been documented at the national level. This documentation does not include abuse which goes beyond a physical nature—emotional and spiritual abuse.

Some fifteen years after Porter wrote *Sex, Power and the Clergy*, having traced the response of the church to instances of sexual abuse by clergy for close to two decades, she published *The New Scapegoats: The Clergy Victims of the Anglican Church Sexual Abuse Crisis*. The focus of *The New Scapegoats* is on the internal measures taken by the Anglican Church in Australia to control and regulate the lives of current clergy. Porter disagrees with Bishop Tom Frame, who declared in his study of Australian Anglicanism that the adoption of the Faithfulness in Service code of conduct "has removed much of the ambiguity about what is and isn't acceptable conduct among Christian leaders and highlighted the consequences of poor pastoral practice."[107] She claims that the code is a harsh new restriction on the lives of clerics, and that the professional standards processes developed in recent years have made clergy vulnerable to intrusive and blaming behaviors by a church seeking to rebuild its severely damaged reputation at their expense. Porter's contention is essentially that the power that the institutional church wields, the same power that was previously used against victims of clergy abuse and their families to protect the standing of the church, has now been turned inward and used against the clergy. She maintains that "the Anglican Church is going to extraordinary lengths to make individual clergy pay the price for the church's good name, making the clergy the scapegoats forced to bear the church's shame."[108] This is a very interesting and telling claim in that, if Porter's assertion is correct, the church is continuing to use the same patriarchal, hierarchical and coercive power tactics in its contemporary internal dealings that it has over time used in the world.

107. Frame, *Anglicans in Australia*, 169. Faithfulness in Service is a National Code for Personal Behaviour and the Practice of Pastoral Ministry by Clergy and Church Workers, overseen by and copyrighted to The Anglican Church of Australia Trust Corporation 2006–2017. It has been adopted by the majority of Anglican Dioceses in Australia.

108. Porter, *New Scapegoats*, 6.

In her study on sexuality, gender, and the human quest for God, Sarah Coakley finds it noteworthy that, even as both the Catholic and Anglican Churches seek to respond to sexual misconduct in the church, there is very little theology being undertaken around the fundamental issue of desire and its outworking in the lives of clergy, church workers, and Christians in general.[109] She points out that a prominent feature of both the Roman Catholic and Anglican response to the sexual abuse crisis has been a major focus of attention on same-sex relationships, whether of a paedophilic, ephebophilic, or mature homosexual nature. Coakley states:

> It is as if, by comparison, no crisis at all has afflicted the *heterosexual* world *vis a vis* church life and what we might call the general 'economy of desire'. But anyone surveying the cultural and political scene with a dispassionate eye would be forced to come to other conclusions.[110]

The church and Western culture encode the worst and the best in the Christian tradition, according to Coakley. She mentions abuse, denial, duplicity, patriarchal dominance, and the arrogant ignoring of gay and feminist voices as the worst. Alongside this, she refers to a longing for sexual justice, for family and social stability, for a balance between pleasure and commitment, and for realism about sexual weakness leading to a standard of forgiveness worthy of Jesus "law of love" as the best.[111] Coakley believes that our age is in a crisis of erotic faithfulness. She concedes this is a far from popular reflection in the light of our current salacious obsession with homosexuality and the diversion it provides from heterosexual failures in what she calls "ascetic self-examination."[112]

Coakley proposes a new asceticism as the answer to the sexual abuse, homophobia, and patriarchal dominance that many still see as pervasive in the Church. Each one is a misuse of power. She acknowledges that her solution will meet with resounding skepticism unless we are able to identify and acknowledge the forms of authoritarianism, based on monarchical models of God as Trinity, that sustained an earlier, counterfeit asceticism.[113]

---

109. Coakley, *New Asceticism*, 31.

110. Coakley, *New Asceticism*, 36.

111. Coakley, *New Asceticism*, 3.

112. Coakley, *New Asceticism*, 38.

113. Coakley, *New Asceticism*, 25. It is notable that Hartshorne, after listing the negative effects of the worship of power in the church, next defines the type of counterfeit asceticism Coakley seeks to transform. He describes it as "the failure to genuinely synthesize 'physical' and 'spiritual' values, as shown above all in the failure of practically all the churches to do justice to the meaning and problems of marriage." Hartshorne, *Divine Relativity*, 149.

It is here that understanding God as a Social Trinity in process gains some real traction in concert with Coakley's notion of transformed desire, for a Trinity modelled through the lens of process theology does not by definition support any practice of living that is enacted in response to domination and punitive measures. Instead, it calls for Spirit-led integration and divine exchange, and a respect for the genuine otherness of the other.

Looking back into the history of Christian practice and comparing the sixth century *Rule of Saint Benedict* with the *Paedagogos* ("The Instructor") written by Clement of Alexandria around the third century, Coakley makes a note-worthy point about genuine self-discipline in the lives of both the clergy and the laity. Her point is that an invitational, life-long, and loving practice like that of Benedict can re-modulate Christian beliefs beneficially, whereas the legalistic and extrinsic commands of Clement will merely provide an ethical touchstone for distinguishing appropriate behavior from inappropriate without any thought of spiritual re-modulation.[114] Fascinatingly, this picks up the same theme as that of Porter in her critique of the Anglican Church in Australia's attempt to repair the reputation of the church in the wake of the sexual abuse crisis. Porter says:

> Perhaps one of the most damaging long-term effects of the Anglican Church's creation of far-reaching controls on clergy behaviour is the imposition of a new mandated Puritanism. While Anglican clergy have always been expected to live up to an idea of sexual morality . . . now any failure to live up to the narrowest interpretations of that standard can see them in real danger of losing their licence to officiate, either for some years or permanently, or even being threatened with deposition from Holy Orders.[115]

In this reference to the current experience of Anglican clergy, along with Licensed Lay Ministers who are subject to the same code of conduct, it seems that Porter makes a very similar appeal to that of Coakley. It is that the church must prioritize attending to the theology of desire generally, and to human sexuality particularly, rather than simply pronouncing commands for living that have little to offer an ongoing and transformative holiness. Attendant to this plea is the recognition that no understanding of God, no renewed trinitarian spirituality, can ever sidestep the profound issue of the nature of sexual desire. It is a divisive issue in contemporary church life and is fundamentally connected with equally conflicted gender

114. Coakley, *New Asceticism*, 115.

115. Porter, *New Scapegoats*, 37.

themes, ideas about women's roles and women's capacity for empowerment, and for professional equality.[116]

Coakley says it is therefore an important task to rethread the strands of inherited tradition in such a way that enacted sexual desire and desire for God are no longer seen in mutual enmity, or as disjunctive alternatives, where the non-celibate woman or the homosexual is cast in the role of the one who blocks attainment of the divine goal. Further, and importantly for this study, she finds that a renewed trinitarian vision of divine desire is required to provide the guiding framework for a renewed theology of human sexuality. Indeed, she finds that godly sexual relations will be grounded in, and *in some way* correspond to the divine relations of Trinity.[117] In her clarity around the idea that the difficulties the church faces with human sexuality can only be met if the Trinity provides the guiding framework, Coakley appears close to describing the divine relations of the Trinity as a model for our relationships, something in the manner of a Social Trinity in process.

Two key elements of a Social Trinity in process, the Trinity understood as a pattern for our relations and the idea of non-coercive shared power, have come together in the development of models of ministry and a transformed understanding of priesthood in parts of the Anglican Church. In his *Transforming Priesthood*, Robin Greenwood grounds this power sharing in a relational trinitarian understanding of God. On his view, it is essential to the good purposes of God for the universe that all relationships echo the trinitarian pattern, and that the church is called to prepare the way for godly relationships in the world and human society. He therefore finds that the ministerial arrangements of the church must echo the trinitarian relationships of loving communion.[118]

A model of ministry based on these ideas was begun to be explored in the Anglican Diocese of Tasmania in 1998. Known as Enabler Supported Ministry, in this way of being the church local people are called to form a collaborative leadership team in a parish or church community, which is supported by an Enabler. The Enabler takes on the responsibility of carrying forward the mission and ministry of the parish or church, along with the whole community of faith.[119] Although it could be argued in pragmatic

---

116. Coakley, *New Asceticism*, 86–87.

117. Coakley, *New Asceticism*, 87.

118. Greenwood, *Transforming Priesthood*, 87.

119. Collins et al., *Reinventing Church*, 15. "An Enabler is a clergy person (usually stipendiary) appointed by a Bishop to be a companion to a parish (or group of parishes) as it develops this way of being church. Regular visits to the parish to encourage, train, mentor and evaluate their mission and ministry are part of the Enablers role. . . . The Enabler is a permanent part of this way of being church. In addition to the role above,

terms that the impetus for embracing a very different way of going about Anglican parish ministry in Tasmania was based on rural decline and the inability to financially sustain the stipended parish priest model, a key factor in the theological underpinnings of Enabler Supported Ministry is the sharing of power. For, as was noted by Vincent Donovan, a Roman Catholic missionary to East Africa, in the parish priest model regnant in the Anglican and the Roman Catholic Church world-wide, power remains very much the preserve of the ordained. Donovan claims that the standard parish model "condense(s) all the hope and dignity and power and glory of Christianity into the narrow confines of a single individual," namely the priest.[120] He makes clear that skewing power towards the clergy is unhealthy and requires a major re-think of the meaning of mission and ministry—particularly if the church is to properly enable vigorous and self-sustaining local Christian communities.[121]

In *Reinventing Church,* James Collins tells the stories of four rural Anglican parishes in Tasmania that rose to the challenge of re-thinking their mission and ministry through the adoption of Enabler Supported Ministry.[122] Collins, who was the Enabler to these parishes, explains two key changes engendered through this model of ministry, both very much to do with broadening the distribution of power:

> First, ESM (Enabler Supported Ministry) shapes the operation of power within the parishes. There has been a marked democratisation in the decision making process. This has resulted in a broader level of participation across the whole parish by parishioners, and also by the wider community as each of the parishes has actively sought to engage with their local communities. In other words, there has been a change from one person, the priest, exercising enormous power within that parish to that power being dispersed throughout the whole parish and,

---

he or she provides a link with the diocese and with other parishes." Collins et al., *Reinventing Church,* 201.

120. Donovan, *Christianity Rediscovered,* 153. Donovan asks, "Isn't the starting point community rather than individual? And it certainly has nothing to do with organization. All Christians, as members of a community, are priests in the true sense of the word. The ministerial priest, by his ordination, does not become a better or holier man for it. He merely becomes essentially a community man, a servant of the community, a sign of the unity of that community, a focal point for that unity." Donovan, *Christianity Rediscovered,* 91.

121. Donovan, *Christianity Rediscovered,* 99.

122. "Enabler Supported Ministry is known in other dioceses as total ministry, mutual ministry, local collaborative ministry, every member ministry, ministry of the baptised and ministering community." Collins et al., *Reinventing Church,* 199.

indeed, shared with the wider community. Second, ESM changes gender dynamics. There has been a significant reorientation
from a male dominated environment within the parishes where
men held most, if not all, of the positions of power to a situation where power is shared equally by all, regardless of age and
gender. Women now participate fully in all aspects of the life of
the parishes and have a voice at all levels of decision making.[123]

In the Enabler Supported Ministry model, the power inherent in the
various roles and ministries of a local church is intentionally exercised in the
understanding that any authority establishes itself as a demand of relationship. This is very much in keeping with Zizioulas' view, discussed earlier,
that the only valid hierarchy in the church, local or universal, is modelled in
the mutual deference of the persons of the Trinity, and based on the require-
ments of relationship in community, rather than simply on power.[124] In this
ecclesiology, order is neither provided nor imposed by a single person or
group permanently set over another, but by the constantly shifting movement in the relationship of the personal participants. This is *perichoresis*
in action. Rather than the church insisting on permanent subordinations
within its life, revealing a refusal to allow the mystery of the Trinity to be
directly related to ecclesiastical concept, the church can operate as a loving *perichoretic* community. It will do this through a self-ordering process
where individual persons will fulfil unique and necessary roles, yet the total
ordering is achieved without any one person being in a permanently subordinate position to another.[125]

A feature of Enabler Supported Ministry that has been contentious
for some is the role of the Ordained Local Minister, who is a member of a
Local Ministry Support Team.[126] An Ordained Local Minister is responsible
for the aspects of the ministry of the local church which require ordination,
such as presiding at the Eucharist or pronouncing absolution or blessing. If
viewed only through the lens of a traditional expectation of Anglican parish ministry, the notion of local ordination and a priest who shares in the
ministry of the church alongside others might appear to be a lesser version

123. Collins et al., *Reinventing Church*, 10–11.

124. Zizioulas, *Being as Communion*, 223–24.

125. Greenwood, *Transforming Priesthood*, 152.

126. "A Local Ministry Support Team (LMST/the Team) is a group of baptised
people identified and called by the local church to lead them in Enabler Supported
Ministry. The Team is made up of people with spiritual maturity and gifts of leadership.
The Team does not undertake all of the ministry. Rather it encourages and enables all
members to discover and use their own particular gifts for ministry in the life and mission of the church." Collins et al., *Reinventing Church*, 200.

of priestly ministry. If a comparison was to be made, however, it could only be between the ministry of an entire Local Ministry Support Team with the Enabler, and the ministry of a stand-alone parish priest, for the same ministry is in one case shared while in another case individual.[127]

In this context, Greenwood suggests that the lens of traditional expectation for Anglican parish ministry is, in fact, distorted. He points out that sharing in the ministry of the people of God, rather than being a new idea specific to parishes where local ordination and overtly collaborative models of ministry feature, is a key characteristic of what it is (or should be) to be ordained in the church:

> Each member of the Church, whatever their particular ministry, is at heart a disciple of Jesus Christ through the work of the Spirit. Alert to the significance of their baptismal commitment and gift, church members share a common responsibility and commissioning to witness to God's love. To root a conceptuality of ordination in an eschatological-trinitarian ecclesiology, mirroring the ontology and the passionate cause of God, provides a coherent path towards the goal of the modern Church of recognising all ministries as equally representative of that of Christ in the character and task of the Church. Ordained ministers should be encouraged to understand the nature of their vital and unique authority in terms of relatedness. They have no existence outside of a relationship with their fellow members of the baptised community; their own uniqueness is created and sustained within relationships of mutuality with their fellow ordained ministers.[128]

127. Enabler Supported Ministry parishes are encouraged to call at least two people into Ordained Local Ministry. Once ordained, they are priests in the Church of God but can only function in the parish in which they were called. Such clergy always exercise their ministry as part of the Team. Collins et al., *Reinventing Church*, 200.

128. Greenwood, *Transforming Priesthood*, 151–52. Donovan shares Greenwood's view, insisting that "no priest can exist without a community—cannot exist and live and work in a meaningful, functional, realistic way—as priest, that is." Donovan, *Christianity Rediscovered*, 151. Pickard couches the same idea in terms of "belonging to each other," saying: "In the world wide Anglican communion we have lost sight of this truth that we belong to each other . . . our ministry is tied up with the ministry of another's. The ministries are bound together. The ministries we exercise can only be gospel ministries as they are in relation to others. It is as if the ministries give life to each other. They animate each other. Furthermore the ministry I exercise only has life as it belongs to others. Not ownership of ministries but truly shared visions of ministry for the common good. And this includes representative leadership." Pickard, *Theological Foundations*, 228–29.

For Greenwood, to understand that all ordained ministry is inseparably interconnected with the life of the whole baptized church membership is to properly understand the *Communio Sanctorum*. In its medieval
and technical sense, the *Communio Sanctorum* refers to participants in the
sacraments; in its proper sense it means a communion of friends, a fellowship of believers. On this basis, Greenwood rightly maintains that there is
nothing that could be said of deacon, priest, or bishop in any setting that is
not true in some way of the whole church.[129] Furthermore, rather than alone
associating the ministry of the ordained with that of Christ, as received
theology has commonly done, Greenwood affirms that the ministry of the
entire church is associated with the ministry of Christ through the Holy
Spirit. In its worship, and in the shape of its relatedness, the local church is
both constituted by and mirrors the trinitarian communion. Separately and
together, therefore, all members are "ministers" invited and equipped by
their mutual recognition of one another as equal participants in the mission
of God.[130] In this, Greenwood and proponents of collaborative models of
ministry look particularly to the "body of Christ" metaphor in 1 Corinthians 12. The Apostle Paul's notion of varieties of gifts in the one Spirit,
varieties of ways of serving the same Lord, and varieties of activities with the
same God activating all of them for the common good, supports the idea of
every member ministry.[131] "For in the one Spirit we were all baptized into
one body—Jews or Greeks, slaves or free—and we were all made to drink of
the one Spirit."[132]

A perhaps surprising contributor to the relational and power sharing
trinitarian ecclesiology that underpins contemporary collaborative ministry models in the Anglican Church is a moderate high church missionary
to North China, Roland Allen. He also looks to the teaching of the Apostle
Paul, referencing Paul's missionary methods in the New Testament. Allen
criticizes the church in the early twentieth century for its belief that ecclesial authority should be the prerogative of a tiny minority. At its heart, his
criticism is all about a refusal to share power.[133] Allen questions the conventional wisdom of only selecting and training for ministry those who can
pass stringent academic tests, claiming that the ministry of the church needs
a wide range of people and abilities. The descriptive phrases Allen uses indicate both his commitment to genuine local ministry and his frustration

129. Greenwood, *Transforming Priesthood*, 141.

130. Greenwood, *Transforming Priesthood*, 142.

131. 1 Corinthians 12:4–7 (NRSV)

132. 1 Corinthians 12:13 (NRSV)

133. Greenwood, *Transforming Priesthood*, 12–13.

at the imposition of leaders from beyond the local context. He says, "They come, as it were, from outside. . . . The natural leaders are silenced. . . . There is no opportunity for the church to find its prophets. . . . Nor for the prophets to find themselves . . ."[134] Allen maintains that a far better way is to be found in teaching and enabling self-supporting local leaders to exercise the ministries that make a church functional, providing leadership and direction from outside the local context occasionally as needed—just as Paul did. Allen explains his vision thus:

> Four things . . . St Paul deemed necessary for the establishment of his churches, and only four. A tradition or elementary Creed, the Sacraments of Baptism and the Holy Communion, Orders, and the Holy Scriptures. He trained his converts in the simplest and most practical form. He delivered these to them. He exercised them as a body in the understanding and practice of them, and he left them to work them out for themselves as a body whilst he himself went on with his own special work. He was ready at any moment to encourage or direct them by messengers, by letters, or by personal visits, as they needed direction or encouragement; but he neither desired, nor attempted, to stay with them, or to establish his ministers among them to do for them what he was determined that they must learn to do for themselves.[135]

Enabler Supported Ministry is informed by Allen's vision of church, and patterned on relational understandings of God, especially social trinitarianism. This is reflected in its emphasis on collegial mutuality and power sharing in ministry, rather than on the authoritarianism which is inherent in monarchical models of the Trinity. These characteristics describe a model of church in which those exercising their ministry within their parish, whether they be members of the Local Ministry Support Team or parishioners, are committed to "journeying with" rather than the "directing of" other people within and beyond the parish.[136] This links very closely with Whitehead's notion of God as the companion we imitate,[137] and so can also be a vehicle

---

134. Allen, *Missionary Methods*, 106.

135. Allen, *Missionary Methods*, 107. Donovan refers to Allen's view of the responsibility of any Christian community for its own life and mission in his reflection on his experience with the Masai people. Donovan's description of the emergence of self-supporting, local Christian leadership (including the one or ones to be ordained) in a Masai community puts Allen's theory into practice. Donovan, *Christianity Rediscovered*, 144–45.

136. Collins et al., *Reinventing Church*, 151.

137. Whitehead, *Religion in the Making*, 40.

for a process vision of the God who enters fully into the joys and sufferings of the journey to inform the ministry and mission of the Church.

These key characteristics of Enabler Supported Ministry can, nevertheless, also be something of an Achilles' heel. As notions of companioning and power sharing in ministry are still counter-intuitive in the church, they can be the cause of misunderstanding and conflict. As Pickard points out:

> It is not unusual for churches to reach agreement on a range of ministry matters: the ministry of the whole people of God; the nature of the Church as a community in which there are a variety of gifts and graces; the importance of ministerial offices amidst a growing diversity of other ministries. . . . Notwithstanding the consensus reached, both formal and informal . . . the unresolved tensions between the ministries remain embedded in the discourse.[138]

These tensions can lead to conflict between clergy and laity, and then to loss of a healthy sense of authority and direction in communities of faith engaged in collaborative ministry. Pickard says that, in parishes that have formerly appealed to a strong christological basis for the legitimization of office and authority, the tendency can be to sidestep the collaborative model and effectively reassert the tradition of clerical leadership. Parishes that have looked to the gifts of the Spirit in the body of Christ as a rationale for sharing ministry tend to do better for longer but may eventually lose momentum and energy for ministry.[139] Pickard suggests that such difficulties surrounding the healthy living out of collaborative ministry models could begin to be addressed over time by locating the ministry of the church in a doctrine of creation. He says:

> Far from undermining the particularity of ecclesial ministries (for example, those in orders) such an approach widens the reach for which such orders have responsibility. It also makes it abundantly clear that the creative and redeeming work of God is much wider than a narrow churchy focus. The baptised are called, in their life, vocation and work, to follow the creative and reconciling work of God and offer their gifts and talents accordingly.[140]

138. Pickard, *Theological Foundations*, 41.

139. Pickard, *Theological Foundations*, 41.

140. Pickard, *Theological Foundations*, 45. Pickard finds the uncovering of the collaborative nature of all work and ministry a crucial factor in coming to terms with ministry models which include the whole people of God. He suggests that "reflection on the nature of ministry becomes a litmus test of our understandings of the relation

This focus on the ongoing creative and redeeming work of God in creation aligns with the theological underpinnings of a Social Trinity in process, and the thinking of both Moltmann and Hartshorne. The full and effective living of the ideals of non-coercive shared power and mutuality in ministry in church and creation remains, however, a work in progress.

In another overt effort to share power in the church, to exercise power "with" rather than "over" others in the trajectory of a process vision of God, the entire structure of the Anglican Church in Aotearoa, New Zealand and Polynesia/ *Te Hahi Mihinare ki Aotearoa ki Niu Tireni, ki Nga Moutere o Te Moana Nui a Kiwa* has been revised constitutionally. This happened in 1992 at the General Synod/*te Hinota Whānui* in Hamilton resulting in the church being organised into three self-governing *tikanga*: *Māori*, *Pākehā* and *Pasefika*.[141] Each now share a common life under the umbrella of a synod that relies on consensus between the *tikanga* and between the houses of the laity, the clergy, and the bishops. Built into the constitution is a requirement for resource sharing between the *tikanga*; each partner and their component parts are expected to ensure that adequate provision and support is available to the other partners.[142]

In speaking of the turbulence of the Anglican journey in New Zealand over two hundred years before the constitutional revision of 1992, John Bluck says:

> Anglicanism . . . began here for its first 40 years as a *Māori* Church, calling itself *Te Hāhi Mihinare*, then rapidly became a Settler Church, including a Native Church as an appendage to be absorbed. The changing names tell the story. In 1857 we became a Branch of the United Church of England and Ireland in New Zealand, then in 1874, The Church of the Province of New Zealand (commonly known as the Church of England). One hundred years later, ever so painfully, that Native Church won the right to be self-determining and finally to become a full and equal partner in a church of three *tikanga* or cultural pathways. In 1992, we agreed on the name we use today, *Te Hāhi Mihinare ki Aotearoa ki Niu Tireni, ki Ngā Moutere o te Moana*

---

between creation and redemption as well as our doctrine of the Church." Pickard, *Theological Foundations*, 45.

141. *Tikanga* means cultural pathways. *Māori* are the indigenous Polynesian people of New Zealand. *Pākehā* refers to European settlers. *Pasefika* are the people of the South Pacific nations of Fiji, Tonga, Samoa, and American Samoa, along with Pacific communities in New Zealand. Bluck, *Wai Karekare—Turbulent Waters*, 10 and 17.

142. Bluck, *Wai Karekare—Turbulent Waters*, 61.

Nui a Kiwa—The Anglican Church in Aotearoa New Zealand and Polynesia.[143]

Bluck notes that the story of Anglicanism in New Zealand, from the very start, "has been a struggle for dominance and the superiority of one culture over another." Indeed, that "Anglicanism has never played on level ground in Aotearoa."[144] Whatever development is still required to balance diverse *Māori* experiences of oppression and empowerment in the Church,[145] the fact that the group with the most power, the *Pākehā*, have agreed to share their power constitutionally with those less powerful, the *Māori* (and the *Pasefika*), is significant theologically. In his essay "The Theological Implications of a Three *Tikanga* Church" Rangi Nicholson notes how critical *Māori* theology is of the history of the New Zealand Church which has often worked in collaboration with the state to oppress and disempower *Māori*. He insists, however, that it is now "mostly concerned with the tradition of Christianity that will assist the struggle for *Māori* liberation."[146] The sources for this are protest theologies, most notably Black Liberation Theology[147] and Feminist Theology.[148] The becoming of a Three *Tikanga* Church in Aotearoa is therefore deeply relevant to issues of power, power both in God and in the community of faith. As John Paterson, a now retired Bishop of Auckland, using the *Māori* word for power (*mana*), explains:

> The absolute key for me lies in the concept of *mana*. . . . Until the *mana* of the Treaty of Waitangi is recognised equally by both *Māori* and *Pākehā*, it will not be possible for *Pākehā* to be truly and authentically Christian *Pākehā* in this place. . . . Whether we like it or not, our identity in relation to our partner has to take the matter of *mana* into serious consideration. What we do simply has to be *mana*-enhancing for our partner. We cannot enhance our own *mana* in isolation. We cannot build more self-esteem for ourselves by ourselves. We can endeavour to enhance the *mana* of our partner and thereby enhance our own.[149]

Mana, as power, is something we all have. It is something best shared. To enhance the power of others in mutuality and service, as the Anglican

143. Bluck, *Wai Karekare—Turbulent Waters*, 10.

144. Bluck, *Wai Karekare—Turbulent Waters*, 11.

145. Nicholson, "Theological Implications," 36.

146. Nicholson, "Theological Implications," 38.

147. Cone, *Black Theology of Liberation*.

148. Adams, *Towards a Reshaped Church*.

149. Bluck, *Wai Karekare—Turbulent Waters*, 19–20.

Church in Aotearoa, New Zealand and Polynesia/ *Te Hahi Mihinare ki Aotearoa ki Niu Tireni, ki Nga Moutere o Te Moana Nui a Kiwa* has sought to do, is to recognize that authentic Christian identity is built through sharing power in partnership "with" rather than through an isolated exercise of power "over" others. Nicholson identifies nine other cultural concepts that contribute to the examination of Maori perspectives on the exercise of power in partnership. These are *whakaiti* (humility), *turangawaewae* (territory), *pono* (truth), *whanaungatanga* (relationship), *whakapapa* (genealogy), *wananga* (learning), *kawa* (protocol), *tika* (justice), and *aroha* (compassion). He notes that a more prominent role for Maori language and culture in the life of the church has served to increase the *mana* (power) of the Maori and Pacific Island partners considerably.[150] This is grounded in the understanding that true Christian identity is found by seeking to relate to one another after the manner of the Triune God, who is an entirely persuasive and loving divine communion.

To consider the implications of imaging God as a Social Trinity in process for the pastoral care offered by the church, I need do no more than cast my mind back some forty years. Back to a school holiday morning in January 1977 when my family caught a train from the Blue Mountains to Sydney for a day in the city. My mother, sister and brother and I had been out earlier to collect two new budgerigars from the pet shop, so we caught a later train than my father did to get to his place of work. Thanks to this delay, the four of us were bussed around the site of the Granville Train Disaster rather than being caught up in it ourselves.

In the city we went to my father's office, but he had not been in that day. I recall turning quietly to my sister as we made our way home, putting into words each of our thoughts. "What if that was Papa's train?" We got home and looked for him. We waited. Friends and neighbors came. My mother phoned the disaster hotline every hour to ask for news. In the early hours of the morning, I fell asleep in my parent's bed. As I was clipping the yellow dishes of seed and water to the side of the shiny new bird cage in the morning, Mama told me that Papa was among the dead. I did not say a word, just quietly continued what I was doing; I did not know how to react. My mother paused behind me, hesitating, before leaving me to attend to the small, colorful birds that had prevented us from being on that disastrous train.

With the post next day cards began to come; the house filled with flowers, food, and people. Newspapers listed eighty-three names, published photographs, and each time they did they spelled our surname incorrectly.

150. Nicholson, "Theological Implications," 37.

Mama stopped us watching the news. Among the visitors was the Curate from the local Anglican church. My first lessons in theology came from him. "All things work together for good for those who love God and are called according to his purposes," he said. I heard that, due to everything that happened anywhere being part of God's preordained plan, we must "give thanks in all circumstances, for this is the will of God."[151] Looking back, I see that the efforts of the Curate who eventually became the Bishop of South Sydney reflected pastoral inexperience and poor theology, but not ill intent. My mother remained polite at the time in her protest but was completely incredulous about all things Christian from that point. I do not believe she ever said thank-you to God for planning the Granville Train Disaster.

I have wondered many times in the four decades that have passed since my father died what a different impact a pastoral theology grounded in an understanding of God as a Social Trinity in process could have made to my family. Especially to my mother, who died thirty-seven years after her husband with her fists still clenched and a silent, but tangible, cry of protest on her lips against the justice of the suffering which God had apparently willed for her, and hundreds of others, affected by the tragedy at Granville. I wonder how she would have responded to a panentheistic God who is with us eternally as a non-coercive influence for good, who in love feels with the pain of the world as "the fellow sufferer who understands."[152] For, even when she was able to acknowledge the possibility of God in the face of her own experience of evil and suffering, she remained weighed down by the idea of God explained to her by the local Curate at the time of my father's death. In the long run, the Curate's pastoral efforts developed into a second wave of tragedy, as there came a time when she could find no hint of love or care at all in a dominant and controlling God who exercises unilateral power over the world and directs every aspect of the course of history. This "tyrant idea of God"[153] is the one that Hartshorne, Moltmann and Tillich[154] all agreed readily leads to atheism, and, in my mother's case, it did. In my case, it led to an early Christian conversion driven largely by fear, a fear which I was not able to quell for many years and which also compounded my grief and sense of loss.

In my ministry as an Anglican School Chaplain, I have called many times on this experience of loss. That the process of grieving was made more

---

151. Romans 8:28 (NRSV) and 2 Thessalonians 5:18 (NRSV)

152. Whitehead, *Process and Reality*, 351.

153. Hartshorne, *Omnipotence and Other Theological Mistakes*, 13.

154. Hartshorne, "Formally Possible Doctrines," 205; Moltmann, *Crucified God*, 236. Tillich, *Courage to Be*, 177.

difficult by an idea of God that is neither pastoral nor life-giving continues to inform my care of students and staff—it can be no other way. When a student or staff member, or one of their family, is diagnosed with a terminal illness; when a friend or loved one ends their own life by suicide; when there is a car accident and multiple people die, an act of violence on school grounds causes someone permanent disability, or a staff member drowns at a school camp,[155] I never maintain that this is God's will for them. I never propose that God's power is so all-encompassing that everything that happens, every aspect of their pain and suffering, is directed by God. I never say these things, not because they are pastorally and theologically inadequate (although they certainly are); I never say them because I do not believe them. In all pastoral situations I say what I believe, and I believe that God cannot and does not make or unilaterally impose a plan per se, but instead has an ongoing *purpose* that is always for the good. I believe that God is all-encompassing, persuasive-suffering love,[156] that God is the fellow sufferer who both understands and feels our griefs.[157] Furthermore, when I am asked "Where is God in all this?" I explain that God is right here with us in solidarity, keeping vigil with us and our sorrow in eternal love, and calling us into a transformed future.

The reformed theologian, Karl Barth (1886–1968), captures the most common argument against this gentler, more incarnational vision of God in a comment he made to Moltmann in 1964. "If you will pardon me, your God seems to me to be rather a pauper,"[158] he said. His criticism of Moltmann's "pauper" God, however, along with any version of the idea that if God does not have the power to control and direct the course of history then God is not worthy of worship, takes us firmly into an ideological trap. The trap is to confine the measure of the worth of the power of God to quantity and not to quality. Indeed, Hartshorne has already insisted based on his process view that God has the maximum possible power, a quantitative measure:

> Instead of saying that God's power is limited, suggesting that it
> is less than some conceivable power, we should rather say: his
> power is absolutely maximal, the greatest possible, but even the
> greatest possible power is still one power among others, is not

---

155. Each of these scenarios have played out in one or another of the schools I have worked in as a Chaplain over the course of seventeen years, some multiple times.

156. Griffin, "Naturalistic Trinity," 26.

157. Whitehead, *Process and Reality*, 351.

158. Moltmann, *History and the Triune God*, 126.

the only power. God can do everything a God can do, everything
that could be done by 'a being with no possible superior.'[159]

So, the quantity of God's power is not the issue at hand, the issue is the
type or quality of the power that God exercises. Somewhere between God
understood to be omnipotent and, at the other end of the spectrum, God
stripped of any power at all, there is an understanding of God's power as
qualitatively different. It is not a choice between sheer and absolute power
or ineffectual weakness. In the space between those two extremes there is a
transformative, gracious power that can and will make all things new and
bring light and love out of darkness and death. When it comes to pastoral
theology, comfort and hope can therefore be found in the so-called "pauper" understanding of God that Barth decries. For this pauper God not
only suffers with us but invites us to participate in the redemptive dance of
the Trinity in creation. This includes exercising our own power in the way
the Triune God does, gently and non-coercively, in and amidst tragedy and
grief, and open to future transformation.

CONCLUSION

This book is founded on my theory that the way we understand and exercise
power in all our relationships is intricately linked with the way we conceive
of God. It represents my commitment to stand in solidary with those whose
bodies and lives have been negatively affected by abuses of power. In the
tradition of liberation and feminist theologians, I can only be open about
my own bias toward those who suffer the misuse of power in the world
and the church, which warrants the acknowledgment that I do my theology
from this point of view.

I began by identifying a key misconception about the power of God,
namely the idea that God is omnipotent in the sense of having unlimited
power "over" all things. Furthermore, I argued that the wrong of understanding God this way has subliminally affected our human exercise of
power in relationship, the standard meaning of power being found in
domination and control. Next, I analyzed power as a concept within society, power being considered in the discourses of sociology, philosophy, and
theology in chapter 1. In this chapter and throughout I have explained and
frequently referred to the two most influential visions of God for Christianity, classical theism, and deism. As they both describe God as omnipotent
over the world and separate from it, together they form a foundation for an

159. Hartshorne, *Divine Relativity*, 138.

understanding of power as domination based in the rule of a transcendent God who controls and directs the workings of the universe. My contention that the way the Church has modelled God shapes the exercise of power in human society finds general support in Max Weber's social theory of power and the notion of power as discipline developed by Michel Foucault. Both theorists find that power understood as domination is embedded as a cultural norm in human society.

When I turned to contemporary theologians of power, I found a consensus of dissatisfaction with explaining the power of God as traditional omnipotence understood as domination and control. I also found that the majority of thinkers about God and power were much less specific about what, in fact, God's power could alternatively be. My response to the dissatisfaction associated with God's power understood as omnipotence, the one that I have promoted throughout this book, is to move beyond both theism and deism and understand God and God's exercise of power panentheistically.

This movement into panentheism necessitates a preparedness to embrace a balance between the immanence and transcendence of God, and to challenge the established cultural norm in society and much of the church that continues to operate on the basis that true power exerts coercive control. For this challenge, I have unpacked the "rebel voice"[160] of process thought within Christianity. The persistent voice of process thinkers, beginning with Whitehead nearly a century ago, has questioned many of our inherited notions of God, particularly those to do with divine omniscience, omnipotence, and immutability.[161] I have made much of the adequate power of God in process thought and traced the motivations and main ideas of both Whitehead and Hartshorne as its founding theorists. This has been with a view to outlining how process thinking about the power of God can contribute to genuinely Christian ideas about the incarnation, resurrection, eschatology, theodicy, and justice.

While Process theology is often understood to have something to contribute to a conversation about God's exercise of power, it is typically seen as limited in its development of a Trinitarian understanding of God. A key goal has therefore been to link process theology with an established theology of the Trinity. Consequently, I briefly outlined the development of trinitarian theology in the early Christian centuries, considering what constitutes a "pro-Nicene"[162] basis for contemporary theologies of Trin-

---

160. Fisher, *Many Voices of Job*, 30.

161. Ford, *Lure of God*, 1.

162. Ayres, *Nicaea and Its Legacy*, 236. A pro-Nicene theology of Trinity is one that

ity. This was in recognition of the importance of connecting a potential process-based model of the Trinity with accepted trinitarian ideals and understandings from the early Christian Councils. Focusing then on the power sharing social trinitarianism of Jürgen Moltmann as a potential orthodox understanding of the Triune God to inform the process theology of Charles Hartshorne, I demonstrated that Moltmann's Social Trinity can be described as a pro-Nicene understanding of Trinity. Through exploring the key links between Moltmann's trinitarian theology and Hartshorne's process understanding of God as the Divine Relativity, I have synthesized the main ideas they shared to explain God as a Social Trinity in process. The result is a fully relational, panentheistic model of God where God is both characterized and constituted by social relations. It is a non-zero-sum model in which the divine power is exercised cooperatively and non-coercively, and therefore one in which the future is genuinely open.

In this final chapter I have concentrated on the relationship between power and the way we model God, considering some implications of explaining the divine nature as a Social Trinity in process. The main consequence of changing our long-held interpretation of the power of God from dominance "over" the world to invitational power shared "with" the world is a convincing response to the problem of evil and suffering. Furthermore, understanding that God as a Social Trinity in process can provide a valid image for healthy relationships in the world and in the church enables the intentional development of mutual, loving relations of shared power wherever tactics of domination and control are replaced with non-coercive power that invites others into the fullness of their being. I am aware, nevertheless, that both the sharing of power with "the other" based on rejecting omnipotence in God and patterning our relationships in the world and the church after a fully relational understanding of the divine, continue to be on the fringes of what many would consider an orthodox version of the Christian faith. Perhaps this is because we have not been able to really listen to the rebel voice?

Since committing myself to listening to the critics of traditional understandings of God, I have become convinced that this frequently ignored rebel voice is, more often than not, a voice of deep faith. From the ancient writers of the book of Job, right through to Hartshorne, and Moltmann, and contemporary theologians of practically every stripe, voice has consistently been given to legitimate questions about the logic and justice of notions of divine omnipotence and models of God in which power is exercised as

accepts as foundational the agreed and orthodox formulations arrived at in the Nicene-Cosmopolitan credal statements.

domination and control. It is therefore with a voice of faith, a voice connected to a long line of faithful questioners, that I respond by submitting the view that the most realistic and faith enabling way to understand God is as a Social Trinity in process, a fully relational God. This model shifts the focus from the quantity of power that God exercises to the quality of God's power, thus pointing towards an understanding of the Triune God as abundantly good rather than as omnipotent in the classic sense. God does not, in fact God *cannot*, unilaterally plan and visit disease or disaster on individual lives or the life of the world. Instead, God suffers with us in love and solidarity, and constantly invites us and the world to take up God's lure of transformative good in all our free choices. Further, a Social Trinity in process calls us to model our own lives and relationships on the image it provides of the love and solidarity of God. When we share power, love mutually, and understand that our life is related to all others and to the life of the world, we collectively enact Emmanuel. God is with us.

BIBLIOGRAPHY

Adams, Susan. *Towards a Reshaped Church: A Feminist Look at Theological Education and the Future of the Church*. Auckland: Auckland Anglican Women's Resource Centre, 1993.

Allen, Roland. *Missionary Methods; St Paul's or Ours?* London: World Dominion, 1962.

Armstrong, Karen. *The Case for God*. London: Vintage, 2010.

Athanasius. *On the Councils of Arminum and Seleucia (De Synodis)*. In *Athanasius: Select Works and Letters*. Translated by John Henry Newman, revised by Archibald Robertson, 41, 43–45. Nicene and Post-Nicene Fathers Second Series 4. Grand Rapids: Eerdmans, 1980.

Augustine. *The City of God*. Translated by Gerald G. Walsh et al. New York: Doubleday, 1958.

———. *On the Trinity*. Translated by A. W. Haddon. Edinburgh: T. & T. Clark, 1873.

Ayres, Lewis. *Nicaea and Its Legacy: An Approach to Fourth-Century Trinitarian Theology*. Oxford: Oxford University Press, 2004.

Barbour, Ian. "God and Nature." In *Religion in an Age of Science*, 243–70. London: SCM, 1990.

———. "Indeterminacy, Holism, and God's Action." In *God's Action in Nature's World*, edited by T. P. Peters et al., 113–29. Aldershot: Ashgate, 2006.

Basil of Caesarea. "Letter 236.6." In *Saint Basil: The Letters, Volume 3*. Translated by Roy J. Deferrari, 276–79. Loeb Classical Library. London: Heinemann, 1962.

Beeley, Christopher A. *Gregory of Nazianzus on the Trinity and the Knowledge of God*. Oxford: Oxford University Press, 2008.

Birch, Charles. *On Purpose*. Kensington: New South Wales University Press, 1990.

Bigongiari, Dino. *The Political Ideas of St. Thomas Aquinas: Representative Selections*. Edited and with an introduction by Dino Bigongiari. New York: Free Press, 1953.

Blau, Peter M. "Critical Remarks on Weber's Theory of Authority." In *Max Weber*, edited by Dennis Wrong, 147–65. Englewood Cliffs, NJ: Prentice-Hall, 1970.

Bluck, John. *Wai Karekare—Turbulent Waters: The Anglican Bicultural Journey 1814–2014*. Auckland, NZ: The Anglican Church in Aotearoa, New Zealand and Polynesia, 2012.

Boff, Leonardo. *Church, Charism and Power: Liberation Theology and the Institutional Church*. New York: Crossroad, 1985.

———. *Trinity and Society*. Translated by Paul Burns. Liberation and Theology Series. London: Burns & Oates, 1992.

Bowman, Donna. *The Divine Decision: A Process Doctrine of Election.* Louisville: Westminster John Knox, 2002.

Bracken, Joseph A. *Christianity and Process Thought: Spiritualty for a Changing World.* Philadelphia: Templeton, 2006.

———. "Incarnation, Panentheism, and Bodily Resurrection: A Systems-Oriented Approach." *Theological Studies* 71 (2016) 32–47.

———. *The One in the Many: A Contemporary Reconstruction of the God-World Relationship and Christianity.* Grand Rapids: Eerdmans, 2001.

———. "Panentheism from a Process Perspective." In *Trinity in Process: A Relational Theology of God,* edited by Joseph A. Bracken and Marjorie Hewitt Suchocki, 95–113, New York: Continuum, 1997.

———. *The World in the Trinity: Open-Ended Systems in Science and Religion.* Minneapolis: Fortress, 2014.

Bracken, Joseph A., and Marjorie Hewitt Suchocki. *Trinity in Process: A Relational Theology of God.* New York: Continuum, 1997.

Broughton, Geoff. *Restorative Christ: Jesus, Justice, and Discipleship.* Cambridge: Lutterworth, 2015.

Brown, Delwin, and Gene Reves. "The Development of Process Theology." In *Process Philosophy and Christian Thought,* edited by Delwin Brown et al., 21–64. New York: Bobbs-Merrill, 1971.

Brown, James, et al. *Process Philosophy and Christian Thought.* New York: Bobbs-Merrill, 1971.

Calhoun, Craig. *Dictionary of the Social Sciences.* Oxford: Oxford University Press, 2002.

Campbell, Jeremy. *The Many Faces of God: Science's 400-Year Quest for Images of the Divine.* New York: Norton, 2006.

Campbell, R. "A Process-Based Model for an Ontology of Activity." In *Creation and Complexity: Interdisciplinary Issues in Science and Religion,* edited by Christine Ledger et al., 147–66. Adelaide: ATF Press, 2004.

Case-Winters, Anna. *God's Power.* Kentucky: Westminster John Knox, 1990.

Cavadini, John C. "Trinity and Apologetics in the Theology of St Augustine." In *Visioning Augustine,* 239–84. Hoboken: Wiley-Blackwell, 2019.

Chan, Michael J., and Brent A. Strawn, eds. "Introducing Fretheim: His Theology and His God." In *What Kind of God? Collected Essays of Terence E. Fretheim,* edited by Michael J. Chan and Brent A. Strawn, 3–17. Winona Lake, IN: Eisenbrauns, 2015.

———. *What Kind of God? Collected Essays of Terence E. Fretheim.* Winona Lake, IN: Eisenbrauns, 2015.

Christ, Carol P. *She Who Changes: Reimaging the Divine in the World.* New York: Palgrave Macmillan, 2003.

Clarke, Bowman. "Two Process Views of God." In *God, Reason and Religions,* 61–74. Dordrecht: Kluwer, 1995.

Clayton, Phillip. "Pluralism, Idealism, Romanticism: Untapped Resources for a Trinity in Process." In *Trinity in Process: A Relational Theology of God,* edited by Joseph A. Bracken and Marjorie Hewitt Suchocki, 117–45. New York: Continuum, 1997.

Clement of Rome. "Letter to the Corinthians." In *Early Church Fathers,* translated and edited by Cyril Richardson, 43–73. New York: Touchstone, 1996.

Coakley, Sarah. *God, Sexuality, and the Self: An Essay "on the Trinity."* Cambridge: Cambridge University Press, 2013.

————. *The New Asceticism: Sexuality, Gender and the Quest for God.* London: Bloomsbury, 2015.

————. *Powers and Submissions: Spirituality, Philosophy and Gender.* Oxford: Blackwell, 2002.

Cobb, John B., Jr. *A Christian Natural Theology: Based on the Thought of Alfred North Whitehead.* Philadelphia: Westminster, 1965.

————. "A Whiteheadian Christology." In *Process Theology and Christian Thought,* edited by Delwin Brown et al., 362–81. New York: Bobbs-Merrill, 1971.

————. "A Whiteheadian Doctrine of God." In *Process Philosophy and Christian Thought,* edited by Delwin Brown et al., 215–43. New York: Bobbs-Merrill, 1971.

Cobb, John B., Jr., and Clark H. Pinnock. *Searching for an Adequate God: A Dialogue between Process and Free Will Theists.* Grand Rapids: Eerdmans, 2000.

Cobb, John B., Jr., and David R. Griffin. *Process Theology: An Introductory Exposition.* Philadelphia: Westminster, 1976.

Collins, James, et al. *Reinventing Church: Stories of Hope from Four Anglican Parishes.* Melbourne: Morning Star, 2016.

Cone, James H. *Black Theology and Black Power.* Maryknoll: Orbis, 1997.

————. *A Black Theology of Liberation.* Maryknoll: Orbis, 1990.

Costa, James T. *The Annotated Origin: A Facsimile of the First Edition of* On the Origin of Species *by Charles Darwin.* Annotated by James T. Costa. Cambridge, MA: Harvard University Press, 2009.

Coutts, Ian A. "A Trinitarian Theology of Family." PhD diss., Charles Sturt University, 2015.

The Creed of Constantinople, 381. In *Early Christian Creeds,* translated by J. N. D. Kelly, 296–322. 3rd ed. Harlow, UK: Longmans, 1972.

Donovan, Vincent J. *Christianity Rediscovered: An Epistle from the Masai.* Maryknoll, NY: Orbis, 1982.

Dostoyevsky, Fyodor. *The Brothers Karamazov.* London: Penguin, 1993.

Edwards, Dennis. *The God of Evolution: A Trinitarian Theology.* Mahwah: Paulist, 1999.

————. *How God Acts: Creation, Redemption, and Special Divine Action.* Hindmarsh: ATF Press, 2010.

Elden, Stuart. *Foucault: The Birth of Power.* Cambridge: Polity, 2017.

Emery, Giles, and Matthew Levering. *The Oxford Handbook of the Trinity.* Oxford: Oxford University Press, 2011.

Epperly, Bruce G. *Process Theology: A Guide for the Perplexed.* London: T. & T. Clark, 2011.

Faber, Roland. *The Becoming of God: Process Theology, Philosophy, and Multireligious Engagement.* Eugene, OR: Cascade, 2017.

Feske, Millicent C. "Christ and Suffering in Moltmann's Thought." *The Asbury Theological Journal* 55 (2000) 85–104.

Fiorenza, Elisabeth Schüssler. *Jesus and the Politics of Interpretation.* New York: Continuum, 2001.

"First among Equals." https://dictionary.cambridge.org/us/dictionary/english/first-among-equals.

Fisher, Loren R. *The Many Voices of Job.* Eugene, OR: Cascade, 2009.

Flannery, Tim. *Here On Earth: An Argument for Hope.* Melbourne: Text, 2010.

Ford, Lewis S. *The Lure of God: A Biblical Background for Process Theism.* Philadelphia: Fortress, 1978.

————. "Whitehead's Differences from Hartshorne." *AAR Studies in Religion* 5 (1973) 58–83.

Foucault, Michel. *The Courage of Truth (The Government of Self and Others II) Lectures at the College de France 1983–1984.* Basingstoke: Palgrave Macmillan, 2008.

————. *Discipline and Punish: The Birth of Prison.* New York: Vintage, 1995.

————. *History of Madness.* Translated by J. Murphy and J. Khalfa. London: Routledge, 2009.

————. *The History of Sexuality: An Introduction Volume 1.* Translated by R. Hurley. New York: Vintage, 1990.

————. "Two Lectures." In *Power/Knowledge: Selected Interviews and Other Writings 1972–1977,* edited by C. Gordon, 78–108. New York: Random House, 1980.

Frame, Tom. *Anglicans in Australia.* Sydney: University of NSW Press, 2007.

Franklin, S. T. "Panentheism." In *The Evangelical Dictionary of Theology,* edited by Walter A. Elwell, 818–19. Grand Rapids: Baker, 1984.

Fretheim, Terence E. "Creator, Creature, and Co-Creation in Genesis 1–2." In *What Kind of God? Collected Essays of Terence E. Fretheim,* edited by Michael J. Chan et al., 195–205. Winona Lake, IN: Eisenbrauns, 2015.

————. *Deuteronomic History.* Nashville: Abingdon, 1983.

————. *The Message of Jonah: A Theological Commentary.* Minneapolis: Augsburg, 1977.

————. *The Suffering of God, An Old Testament Perspective.* Philadelphia: Fortress, 1984.

————. "What Biblical Scholars Wish Pastors Would Start or Stop Doing about Ethical Issues in the Old Testament." In *What Kind of God? Collected Essays of Terence E. Fretheim,* edited by Michael J. Chan et al., 382–91. Winona Lake, IN: Eisenbrauns, 2015.

Giles, Kevin. "The Orthodox Doctrine of the Trinity." *Priscilla Papers* 26 (2012) 12–23.

Gilkey, Langdon. *Reaping the Whirlwind: A Christian Interpretation of History.* New York: Seabury, 1976.

Goetz, Stewart. "The Argument from Evil." In *The Blackwell Companion to Natural Theology,* edited by William Lane Craig et al., 449–97. Chichester: Wiley-Blackwell, 2012.

Good, Roger. "*El Shadday*: Its Meaning and Implications." *Glossa* 12 (2007) 67–71.

Greenwood, Robin. *Transforming Priesthood: A New Theology of Mission and Ministry.* London: SPCK, 1994.

Gregersen, N. H. "A Primer on Complexity: Definitions, Theories, and Theological Perspectives." In *Creation and Complexity: Interdisciplinary Issues in Science and Religion,* edited by Christine Ledger et al., 3–16. Adelaide: ATF Press, 2004.

————. "A World Made to Flourish: Divine Design and the Idea of Natural Self-organisation." In *Creation and Complexity: Interdisciplinary Issues in Science and Religion,* edited by Christine Ledger et al., 110–11. Adelaide: ATF Press, 2004.

Gregory of Nyssa. "On "Not Three Gods"—To Ablabius (Quod non sint tres dii)." In *Gregory of Nyssa: Dogmatic Treatises,* translated by H. A. Wilson, 331–36. Nicene and Post-Nicene Fathers Second Series 5. Grand Rapids: Eerdmans, 1980.

Griffin, David. "Hartshorne's Differences from Whitehead." *AAR Studies in Religion* 5 (1973) 35–57.

————. "A Naturalistic Trinity." In *Trinity in Process: A Relational Theology of God,* edited by Joseph A. Bracken and Marjorie Hewitt Suchocki, 23–40. New York: Continuum, 1997.

Gunton, Colin E. *Becoming and Being: The Doctrine of God in Charles Hartshorne and Karl Barth.* Oxford: Oxford University Press, 1978.

Gutierrez, Gustavo. *A Theology of Liberation: History, Politics, and Salvation.* Translated and edited by Caridad Inda and John Eagleson. Maryknoll, NY: Orbis, 1973.

Hamilton, Peter N. "Some Proposals for a Modern Christology." In *Process Theology and Christian Thought,* edited by Delwin Brown et al., 362–81. New York: Bobbs-Merrill, 1971.

Hartshorne, Charles. *Beyond Humanism: Essays in the Philosophy of Nature.* New York: Willet Clark, 1937.

————. *Creativity in American Philosophy.* Albany: State University of New York Press, 1984.

————. *The Divine Relativity: A Social Conception of God.* New Haven: Yale University Press, 1948.

————. "The Formally Possible Doctrines of God." In *Process Philosophy and Christian Thought,* edited by Delwin Brown et al., 188–214. New York: Bobbs-Merrill, 1971.

————. "Ideas and Theses of Process Philosophers." *AAR Studies in Religion* 5 (1973) 100–103.

————. *The Logic of Perfection and Other Essays in Neo-Classical Metaphysics.* La Salle: Open Court, 1962.

————. *Man's Vision of God.* Hamden: Archon, 1937.

————. *Omnipotence and Other Theological Mistakes.* Albany: State University of New York, 1984.

————. "A Philosopher's Assessment of Christianity." In *Religion and Culture,* edited by W. Leibrecht, 171–89. New York: Harper & Row, 1959.

————. *Philosophers Speak of God.* Chicago: University of Chicago Press, 1953.

————. *Reality as Social Progress.* New York: Collier-Macmillan, 1963.

————. *Wisdom as Moderation: A Philosophy of the Middle Way.* Albany: State University of New York Press, 1987.

Hasker, William. *Metaphysics and the Tri-Personal God.* Oxford: Oxford University Press, 2013.

Haught, John F. *Christianity and Science: Toward a Theology of Nature.* Maryknoll: Orbis, 2007.

"Hemopoiesis." https://medical-dictionary.thefreedictionary.com/hemopoiesis.

Hensley, Jeffrey. "Trinity and Freedom: A Response to Molnar." *Scottish Journal of Theology* 61 (2008) 83–95.

Heyward, Carter. *The Redemption of God: A Theology of Mutual Relation.* Lanham, MD: University Press of America, 1982.

————. *Staying Power: Reflections on Gender, Justice, and Compassion.* Cleveland, OH: Pilgrim, 1995.

Hunt, Anne. *The Trinity: Insights from the Mystics.* Collegeville, MN: ATF Theology, 2010.

Husbands, Mark. "The Trinity Is *Not* Our Social Program: Volf, Gregory of Nyssa and Barth." In *Trinitarian Theology of the Church: Scripture, Community, Worship,* edited by J. Daniel et al., 120–41. Downers Grove: InterVarsity, 2009.

Ignatius. "The Letters of Ignatius." In *Early Church Fathers*, translated and edited by Cyril Richardson, 87–120. New York: Touchstone, 1996.

Inbody, Tyron L. *The Many Faces of Christology.* Nashville: Abingdon, 2002.

Irenaeus. "Against Heresies." In *The Apostolic Fathers with Justin Martyr and Irenaeus*, translated by M. Dods, 315–567. Buffalo: Christian Literature, 1885.

James, Ralph E., Jr. "Process Cosmology and Theological Particularity." In *Process Theology and Christian Thought*, edited by Delwin Brown et al., 188–214. New York: Bobbs-Merrill, 1971.

Janzen, Gerald. *At the Scent of Water: The Ground of Hope in the Book of Job.* Grand Rapids: Eerdmans, 2009.

Johnson, Elizabeth A. *Ask the Beasts: Darwin and the God of Love.* London: Bloomsbury, 2014.

———. *She Who Is: The Mystery of God in Feminist Theological Discourse.* New York: Crossroad, 1992.

Justin Martyr. *The First and Second Apologies.* Translated by Leslie Barnard. Ancient Christian Writers. New York: Paulist, 1997.

Kelly, J. N. D. *Early Christian Doctrines.* 5th rev. ed. London: A. & C. Black, 1977.

Kilby, Karen. "Perichoresis and Projection: Problems with Social Doctrines of the Trinity." *New Blackfriars* 81 (2000–2011) 432–45.

———. "Trinity, Tradition, and Politics." In *Recent Developments in Trinitarian Theology: An International Symposium*, edited by Christophe Chalamet et al., 73–86. Minneapolis: Fortress, 2013.

King, C. M. "Interpretations of Complexity in Nature: Teilhard to Maynard Smith." In *Creation and Complexity: Interdisciplinary Issues in Science and Religion*, edited by Christine Ledger et al., 51–81. Adelaide: ATF Press, 2004.

———. "Models of Invisible Realities: The Common Thread in Science and Theology." In *Creation and Complexity: Interdisciplinary Issues in Science and Religion*, edited by Christine Ledger et al., 17–50. Adelaide: ATF Press, 2004.

Kung, Hans. *The Beginning of All Things: Science and Religion.* Grand Rapids: Eerdmans, 2007.

Kushner, Harold S. *When Bad Things Happen to Good People.* London: Pan, 2002.

LaCugna, Catherine M. *God for Us: The Trinity and the Christian Life.* San Francisco: Harper, 1991.

Lee, Bernard J. "An 'Other' Trinity." In *Trinity in Process: A Relational Theology of God*, edited by Joseph A. Bracken and Marjorie Hewitt Suchocki, 191–214. New York: Continuum, 1997.

Leftow, Brian. "Classical Theism." https://www.rep.routledge.com/articles/thematic/god-concepts-of/v-1/sections/classical-theism.

Long, Eugene T. *Twentieth Century Western Philosophy of Religion 1900–2000.* Dordrecht: Kluwer, 2000.

Loomer, Bernard J. "Christian Faith and Process Philosophy." In *Process Philosophy and Christian Thought*, edited by Delwin Brown et al., 70–98. New York: Bobbs-Merrill, 1971.

Lowe, Victor. "Whitehead's Metaphysical System." In *Process Philosophy and Christian Thought*, edited by Delwin Brown et al., 3–20. New York: Bobbs-Merrill, 1971.

Lucas, George R. "Whitehead: The Next Generation." In *Beyond Superlatives: Regenerating Whitehead's Philosophy of Experience*, edited by Roland Faber et al., ix–xviii. Newcastle on Tyne: Cambridge Scholars, 2014.

Macquarrie, John. *In Search of Deity*. London: SCM, 1984.

Masterton, Patrick. *Atheism and Alienation*. Dublin: Gill and Macmillan, 1971.

Martin, Douglas. "Charles Hartshorne, Theologian Is Dead; Proponent of an Activist God Was 103." *The New York Times*, October 13, 2000. http://www.nytimes.com/2000/10/13/us/charles-hartshorne-theologian-is-dead-proponent-of-an-activist-god-was 103.html.

McDougall, Joy A. "The Return of Trinitarian Praxis? Moltmann on the Trinity and the Christian Life." *Journal of Religion* 83 (2003) 177–204.

McFague, Sallie. *The Body of God: An Ecological Theology*. Minneapolis: Fortress, 1993.

————. *Life Abundant: Rethinking Theology and Economy for a Planet in Peril*. Minneapolis: Augsburg Fortress, 2000.

————. *Metaphorical Theology: Models of God in Religious Language*. Philadelphia: Fortress, 1982.

————. *Models of God: Theology for an Ecological, Nuclear Age*. Philadelphia: Fortress, 1987.

McGrath, Alister E. *Christian Theology*. Chichester, West Sussex: Wiley-Blackwell, 2011.

Mennell, Stephen. *Sociological Theory: Uses and Unities*. Sunbury-on-Thames, UK: Nelson, 1974.

Migliore, Daniel. *The Power of God and the Gods of Power*. Louisville: Westminster John Knox, 2008.

Molnar, Paul D. *Divine Freedom and the Doctrine of the Immanent Trinity*. London: T. & T. Clark, 2002.

Moltmann, Jürgen. *The Crucified God*. Translated by R. A. Wilson and John Bowden. Minneapolis: Fortress, 1993.

————. *Experiences in Theology: Ways and Forms of Christian Theology*. Translated by Margaret Kohl. Minneapolis: Augsburg Fortress, 2000.

————. *God in Creation: An Ecological Doctrine of Creation*. Translated by Margaret Kohl. London: SCM, 1985.

————. *History and the Triune God: Contributions to Trinitarian Theology*. Translated by John Bowden. New York: Crossroad, 1992.

————. "The Question of Theodicy and the Pain of God." In *History and the Triune God*, 26–30. New York: Crossroad, 1992.

————. "Reflections on Chaos and God's Interaction with the World from a Trinitarian Perspective." In *Chaos and Complexity: Scientific Perspectives on Divine Action*, edited by Robert J. Russell et al., 205–10. Vatican State: Vatican Observatory, 1997.

————. *The Spirit of Life: A Universal Affirmation*. Translated by Margaret Kohl. London: SCM, 1992.

————. *Theology of Hope, On the Ground and Implication of a Christian Eschatology*. New York: Harper & Row, 1965.

————. *The Trinity and the Kingdom of God*. Translated by Margaret Kohl. London: SCM, 1981.

————. "The Unity of the Triune God." *St. Vladimir's Theology Quarterly* 28 (1984) 157–71.

Moltmann, Jürgen, and Elisabeth Moltmann-Wendel. *Humanity in God*. London: SCM, 1984.

Mosser, Carl. "Fully Social Trinitarianism." In *Philosophical and Theological Essays on the Trinity*, edited by T. McCall et al., 131–50. Oxford: Oxford University Press, 2009.

Müller-Fahrenholz, Geiko. *The Kingdom and the Power: The Theology of Jürgen Moltmann*. Translated by John Bowden. London: SCM, 2000.

Nadler, Steven. *The Best of All Possible Worlds: A Story of Philosophers, God, and Evil*. New York: Farrar, Straus & Giroux, 2008.

Neuner, Roos, et al. *The Teaching of the Catholic Church*. Translated by Geoffrey Stevens. Staten Island: Society of St Paul, 1967.

Nicholson, Rangi. "The Theological Implications of a Three *Tikanga* Church." In *Proceedings of Theology in Oceania Conference Dunedin (1996): Doing Theology in Oceania: Partners in Conversation*, by Clive Pearson, 36–41. Dunedin, NZ: Centre for Contextual Theology, School of Ministry, Knox College, 2000.

Nowak, Martin A., and Sarah Coakley. *Evolution, Games, and God: The Principle of Cooperation*. Cambridge: Harvard University Press, 2013.

O'Collins, Gerald. *The Tripersonal God: Understanding and Interpreting the Trinity*. New York: Paulist, 1999.

Ogden, Schubert M. *The Reality of God*. New York: Harper & Row, 1963.

———. "Towards a New Theism." In *Process Philosophy and Christian Thought*, edited by Delwin Brown et al., 173–87. New York: Bobbs-Merrill, 1971.

Ogden, Steven. "Power: Michel Foucault, Human Identity and the Church." In *Speaking Differently*, edited by Phillip Tolliday et al., 127–44. Canberra: Barton, 2013.

Onions, C. T. *The Oxford Dictionary of English Etymology*. Oxford: Oxford University Press, 1966.

Origin. *On First Principle*. Translated by G. W. Butterworth. Gloucester: Smith, 1973.

Orr, Matthew. "What Is a Scientific Worldview and How Does It Bear on the Interplay between Science and Religion?" *Zygon Journal of Religion and Science* 41 (2006) 435–44.

Partridge, Eric. *Origins: A Short Etymological Dictionary of Modern English*. London: Routledge & Kegan Paul, 1959.

Pasewark, Kyle A. *Theology of Power: Being Beyond Domination*. Minneapolis: Fortress, 1993.

Pickard, Stephen. *Theological Foundations for Collaborative Ministry*. Farnham: Ashgate, 2009.

Pittenger, Norman. *Process-Thought and Christian Faith*. New York: Macmillan, 1968.

———. *The Word Incarnate: A Study of the Doctrine of the Person of Christ*. New York: Harper, 1959.

Plantinga, Cornelius, Jr. "Social Trinity and Tritheism." In *Trinity, Incarnation, and Atonement*, edited by R. J. Feenstra et al., 21–47. Notre Dame: University of Notre Dame Press, 1989.

Polkinghorne, John C. *Belief in God in an Age of Science*. New Haven: Yale University Press, 1998.

———. "Quantum Theology." In *God's Action in Nature's World*, edited by T. P. Peters et al., 137–46. Aldershot: Ashgate, 2006.

Porter, Muriel. *A New Exile? The Future of Anglicanism*. Northcote: Morning Star, 2015.

———. *The New Scapegoats: The Clergy Victims of the Anglican Church Sexual Abuse Crisis*. Melbourne: Morning Star, 2017.

———. *Sex, Power and the Clergy*. South Yarra: Hardie Grant, 2003.

Reuther, Rosemary Radford. *Sexism and God-Talk: Toward a Feminist Theology*. Boston: Beacon, 1983.

Reeves, Gene, and Delwin Brown. "The Development of Process Theology." In *Process Philosophy and Christian Thought*, edited by Delwin Brown et al., 21–64. New York: Bobbs-Merrill, 1971.

Russell, Robert J. *Cosmology, Evolution, and Resurrection Hope.* Kitchener: Pandora, 2006.

Sideris, L. H. *Environmental Ethics, Ecological Theology and Natural Selection.* New York: Columbia University Press, 2003.

Smith, S. M. "Perichoresis." In *Evangelical Dictionary of Theology*, edited by Walter A. Elwell, 843–44. Grand Rapids: Baker, 1984.

Smith, Walter C. "Immortal, Invisible." https://www.hymnal.net/hymn/h/14.

Socrates. "Ecclesiastical History." In *Socrates, Sozomenus: Church Histories*, translated by A. C. Zenos, 1–178. Nicene and Post-Nicene Fathers Second Series 2. Grand Rapids: Eerdmans, 1980.

Solch, Dennis. "Metaphysical Creativity and Creative Metaphysics: An Emersonian Perspective." In *Beyond Superlatives: Regenerating Whitehead's Philosophy of Experience*, edited by Roland Faber et al., 2–17. Newcastle on Tyne: Cambridge Scholars, 2014.

Suchocki, Marjorie Hewitt. "Spirit in and through the World." In *Trinity in Process: A Relational Theology of God*, edited by Joseph A. Bracken and Marjorie Hewitt Suchocki, 173–90. New York: Continuum, 1997.

Sykes, Stephen. *Power and Christian Theology.* London: Continuum, 2006.

Tanner, Kathryn. *God and Creation in Christian Theology: Tyranny or Empowerment?* Oxford: Basil Blackwell, 1988.

———. "Social Trinitarianism and Its Critics." In *Rethinking Trinitarian Theology*, edited by Robert J. Woźniak et al., 368–86. London: T. & T. Clark, 2012.

Terrien, Samuel. *Job: Poet of Existence.* Eugene, OR: Wipf & Stock, 1957.

Tertullian. *Treatise Against Praxeaus.* Edited with an introduction and commentary by Ernest Evans. London: SPCK, 1948.

Tillich, Paul. *The Courage to Be.* London: Collins, 1952.

———. *Love, Power and Justice.* London: Oxford University Press, 1954.

Volf, Miroslav. *After Our Likeness: The Church as the Image of the Trinity.* Grand Rapids: Eerdmans, 1998.

———. "'The Trinity Is Our Social Program': The Doctrine of the Trinity and the Shape of Social Engagement." *Modern Theology* 14 (1998) 412.

von Neumann, John, and Oskar Morgenstern. *The Theory of Games and Economic Behaviour.* Princeton: Princeton University Press, 1944.

Warren, Rick. *The Purpose Driven Life.* Grand Rapids: Zondervan, 2002.

Weber, Max. *Economy and Society: A New Translation.* Edited and translated by Keith Tribe. Cambridge, MA: Harvard University Press, 2019.

———. *Essays in Sociology.* Translated, edited, and with an introduction by H. H. Gerth and C. Wright Mills. London: Routledge & Kegan Paul, 1948.

Weber, Max, et al. *Economy and Society.* 3 vols. New York: Bedminster, 1968.

Wegter-McNelly, K. "Atoms May Be Small, But They're Everywhere: Robert Russell's Theological Engagement with the Quantum Revolution." In *God's Action in Nature's World*, edited by T. P. Peters et al., 93–111. Aldershot: Ashgate, 2006.

Whitehead, Alfred North. *Adventures of Ideas.* New York: Macmillan, 1933.

———. *Essays in Science and Philosophy.* New York: Philosophical Library, 1947.

————. *Process and Reality.* Edited by David R. Griffin and Donald W. Sherburne. New York: Free Press, 1978.

————. "Religion and Metaphysics." In *Process Philosophy and Christian Thought,* edited by Delwin Brown et al., 67–69. Indianapolis: Bobbs-Merrill, 1971.

————. "Religion and Science." In *Process Philosophy and Christian Thought,* edited by Delwin Brown et al., 431–40. New York: Bobbs-Merrill, 1971.

————. *Religion in the Making.* New York: Macmillan, 1924.

————. *Science and the Modern World.* New York: Macmillan, 1926.

Williams, Rowan. *Arius: Heresy and Tradition.* London: SCM, 2001

Wrong, Dennis. *Max Weber.* Englewood Cliffs, NJ: Prentice-Hall, 1970.

Zizioulas, John D. *Being as Communion: Studies in Personhood and the Church.* London: Darton, Longman & Todd, 1985.

SUBJECT INDEX

Made in the USA
Middletown, DE
01 May 2023